The Forerunner

The Forerunner

A STORY OF PAIN AND
PERSEVERANCE IN AMERICA

Cori Bush

ALFRED A. KNOPF   NEW YORK 2022

THIS IS A BORZOI BOOK
PUBLISHED BY ALFRED A. KNOPF

Copyright © 2022 by Cori Bush

www.aaknopf.com

Knopf, Borzoi Books, and the colophon are registered
trademarks of Penguin Random House LLC.

Library of Congress Control Number: 2022935862

ISBN: 9780593320587 (hardcover)
ISBN: 9780593320594 (ebook)

Jacket photograph by Joe Martinez
Jacket design by Janet Hansen

Manufactured in the United States of America

First Edition

To my kids, Zion and Angel

To all my readers—

In the pages ahead, you will find sometimes traumatic stories of abuse and assault, racism and misogyny. Everything you will read relays the events of my life exactly as they happened, although some people's names and identifying features have been altered to protect their individual privacy. As difficult as my story may be, I share it with you in the hopes that it will bring you solace and will help you feel heard. I write it all with love, every word.

Your congresswoman loves you.

Prologue

SOME PEOPLE START THEIR political careers with a run for the local school board or a statewide seat. Not me. That's not my story.

In 2016, I ran for the U.S. Senate, challenging Missouri's then secretary of state in the Democratic primary. That August, I lost the race. But I'd gained invaluable experience that would later serve me in the two subsequent runs for Congress I'd make before winning my seat representing Missouri's First Congressional District. Twenty sixteen wasn't my time to win. I licked my wounds and went on with my life. I had two beautiful children, Zion and Angel, to parent as a single mom, and I was working full-time as the nursing supervisor at a community mental health agency. But four weeks after I lost that Senate race, I experienced something much more devastating than a political setback. I was raped.

Two years prior, I was fighting on the front lines of the Ferguson uprising, which rose up in the aftermath of the killing of Michael Brown Jr. when he was just eighteen years old. Being out in the streets, protesting the needless killings of Black folks by the police, the very people who are meant to protect us, made me a target of harassment.

I'd had my tires slashed while my car was parked in front of the complex in which I lived. I'd come home to find the doorknob tampered with, my front door left ajar. On one occasion, my daughter had been home when someone entered our first-floor apartment. That day, I came home from work to find paper scraps strewn about the floor of our living room and kitchen. Angel was in her bedroom, mercifully unaware that she hadn't been alone. I, on the other hand, was coming to the growing realization that my family and I were no longer going to be safe in our home.

So when a local faith leader posted to social media that he had a house for rent, I quickly replied to him, asking to set up an appointment to take a look. That day started off rough. A member of our protest family was found murdered that morning. When I heard the news, I was in disbelief. The last time I saw him we were at an event unrelated to protests. He saw me come in the door, smiled at me, and came over and gave me a hug. We chatted for a few minutes, and then he went back to his seat. If only I would have known I'd never see him again, I would've hugged him longer and taken more time to talk. I would've said, "I love you, bro," while looking him in his eyes instead of saying it while we were hugging. I can think of so many things I would've done differently.

I cried getting ready for work, on the drive to work, and even in my office. I ended up on a call with my friend Chris Phillips, a talented, young Black filmmaker whom I met on the streets of Ferguson during the uprising. He would be in the midst of the tear gas collecting footage in the heat, rain, or snow. Chris allowed me to cry and vent as he listened and tried to console me. Later that afternoon, I checked my Facebook timeline to see if there was any new information on my murdered protest brother. I began to cry all over again seeing the posts that made it all the more real. He was one of us, and he was gone.

I didn't have many details about what happened to our protest brother, but I felt even more unsafe than I had. Seeing the social media post from the faith leader, I felt this could be a quick way to a safer living situation. That faith leader was someone I had known for more than a year and we had done community work together before. The idea of renting from someone who knew me and might be willing to waive a credit check so that my name wouldn't be connected to my new address was appealing. The death threats on account of my activism were real.

At that point, I'd lived through several evictions, the result of periods in my life when I'd made poverty wages and when domestic violence shaped my entire world. Plus, a credit check would allow my new address to be searchable for someone who's looking for it. This faith leader and I decided that I would meet him at the rental he was offering after I finished up work at the clinic for the day.

I was back on the phone with Chris for the drive from work. I updated him on how the rest of my workday went and filled him in on the news that I was on my way to look at a home for rent. When I approached the address and parked in the driveway in the back of the home, I told him I would call him back as soon as I finished looking at the house.

I had on a white scrubs top, blue scrubs pants, and sturdy Nike boots as I walked up the back steps at the address the faith leader had given me. The two of us walked through the one-and-a-half-story house together, alone. The truth was that I wasn't crazy about the place. But I wanted to hear what he was asking for it before telling him I wasn't interested.

We talked money while standing in front of a table where I'd set down my phone and keys. My phone rang, the screen displayed the name Chris Phillips and I reached for it, but the faith leader also looked at the screen, grabbed first my arm and then both of my wrists. He pulled me toward him, and continued to pull me with him, as he walked backward toward a bedroom. "What are you doing?" I asked him. "Where are we going?" When we got to the threshold of the door, I saw the bed. I wasn't confused anymore and struggled to break free. I couldn't. "What are you doing?" I asked in panic. "I would've done this a long time ago if I didn't know your history," he responded.

I looked at him and understood in that moment that I was looking not at a man but at a monster. He twisted me around and pushed me face-first onto the bed. I scrambled, trying to get on all fours and then stand, but to no avail. He pulled my scrubs pants and panties as far down my legs as they could go, just above my boots. He forced himself into me. At first, my body struggled against his. But the more I tried to get up, the harder he would thrust his body into mine. Eventually, I stopped fighting, and my mind floated away. There was a window off to the side of the bed, and I stared out of it. I whimpered through the pain. It seemed like forever. I felt like dying. I wanted to die.

When he finished, I rushed to pull up my clothes, scampered to the other room to grab my keys and phone, and made a move to run out of the room toward the door. Instead, the faith leader grabbed me and asked me why I was crying. I was afraid of what he would do next. Boundaries were broken. I didn't think he would let me leave alive. "I'm hurt," I said to him through my tears, not wanting to upset him more. "Why are you hurt?" he asked. I could be his girlfriend, he told me. We could do this all the time.

.   .   .

THE HOURS, DAYS, AND weeks that followed were a nightmare. After I made my escape from the house and drove away, I called Chris frantic and crying. He told me to drive straight to his house. He happened to be on the phone with someone from Ferguson Frontline who was together with others from the group. They were gathered at the site where our protest brother had been found dead early that morning, his body charred inside a burning car. Mourners were grieving together.

I confided in Chris that day and told him what had happened to me. The person he was on the phone with announced news of my assault to the others. They sprang into action to care for me. News of my rape spread wider. Instead of taking a moment in privacy and quiet to process what happened to me, within minutes I was surrounded by my protest family in the parking lot at Chris's home.

I felt embarrassed, ashamed, dirty while managing a great deal of pain, and I was devastated by the lack of discretion afforded me. A caravan of people followed me to the hospital, and dozens of activists sat in the hospital lobby as I was ushered away and subjected to the pain and humiliation of a rape kit.

I'd spent many years working as a nurse to the people of St. Louis, and I'd administered rape kits to patients. But I'd never myself been examined in this manner. I was given Percocet to dull the searing vaginal pain. Then a stream of people began to pour into my room at the hospital: my beloved parents, heartbroken by what had happened to me; protesters and clergy members, who must have expected to see me with black eyes and bloodied lips, because they were skeptical after realizing my wounds weren't going to be visible to them, especially not on day one (people of my skin tone don't show bruising as easily as those with lighter skin); St. Louis police officers, who came in to show me mug shots and ask me to identify my perpetrator, and to my surprise his mug shot was in the stack; and finally, the hospital's rape advocate, who brought me the softest clothes I'd ever felt and introduced an element of calm and comfort in a chaotic time.

It took me four months to reenter society. There were days upon days when I screamed and cried through the night. For two weeks, I couldn't go near my bedroom. The idea of being in a room with a bed and a window immobilized me. Once I finally felt strong enough to cross the threshold of the bedroom for the first time, I took comfort inside this private room where I controlled what happened within it. I refused to leave. I couldn't eat or sleep. I couldn't be around other people. I couldn't work. I couldn't cook or wash clothes. Chris helped out with my daily tasks and cared for me during my emotional outbursts. My mind often wandered mid-task, and I'd let a pot burn on the stove. I wasn't in control. I was paralyzed, fixed on that fateful moment. I grew paranoid and depressed. I also felt shame.

I had just turned forty a couple months before I was raped. I kept thinking, "How does this happen now? At this age? Under these circumstances?" I had compartmentalized the assaults I'd experienced in my teenage years and in my early twenties. On some level, sadly, I believed I'd played a role in the abuse I had endured when I was young. I told myself that it was because I'd been out there with my booty hanging out of my shorts. I told myself it was because I'd been drinking. I'd let a guy I didn't know get too close. I told myself it had been my fault, that I'd put myself in those positions. But this time? I was a mom, in my scrubs, visiting a house I was considering renting from someone I thought I knew. How had this happened?

·   ·   ·

CHRIS FOUND ME A therapist who helped lead me away from self-blame and away from questions that have no answers. Instead, she turned my attention to healing. For a year and a half, I met and talked with her regularly. She helped me see how I'd internalized my previous experiences and assaults, those years of violence I'd endured. In my mind, I had moved on. I no longer worked low-wage jobs and had become a registered nurse. I was a parent, a pastor, a leader in my community. I wanted to believe that these changes in my life would make earlier hurts fade away. But they hadn't. Instead, deep inside me they'd compounded, and they were all rising to the surface now, triggered by this latest violation. Slowly, over the course of the next year, I learned to understand that grief in the face of tragedy was reasonable. My grief was reasonable. My grief was warranted by the life I'd lived. My mom, my sister, Kelli, and Chris would take shifts caring for me, and my going to therapy gave them all a break.

I learned practical tools. I started going outside every day, if only for fifteen minutes. When my rage boiled up inside me, I allowed myself to release it on the pillows in my bedroom. Meanwhile, Chris was there for me when I had a panic attack in Saint Louis Bread Company, or Panera. He was there every time my efforts to see my rapist prosecuted or otherwise held accountable hit a roadblock. He was there as my rape kit sat on a shelf, ignored, for four months. He was there when my kids needed rides to school. He was there for every doctor's appointment. During every follow-up, he held my hand. He was there to console me when the doctor who finally reviewed my forensic exam declared that the encounter could have been an assault or, as the rapist had claimed, consensual rough sex. He was there with me each time I went to court to try to get an order of protection against the pastor. He was there each time the court failed me, allowing the perpetrator's rights to trump my own rights. Along this journey, my therapist listened and taught me the tools to help me back to living again. These folks saved my life.

. . .

IN THE PAGES THAT follow, I recount other times I've been brutalized. These are a part of my story and who I have become. They are a part of why I fight for the rights of all of my people—no matter who they are or what the circumstances of their lives are like. I know what it's like to struggle to live after a sexual assault. I know what it's like to not be believed, to be told to be quiet, to move on and get over it. I fight for the rights and dignity of victims and survivors of sexual assault the way that I do partly because I've been there myself.

For me, reproductive justice isn't abstract. As someone who has had to end pregnancies, I know what a difference it would have made to have been met with quality, compassionate, culturally responsive care when I decided to terminate. It's part of the reason why I fight so hard for comprehensive reproductive health care, including family planning and abortion care, because I believe the right of a person to make their own decision should be protected for everyone.

As a mother of two, I know what it's like to endure health complications during childbirth, to deliver a baby four months premature and watch him spend the first months of his life in the neonatal intensive care unit. It's one reason I fight so hard to end the Black maternal health crisis in our country that kills too many Black women and birthing people.

As someone who has been either uninsured or underinsured for most of my adult life, I know what it's like to be burdened by thousands of dollars in medical debt and to have to seek out routine medical care in an emergency room rather than with a primary care doctor. And as a nurse, I've seen too many patients forgo mental health services or be forced to ration their insulin because they couldn't afford the cost of treatment or medication. It's also why I fight for Medicare for All, including for easy access to comprehensive mental health services and affordable prescription drugs, because health care is a human right and must be guaranteed for everyone.

As an organizer and activist in the movement working to save Black lives, I've seen too many Black children die at the hands of police officers. I've personally been brutalized and assaulted by law enforcement officers during protests and have watched other activists' rights violated while protesting for justice. It is why I hold fast when I fight to fundamentally transform our approach to public safety in our country, so we can save lives and finally achieve true justice and accountability.

And as someone who has been evicted, has been unhoused, and has worked low-wage jobs, I know what it's like to struggle to pay rent, keep the heat on, and put food on the kitchen table. In part, it's why I fight so hard for a social safety net that actually meets the needs of those most marginalized by our society so we no longer have to just survive, but so we can thrive. I fight so hard for transformational change because it's right and it's necessary, but also because I've lived through the harms and devastation of police violence, and I know that with more people in positions of power who have an understanding, personally or not, of what it's like to struggle to survive, we can build a more just and equitable world that meets the needs of regular, everyday people like me.

Growing up in the church, I was often reminded of the importance of the figure of the forerunner, that person who blazes a clear path where there was none before. In the New Testament, Jesus shows his followers the way to everlasting life, and John the Baptist was his forerunner—he readied the world for Jesus's coming. Because the forerunner goes before the others, he takes on whatever lies ahead and withstands the pains and pressures of the journey. The forerunner prepares hearts and minds to receive what comes next, and eases the way. Of course I am not a Biblical figure. But I would not be the leader I am if it were not for the challenges I've faced to be where I am, and today, I work to make that path easier for others.

This is not your typical political memoir. I have no problem challenging our notions of what is proper or what is respectable. I have no problem being vulnerable and sharing episodes from my life that might make some readers uncomfortable. I know that for every reader who can't relate to the struggles I've been through, there are at least two more who have lived through something similar.

Not everyone is able to tell their story. If my telling mine helps others and makes them feel seen, then my own self-exposure will be worth it. If telling my story helps others in positions of power better understand how their decision making affects regular, everyday people, people like me, then my own self-exposure is worth it. When people in power can claim that they don't know the truth of our experiences, they can continue building a world in which there's no room for us to thrive. I want to put an end to that.

I'm sharing my truth because I feel an urgency to put my mind, my body, and my reputation on the line to make sure our communities get what we need. I hope that by being open about my own journey, I can help ease others' pain. My work is to move with purpose, knowing that every minute people in our country are walking into new instances of preventable hurt and that I have a responsibility to dismantle the systems of violence that too often cause that hurt.

May the words that follow be a salve to all those who need it:
We are not alone. Our stories are not anomalies.

Part One

Chapter 1

I LIKE TO WEAR a T-shirt that reads "St. Louis Built" because this place built me as hard as it has the fired bricks that make up the walls of the homes seen throughout the community. Fired bricks can withstand heat and overwhelming force. I liken them to the hardest, grittiest parts of my own person. For me, the majestic structures that make up my hometown symbolize beauty in the midst of the storms that life brings.

The asphalt reminds me of the pain and trauma I've lived through. I can vividly remember every time my face was pressed up against it, burning hot from the summer sun—my childhood playground falls, the times when my domestic assaults spilled out onto the sidewalk, when the police tyrannized us when we protested. So much of what I've seen and experienced here helped shape me. St. Louis is my soul and my heartbeat.

Ask most people in the United States what they know about St. Louis, and they will mention the iconic arch that stands regally over the wide and winding Mississippi River. The St. Louis that I know is alive and humming with a diversity of peoples, cultures, and culinary traditions.

Soul food from places like Sweetie Pie's, Mom's Soul Food Kitchen, Kingz Turkee Shack, and Mother's Fish makes me feel connected to my family's roots. The meat served at Red's BBQ in Ferguson takes me back to the family cookouts my parents used to host. I head to Cherokee Street for Mexican restaurants like La Vallesana and Black-owned places like Burger 809 for the salmon melt, greens, and mac and cheese. At Yaquis, you can find me grabbing slices from a warm pizza with friends. In the Tower Grove neighborhood, I sometimes walk blocks before I decide what I'm in the mood for. There's a bounty offering Thai, Mediterranean, Mexican, vegetarian, Vietnamese, Persian, sushi, breakfast, Indian, or shakes and protest signs at MoKaBe's Coffeehouse.

I love to be reminded of all the people who make up the melting pot that is my hometown. St. Louis has been home to artists like Miles Davis, Ike and Tina Turner, Chuck Berry, Scott Joplin, Josephine Baker, Donny Hathaway, Angela Winbush, Huey, Nelly, and the St. Lunatics. Today, we are home to rising femme rap artists like Bates. These folks make up the vibrant character of this area. Whenever I'm home, I feel this vibrancy and flavor in the wind. We are a sports town with the best fans. We are home to the St. Louis Cardinals, St. Louis Blues, St. Louis Surge Pro Women's Basketball, plus a host of great college and high school teams. Next up, major league soccer.

But despite this richness of culture, the truth is that we live in a lethal environment in St. Louis, and we're dying. The St. Louis Metropolitan Police Department kills more people per capita than any other metropolitan police force in the country. We consistently have some of the nation's highest homicides for our population size. A child is more likely to die of gun violence in St. Louis than anywhere else in America. It's as I said. We're dying.

Some people think that St. Louis is in the South. It's not, it's in the Midwest, but Missouri *was* a slave state. The legacies of slavery and de jure segregation affect every aspect of society here. Delmar Boulevard, nine miles long, divides Black St. Louis to the north from wealthy and white neighborhoods to the south. The redlining and restrictive covenants that were put in place in the early twentieth century determine where we live to this day. Oppression, division, and separation are threads in our culture.

Many people arrived in St. Louis during the Great Migration, when around six million Black Americans moved north in the early to mid-twentieth century, fleeing persecution, segregation, and discrimination in the South. Some of them intended to only pause in St. Louis before continuing farther north, and stayed. If you ask Black people in St. Louis where our roots are, many of us will say Mississippi, Tennessee, Alabama, or Louisiana, a history that you can find in our soul food and in the patterns of our speech.

My paternal great-grandparents came to St. Louis from Starkville, Mississippi, as part of the Great Migration. My maternal grandfather arrived from Pageland, South Carolina, where a cemetery, shopping center, and several streets still bear his family name: Blakeny. As is the case with many who moved north in that period from 1915 to 1970, racial terror, or at least the threat of it, preceded my maternal grandfather's move to St. Louis.

My grandfather was a dark-brown-skinned child of a biracial mother, and his family lived on the Pageland plantation where they'd been enslaved. I was told that when he returned home after serving in World War II in the Army Air Corps on the Solomon Islands of the South Pacific, he was accused of having looked at a white woman. He got wind that a mob was amassing to come for him, and he hopped on the first bus he could catch headed to St. Louis, where his best buddy from the war lived. There he met, and fell in love with, his friend's sister, a quiet and jolly spirit. He married her, and she would become my grandmother. Her family had moved to St. Louis from Greenwood, Mississippi, when she was eighteen years old, motivated by a similar situation. I don't know the particulars of that story, but I do know that the Klan and a white woman were involved. Whatever happened, my grandmother's brother was never seen or heard from again, and the surviving family packed up for Detroit, where other family lived. They made it only as far as St. Louis.

.   .   .

WHEN I WAS GROWING up, my immediate family consisted of my parents, a brother, Perry, who's two years older than me, and a sister, Kelli, who was born a few months shy of my sixth birthday. My father, Errol Bush, worked as a union meatcutter. I loved seeing him at the local grocery store when my mom sent my brother and me on an errand. He wore a long red coat and smock, white hat, and white cloth gloves that would often be tinged pink from the hours he spent handling meat. My dad was popular. Everyone seemed to know him. And he wasn't popular only at the grocery store where he worked.

Over the years, I watched my dad lead in every group or institution he was a part of. He was president of our family reunion planning committee, and as such he gathered more than a hundred of our family members from all over the country in St. Louis when I was a child. He was president of the PTA at the Catholic elementary school I attended. I watched him be elected alderman in the City of Northwoods, in St. Louis County, when I was ten. Later, he would be elected mayor. I watched him put his mind to something, work hard, and accomplish it. In my eyes, my dad was a giant.

I watched my mother, Barbara, hard at work every day, juggling home and career. But my mom was also the nurturer who enveloped me in love, with all the hugs and kisses I could want. She called me "tweetie bird," because I was always hanging around her neck. Once I was old enough to attend school, she became a computer analyst. She worked 8:00 to 5:00 every weekday and some weekends, then came home to take care of us three kids. Each evening, making it all seem effortless, she cooked us a full meal. She made sure we did our chores: we would iron our clothes, clean the kitchen, and otherwise help out around the house. She was never too tired to help with homework. And, oh, how I remember the long sessions poring over my math assignments!

To me, my mother was the smartest person in the world. She always knew how to find the right answer. And not only was she smart, but she was also pretty and stylish. She would answer my questions about clothing and style and then care for me when I complained of a tummy ache. She could bake, cook, clean, and take care of us all while being a professional and excelling at her career.

When I was born in 1976, my family lived in a duplex on the west side on a street named Ashland Avenue, or "The Horseshoe," before we moved to the northside, to Richard Place. My dad likes to say that he learned in those days that if you have small kids, you should never live upstairs from your landlord. My brother and I were small children then, and our landlord would knock on his ceiling when the patter of us playing bothered him. An older neighbor, Mr. Sites, was retired and spent much of his time wiping down his car in front of his house. One day, he asked my dad if he'd ever considered buying his own home. Didn't he want to give my brother and me more living space and our own yard to play in? My father, who was twenty-two at the time, asked innocently, "How much does a house cost?" The answer was $30,000.

Mr. Sites introduced my parents to a real estate agent with an office in the suburbs, just north of the St. Louis city limits in North County, who took them under his wing and showed them properties around the city. At first, my parents had their eyes on a big house in Lafayette Square, a neighborhood populated by Victorian town houses that today sell for upwards of half a million dollars. Back then, many of the homes were gutted, and my parents wanted to buy such a place, take out a loan, and rehab it. But at the bank, my dad was told that loans weren't being given in that neighborhood. What the banker really meant was that they weren't giving loans to *Black people* in that neighborhood. My parents, young and inexperienced, didn't recognize the signs of housing discrimination and went on about their business, happy to look at the next house their real estate agent had lined up for a viewing. That's how we ended up in Northwoods.

The City of Northwoods is a suburban community less than five minutes from St. Louis city, but it was still a different community in my father's eyes. The homes weren't as tall or as close together as they were on the northside, where we had moved from. Trees lined the streets, and green grass blanketed the front lawns. Many of my earliest memories of childhood were in that home, a three-bedroom ranch style that we didn't have to share with another family, as we had the duplex. In Northwoods, only one family per home. Our driveway was ours alone. The brick that covered the outer walls of the house was an orange color, lighter than the deep red brick of the duplex where we used to live.

In 1980, Northwoods was a majority white community, and I watched the racial makeup change over the years as white families took flight. Today, the neighborhood is nearly all Black. At the southwestern edge of the small city was Normandy Shopping Center. It was a ten-minute walk from my childhood home, and it was our neighborhood hangout when I was growing up there. There was the National grocery store where my dad worked, Normandy Bank, a hair salon, shoe repair, Chinese restaurant, Walgreens, Laundromat, beauty supply store, a popular bowling alley, Ben Franklin five-and-dime stores, and a Velvet Freeze ice cream shop, where you would find me most. They sold penny candy galore, Big League Chew gum, Pop Rocks, cigarette candy, bubble gum ice cream, and the whole deli pickles where I would put my Now and Laters or Jolly Ranchers inside. When I had scrounged enough money for food when out with friends, I would go for a true St. Louis favorite: chicken fried rice. I would treat myself to a chicken St. Paul sandwich, egg rolls, or crab rangoon with a grape or fruit punch Vess soda.

Trips to the store for penny candy or ice cream or to turn in the glass Coca-Cola bottles for a deposit were sprinkled throughout the many hours my brother and I spent playing together outside, him on his Batman Big Wheel and me pedaling alongside him on my

Robin Big Wheel. We would ride for hours on end. I would beg him for a chance to ride his Big Wheel. On my fifth birthday, I finally graduated to a pink-and-white bike that came adorned with a basket and training wheels.

We had a nice-sized yard and over the next few years played hide-and-seek, tag, and touch football with the other kids in our neighborhood. "I Can't Live Without My Radio" by LL Cool J and "La-Di-Da-Di" by Slick Rick made up our soundtrack. As long afternoons turned to dusk, we knew to be home when the street-lights came on if we hadn't already been called in for dinner. All of the parents on the street knew us kids, and it was easy to be in trouble with any one of them. Northwoods was a village.

Everyone came out for the neighborhood's much anticipated annual picnic, an event that punctuated my childhood in North-woods. For years, my dad helped organize the event and made my brother and me work. We set up tables, handed out hot dogs, and served sodas. We didn't get to partake in the fun until later in the day, once our tasks were completed. Often, at that time, I felt enveloped by a sense of loneliness, because my neighborhood and school friends didn't typically attend. But all day, activity buzzed around us: The Bosman Twins played their saxophones onstage. Young kids took pony rides, squealed with delight at the petting zoo, or ran around as part of the Police Athletic League T-ball game. Barbecue was plentiful. And the teenagers and young men, many of them with Jheri curls and bare torsos, huffed and puffed on the basketball court.

That's how I remember the community that surrounded our Northwoods home. Inside, we created our own world. Until kindergarten, my family and neighbors were my everything. My mom didn't work at that time and took care of me at home. I was never the little girl who played house. While I performed my chores diligently, I never pretended to iron, cook food, grocery shop, or anything like that. I liked to play teacher, or "school" as I called it. I would line up all of my dolls and stuffed animals around the perimeter of my room and give them pencil and paper or chalk and a chalkboard. For hours, I would sit with them on the floor and pretend to teach.

To me, these baby dolls and stuffed animals were alive. Each one had a name and personality, and I was there to pass on what my mom had taught me, which consisted mostly of the alphabet, numbers 1–10, and how to spell my own name. I pulled from what I'd seen on television on *Sesame Street, The Letter People,* and *The Electric Company.* I taught them to write the letter *A,* and I fussed and scolded them, directing my students to look at the chalkboard, stop talking, and sit up straight. I took breaks to change a stuffed animal's clothes or talk to a student's parent. I often had to readjust my fluffy white snail that played "You Are My Sunshine" when wound up. It was top heavy and often fell over, causing me to stop class and set it right side up. When I was lost in the world of school, nobody bothered me. My brother didn't interrupt, and my parents let me stay focused on my play. That was my time.

Other times, I played with Tonka trucks and World Wrestling Federation figurines with my brother, Perry. This was my way of spending time with him because I knew Perry was not going to help me with my dolls' hair or play school with me. I did not like playing in dirt, but I liked to watch my brother feed dirt into his concrete-mixer truck and act out Ric Flair, Randy Savage, and the Road Warriors wrestling matches. But what I really craved for my own toy collection was Strawberry Shortcake, Jem, Barbie, and Cabbage Patch Kids dolls. My dad forbade it. I needed to have toys that looked like me, he said. At Christmas, he'd search high and low to find dolls whose complexions matched mine. My skin color was perfect, he told me, and Black is beautiful.

I never got the Strawberry Shortcake poster that I so desperately wanted for my bedroom. Instead, our house was adorned with a photograph of Dr. King and large posters, including one of "The Great Kings and Queens of Africa." I think my daddy bought every Black history book he could find. When we were growing up, he wanted us to know about people like Rosa Parks, Shirley Chisholm,

Fannie Lou Hamer, W. E. B. Du Bois, Frederick Douglass, Marcus Garvey, Harriet Tubman, and Sojourner Truth. He believed he couldn't leave it to anyone else to teach us these things. And if we didn't know our own history, we would lose ground, he told us. We would fall back into the oppressive conditions that our ancestors had worked hard to change but many of which remain with us today. When we watched television with my dad, it was *Eyes on the Prize, Roots, Shaka Zulu,* or *A Raisin in the Sun.* These were difficult to watch oftentimes. I couldn't make sense of why the white people on the TV were angry and violent toward Black people. But I did know, even as a child, that I was going to fight back. My brother and I wanted to watch cartoons, something fun, while my dad was diligently fortifying us, steeping us in culture that would help us recognize the Black excellence inside us.

My father also made sure we felt connected to our own family's legacy and traditions. We had a huge heirloom Bible that had belonged to my paternal great-grandfather, and my dad would give us big silver dollars—he called them "bo dollars"—that his own grandfather had given him. He insisted we give them right back so he could store them alongside the pocket watch and cuff links that had been passed down from his uncle. It was important for my father to feel that he had something to pass on to us.

As a child, my father had loved miniature trains, and he held on to this appreciation as an adult. He had an old, heavy set that ran on a rail around the base of our Christmas tree. Choosing the tree together as a family kicked off the holiday traditions every year. We would drive thirty or forty miles to a farm outside the city to find the perfect tree, then cut it down ourselves. We'd visit the little Santa's village and buy homemade gifts and ornaments while snacking on cocoa and popcorn. Once home, my mom cooked a big lunch that we ate before decorating the tree. On Christmas morning, my parents made a big breakfast, and later in the day my dad would take us to the movies. The next day, Kwanzaa began.

In the early 1980s, most people weren't yet familiar with the holiday, but that was when my dad started taking us to Kwanzaa celebrations, an opportunity to celebrate the Afrocentric holiday created by Black American activist and author Maulana Karenga in 1966. Southern Illinois University Edwardsville has an educational center in East St. Louis, and my dad would drag us there in December to watch performers of African dance. I preferred Christmas and our trips to see Black Santa, but my father also instilled a connection to the culture and ideas of the African Diaspora. As I got older, I came to appreciate the display he put up in our home, the woven *mkeka* mat and kinara, or candelabra, that held red, black, and green candles. We learned about the importance of unity, self-determination, cooperative economics, and the other principles that Kwanzaa recognizes, and gave *zawadi,* or gifts, that we'd made or nurtured ourselves.

My father was pro-Black, and if there was a boycott in the community or any effort to defend Black interests, he was going to be a part of it. A portrait of Jesse Jackson hung in our hallway. At the time, Jackson was running for president on the Democratic ticket for the second time, and his campaigns inspired my father. In the days leading up to the Democratic National Convention in 1988, my dad reached out to Missouri congressman Bill Clay's right hand, the activist and strategist Pearlie Evans, and was able to secure a place on the floor of the convention as an usher. He tells the story about how he got into a heated exchange with the Atlanta mayor and former UN ambassador, Andrew Young, who couldn't find his credentials and so couldn't make his way past my dad. Our whole family made the trip to Atlanta for the convention, sleeping on my cousin Margie's floor. We toured Ebenezer Baptist Church, where King had co-pastored, and the Martin Luther King Jr. Center for Nonviolent Social Change, the institution dedicated to keeping King's legacy alive.

I grew up around politics and public service. While other kids went to daddy-daughter dances, I tagged along for campaign functions and Board of Aldermen meetings. Because of my dad's position, state representatives, state senators, and mayors were always around. When he was running for office, I came along to coffee klatches. He would take me with him to canvass and send me up to people's doors, with a flyer promoting his candidacy in my hand. "When they come to the door, tell them you want to talk to them and you want them to vote for your daddy," he'd say, coaching me. He'd be standing several feet behind me, and I'd be the cute kid who would greet someone when they opened the door. I was bait.

When my dad was an alderman, the mayor of our municipality at Northwoods decided to run for the county executive seat. He won. St. Louis County is composed of more than ninety municipalities: Northwoods is one; Ferguson is another. The county executive is essentially the head of our county government. His was a huge victory for many, because he was to be the first Black person to lead the county's government. With the Northwoods mayoral seat open, my dad ran for it, and also won. Later, he worked on the campaign of Freeman Bosley Jr., who became St. Louis's first Black mayor in 1993.

My father was a powerful force in our home as well as in the community. He was very serious about my appearance, and what he said went.

When I was young, I had big, long, Rudy Huxtable hair. Other kids in my elementary school used to call me "Big Bush." I started getting relaxers when I was three, and my mom would press my hair on top of the perm. First, she would give me a hot oil treatment. Afterward, I spent hours seated next to the kitchen stove, near the blue Crisco can, waiting for the next tug of my hair followed by the crunch-and-sizzle sound the hot comb would make as it made its way through my hair. Back and forth, my mom would place the pressing comb on the orange and blue flames to maintain the right amount of heat. She would have the kitchen window open for the heat and smoke as the hot comb singed the oil she had previously massaged into my curls. I would be so hot I would sweat out the freshly pressed side of my head by the time my mom finished the other side.

I started going to the hair salon when I was five, and by the time I was seven, I was going every two weeks. Even into adulthood, I wouldn't leave home without my hair looking just so. My dad's words are ingrained in me. He stressed to me all the time, like a broken record, to always look presentable: a clean face with Vaseline, clean teeth, and neat and nicely combed hair. Never go outdoors with rollers in your hair, he'd tell me, and never use a hat to cover messy hair. To this day, my sister, Kelli, and I never let him see us without our hair together.

As a child, I loved dresses, jewelry, makeup, and high heels. My mother's closet was my portal into her world. She didn't mind. I would put on her heels, her necklaces and bracelets, her clip-on earrings, and her belts and walk around the house feeling just as fabulous as I thought she always looked. I wanted to smell like her, too. At her dresser, I would dip the puff into her shimmery, perfumed Gloria Vanderbilt powder and then dab myself with the scent.

My mom was my model for timeless elegance and beauty, while my dad's style reflected his Afrocentrism and marked him as a man of his time. During my childhood, he wore an Afro. If he wasn't at work, a black pick with a Black Power fist for a handle stuck out from the top of his cloud of black hair. I often saw him in the clothes he wore behind the meat counter at National, but he also wore fitted shirts and blue jeans (short cutoffs in the summer months), tube socks pulled way up, and white Converse tennis shoes. His orange-colored boots were reserved for special occasions.

He worked the later shift, and when I could get away with it, I tried to stay up until he came home, usually just after ten o'clock. I would hear him coming and scamper onto the black-and-white-checkered recliner, his favorite seat in our living room. I knew that the first thing he'd do after coming into the house would be to take off his jacket and hat and sit in that chair to watch the news. And I wanted his attention. I loved to get there first and greet him by taking up the entire seat. Still, he would squeeze in next to me. That was our daddy-daughter thing, and I treasured those moments. If I couldn't stay up late enough to scramble into that chair, I would try to fall asleep in my parents' bed so that when he came home, he would have to pick me up and carry me to my bed. I craved any time with him I could get.

Since he didn't have to be at work until the afternoon, my dad was home in the mornings and made us a big breakfast every day before we went to school. Sometimes, he would give us a Black history lesson while he squeezed oranges for juice. Looking back, I think this was his way to grab and hold our attention. We always had meat at home because he was a meatcutter, and sometimes breakfast would include leftovers from the night before. My mom made pork chops and rice and corn, or spaghetti and fried chicken and salad. Friday we'd have fried catfish or buffalo and jack, again with spaghetti. On Sundays, there was beef roast or meat loaf with greens, mac and cheese, and corn bread. If my daddy cooked Sunday dinner, one of my favorites of his meals was pork roast, cabbage, candied yams, and hot-water bread.

Meals were important in our home, and while the kitchen wasn't big, we all found a way to sit at the table there and eat dinner together. Even on holidays when my grandmothers and my dad's sisters would join us, we all gathered around that table. On the days we'd celebrate with a big meal, I'd wake to the sound of my parents up early, clanging pots. After some time, the smells of the delicious food bubbling on the stove and baking in the oven wafted to my room.

The only night my mother didn't typically cook was Thursday. Thursday was pizza night. We'd order Domino's Pizza and watch *The Cosby Show* and *A Different World* together. For years, every Thursday night, we crowded in our living room with its beige and blue couches. Nearby, my dad kept his stereo and the crates from Peaches Records and Tapes where he kept his albums, his prized possessions.

He would put one on—the O'Jays, Commodores, Gladys Knight & the Pips, or Earth, Wind & Fire—and we would dance. These were such happy days, when my family was together in those early years.

·　　·　　·

WHEN PERRY FIRST WENT to kindergarten, I thought he was abandoning me. School was shrouded in mystery. He left me for a world that I didn't quite understand. Why did he want to go there so much? Why did he have to wear the same ugly outfit every day? Why couldn't I get a book bag too? Why can't I have dittos? I wanted homework dittos! My brother and I were close, and you didn't usually see one of us without the other. I wanted to do what he did and be where he was, so I didn't understand why he got to go to school when I couldn't. He was making friends in a world that I was not a part of, although I did develop an early crush on a light-skinned classmate of his who lived down the block. That was a perk.

When I did finally go to kindergarten, wearing the green plaid top and skirt that was the uniform, I was so happy and proud to be joining Perry. My mom bought me a Strawberry Shortcake lunch box to mark the occasion; it was unclear to me if my dad knew initially about its existence. But once at school, I was overcome with separation anxiety. I'd never been away from my mother before. After she dropped me off, I cried in my classes that first week I was there. But I adjusted. And once I did, I reveled in school.

I remember the Christmas and spring programs. I remember singing and dancing onstage in front of my family for the first time, beaming. In class, each of us students made the first initial of our first name in pancake batter, and then we ate the results. I learned to count to a hundred. I was amazed that I had the opportunity to learn all that was presented before me. I felt as if I were receiving a winner's prize, as if I were part of some special group honored enough to learn such secrets as the names of the secondary colors.

A world of information opened up before me, and I wanted to soak every piece of it up.

I attended Ascension, a small Catholic school. Ascension was housed in a two-story brick building on a residential street near our home. A regal archway shielded the front entry from the elements. The school reflected our neighborhood's demographic changes. When I started there in 1981, there were still a few white students in my class. By the time I was in eighth grade and preparing for high school, Ascension's student body was 100 percent Black. Meanwhile, the parish connected to the school remained majority white. Most of the people who made up the school's administration were white. On Wednesdays, when we attended Mass along with the parishioners, the adults in the sanctuary with us were almost all white. Our next-door neighbors, the Bells, were part of the small number of Black parishioners. I remember thinking to myself at the time, "These people sure don't live around here."

The teaching staff was homogeneous, too. I remember the first time I had a Black teacher. Ms. Whitfield was a substitute in the second grade. She was slim, dark-skinned, with a relaxer and roller set. She walked in wearing gold jewelry with makeup beat, hair laid, a cute dress, and heels. The first time she walked into my class, my classmates and I couldn't believe she was there to teach us. We were already under the impression that only white people had knowledge and authority at school, because that's all we had ever seen. White people were the ones who taught us and told us what to do.

Ms. Whitfield was different. She didn't try to put on airs or fit into any mold. I so wanted to be like her. I wanted her to be our permanent teacher. The following year, we had a Black teacher by the name of Ms. Joiner. Being in class with Ms. Joiner was like being in class with my mom. She was nurturing and took the time to understand why we were struggling, or what else we needed from her as we diagrammed sentences or wrote out our math equations on the chalkboard. If someone was being disruptive, she would point her finger, put her hand on her hip, and roll that neck. With her, I felt understood. Our white teachers didn't have much spunk or sass. But having a Black teacher in the front of the class showed me that it was okay for me to be who I was and to bring the full fire of my personality and mannerisms into the classroom.

We weren't Catholic, but Catholic school was all I knew. My principal was a nun, and these were the years when nuns would spank you. One day, I happened to be in the principal's office just as she was preparing to spank another student. I saw her pick up the paddle and tell the child to lean over the desk. I screamed and threw the books I was holding to the floor. "You can't do that!" I shouted. I didn't know that indeed they could. I was heartbroken. I lost all respect for my principal. I wouldn't speak to her unless I had to. The practice ended while I was still at Ascension, and I was glad to see it go. A little bit later, that principal was replaced, and I was glad to see her go.

My family went to a Baptist church where the service was lively. There was hand clapping, foot stomping, tambourines, drums, soulful gospel singing, and sometimes Holy Ghost shouting. Mass at Ascension was not that way at all. It was quiet and ritualistic. The priest would speak in Latin. I couldn't understand a word of what he was saying. In religion class, every picture in every book we read and on every wall in our classroom depicted white people. Every statue was of a white person. The angels were white, Jesus was white, Mary was white. I didn't understand this, because at home we had no images of a white Jesus. My dad had told me that Jesus was a Black man. At my family's church, I saw mostly Black sacred figures. But at school, it was impressed upon me that there was a religious hierarchy, and I wasn't anywhere near the top of it. The supreme people, white people, were a part of the most amazing story in the history of the world. This version of religious teaching removed us from something that our ancestors actually were a part of. I wouldn't understand until much later how much harm was inflicted on us by whitewashing the Bible and the story of Jesus in that way. At the time, it all created a strict separation in my mind: This is white people's religion as opposed to the Black people's religion that I saw at the Baptist church.

It wasn't just religion class. Our social studies books at Ascension told a white-oriented version of history, one that was very different from what my dad taught me. In the 1980s and 1990s, school textbooks didn't even make an attempt at nuance. They were blatantly racist. You could easily find a children's book with a matching exercise that prompted kids to link the word "good" or "bad" with a picture of a little white boy playing with a toy or a picture of a little Black boy doing something sinister. Workbooks featuring racist overtones were sold widely at our local grocery store. I eagerly asked my mom to buy me these whenever I noticed a new one was available, because I wanted to access the knowledge that I believed was contained in these books. I thought I would learn something from them that I hadn't yet learned in school. I was so accustomed to those racist images I didn't notice anything wrong with them.

When I was in fifth or sixth grade, every so often a community-based group visited our classroom for about twenty minutes per session to talk with us about Black culture and the Black family. Any discussion of race in school was confined to that short-lived program or Black History Month. But despite its shortcomings, Ascension was a place where Black children were nurtured and Black families supported each other. All the students celebrated on the honor roll were Black. The list of kids excelling in sports was all Black. The science fair winners were Black. At Ascension, Black excellence was all I knew.

I aspired to be excellent. I wanted to make my parents proud. Every morning before taking us to school, my dad would sit my brother and me down and talk to us about responsibility, clapping his hands to emphasize every syllable of the word. "Cori, you are a leader," he would tell me. "But what makes a good leader is someone who knows how to follow. So be responsible, be accountable." He taught us about Black historical figures so that we had models as we strove to leave our marks on the world. There was no room to be regular, because regular wasn't going to change a status quo that desperately needed changing. My dad's consistent message was that I had to be better than what I thought I could be. I had to push myself further.

I tried to live up to those expectations. I was the kid who wanted all As, even an A in conduct, which was how our behavior was evaluated. I didn't want to see my name on the board or be kept in from recess. I wanted to have all the perks that came along with being in school. After my school day ended, I would come straight home, eat a snack, and go to my room to begin my homework. I loved doing my homework. I finally had those dittos that I had coveted when I watched my brother bring them home. As I got older and started using textbooks instead of worksheets, I loaded those books and my well-organized Trapper Keeper into my big off-brand Esprit-like bag and lugged home my work for all of our dozen or so subjects with eagerness.

My dad had dreams of where all that hard work would take me. Oftentimes, he would look across the table and say to me, "You're going to graduate from high school, get scholarships. You're going to go to Howard University. You are going to be attorney general of the United States one day." Just as my father pushed me at home, my teachers pushed me at school, calling on me to do things and helping me believe that I was a natural leader. I knew that if I ever got in trouble there, my teachers would be on the phone to my dad. I didn't want that. I didn't want to risk him thinking that I hadn't understood the mission he'd set out for me—to learn and to become great. So I worked hard, and I stayed on the honor roll.

The teachers would have known to call my dad because he became a near-constant presence at the school. Ascension had an active parents club, and high participation in it earned families a percentage off tuition. It was through the turkey shoots and chili suppers that he helped put on that he got to meet other Northwoods families. He met the mayor of our neighborhood, as well as other elected officials. Those gatherings and connections turned him on to the idea of running for office himself. My dad credits Ascension for giving him his start in politics.

My brother and my little sister went to Ascension, too. When my sister was born, I wasn't upset about being replaced as the youngest in our family. Instead, I was intrigued by the changes her arrival brought. I watched my mom's belly grow big, and I could place my hand there and feel the movement. I understood that soon I would no longer be the baby in the family.

Our house changed to accommodate our growing family. My dad had the basement finished and remodeled, putting tile and carpet down over the concrete floor and carpeting the wooden stairs I'd tumbled down so many times. What had been a storage space became a family room, two bedrooms, a bathroom, and a laundry room. My brother and I moved down to the basement bedrooms to make room for Kelli. For hours, my mother would sit in the living room in a wicker and bamboo rocking chair, soothing our new baby sister. She was a silly baby who eventually figured out how to climb out of her crib and hide beneath it, giggling as we called for her. When she got old enough for solid foods, she ate up all the bacon and all the bread that had never before seemed in short supply.

My social life was beginning to blossom outside our tight-knit family unit. In second grade, I met my first best friend, Tonya. Our families were close, and among the things we had in common were a desire to excel in school and big hair. We had the usual sleepovers and spent as much time as possible with each other. Tonya's parents were separated, and I thought she had it good. I figured when her mom was gone, she imagined that she could do whatever she wanted. Tonya and I loved doing hair and walking to the store for Jolly Ranchers and Now and Laters. We grew into preteens together and shared a love of jewelry, purses, clothes, and music. When we were in seventh or eighth grade, we joined forces with two of our friends, Carla and Juanita, for the school talent show. In coordinated outfits, we performed a dance we'd choreographed to "Poison" by

Bell Biv DeVoe. We would spend hours on the phone going over homework together. As we got older, the topic of conversation often turned to boys and our crushes at school.

When I was twelve and in seventh grade, a cute brown-skinned boy who was a year ahead of me at Ascension asked me to be his girlfriend. I said yes. After school, we would walk together to the nearby shopping center. By then, our school uniforms had changed, and I knew I looked cute in the Eastland shoes my parents had stretched their budget to buy me. I paired my precious Eastlands with a pleated green plaid dress I wore over a white collared button-down shirt. My boyfriend was one of the star basketball players in his grade and I was a cheerleader. At games I would perform a special jump, cheering every time he made a basket. I was crushed when, after a few months, I found out he was also dating another girl in his own class. He hadn't told me, and the news stung all the more when I learned that seemingly everyone else in our school knew. I was humiliated. It wouldn't be the last time a boy made me question my self-worth.

During those middle school years, I also had a new interest that took up my time and attention: sports. I had started playing volleyball at our family reunions. My dad helped plan these events and took painstaking care to make sure we had the right net for our games. We kids loved to play on our block. We raced up and down the street to see who was fastest. Epic games of tag took us into each other's yards, behind houses, and up in trees. As a preteen, I wanted to play organized sports with my friends at school too. But Ascension did not have enough resources for a big sports program.

I had a good relationship with the principal at the time, a white woman who was so skilled at her job that she oversaw a homeroom class and had full teaching duties while also serving as an administrator. She had a reputation for being stern and serious but was unquestionably dedicated to her roles as a white leader in a Black school, meticulously making sure we had opportunities available to us. She wanted to help us be well rounded and equipped for society. So when my friends and I approached her about starting various teams, she was game.

We formed a volleyball team and joined the local league with other Catholic schools. There was no budget for a coach, so one of our teachers volunteered to play the part the best she could. Ascension acquired a pom-pom squad much the same way. I loved cheerleading, and after some cajoling, the school let us start a team. Our parents, who paid out of pocket for our uniforms, and school staff were concerned about what our outfits would look like and worried they would be too revealing—a distraction to the boys playing basketball. But we settled on a cute but comfortable look: white sweatshirts we got airbrushed to read "Ascension Flames Pom Pom" on the front and our names on the back. We wore black leggings and "white girl" tennis shoes with green-and-white pom-poms on the shoelaces to match the green-and-white pom-poms we shook while we cheered.

I was fast and liked running, but an experience at a track meet when I was in seventh or eighth grade soured me on the sport. One spring afternoon, we dressed in our Ascension Flames track uniforms—a green V-neck shirt and matching shorts, both emblazoned with a yellow stripe—for a track meet at another Catholic school. We walked around admiring their field. It was huge, and I immediately noticed the equipment we were missing at Ascension: a high jump mat and bar, a long jump pit, hurdles stacked to the side of the track. As the competition was about to begin, I looked up into the stands and saw a sea of white faces. The few Black faces in the crowd I recognized as my and my friends' family members. We were the only Black school at the meet.

That morning, our coaches informed us of which events we'd be running that day, and I was given 400-meter hurdles. It would be my first time with that event. We didn't practice with actual hurdles, and I needed some guidance. How do I do it? I asked. I wasn't confident as I approached the starting blocks, but I figured I'd give it my best shot. As I crossed the finish line, clearly ahead of the others and in first place, I beamed. I walked over to my coach, my smile wide with joy and surprise. "I won!" I cried, jumping up and down.

In earshot was the adult keeping time for the meet. "You didn't win," he shot back. He gestured to a white girl who had finished in second place well after me. "She won. You may have crossed first but she had better time." I pressed him to explain. How could she win if I crossed first? "She had better time," he repeated. White parents in the stands could hear me as I continued to press him and started to boo. The logic wasn't clear, and I genuinely didn't understand why I hadn't won. But my coach shrank in response and urged me to back down. "Cori, just stop. Let it go. It's not right what he's doing, but let's walk away." I was deflated. I knew the accomplishment had been snatched away from me. I never ran competitively again.

Despite this and a few other crushing incidents, as a whole sports eased my transition from girlhood into adolescence. I'd never gotten the message at home that there were things I couldn't do because I was a girl. I knew my parents had faith in my abilities, and I knew my teachers did, too. But volleyball, cheerleading, and even track built my self-confidence and gave me a sense of independence. I learned how to lean on and trust my teammates.

Ascension was a small parochial school, and we didn't change classes. I had come up with the same group of kids since kindergarten. The teachers knew us intimately. But my time on the sports teams felt different. I got to articulate new elements of my personality and abilities. At the net or with my pom-poms, I got to see that there was more to me than even I had previously understood. Building physical strength and agility over time helped me see I had more than book smarts. Getting these new groups started for the school showed me that my leadership abilities were real and rooted in my own courage and actions, not just in people's perceptions of who I was because I was my father's daughter.

. . .

IT WAS AROUND THIS time that I started to have glimpses into who I might be in the future. I realized how much I loved working with children. At Ascension, sixth graders were paired with younger students and acted as big siblings for kindergartners who were still adjusting to the school. I took this role seriously and cherished it, especially since my own sister, Kelli, was in that cohort. I knew I wouldn't be assigned to her, but I was excited that someone my age would help her transition to the school that I loved.

My classmates and I felt we knew everything there was to know about our school. We knew where all the bathrooms were, which teachers were fun and which were mean, and which ones would let you stay at recess a little longer. When I met the shy little sister I was assigned to near the beginning of that school year, I let her know I was there for her, that if she felt alone or overwhelmed, all she had to do was tell her teacher she needed her big sister. I wanted to protect her the same way I wanted Kelli to feel protected. As a welcome gift, I made her a teddy bear out of a yellow sponge I'd cut and colored myself. I just wanted to give her something that might bring a little joy in a strange new environment.

That same year, our administration transformed what had once been a convent into an early childhood development center. My dad had instilled in us that it was important to volunteer our time, and when I had the opportunity to help out at the new preschool, I took it. After my school day ended, I played with the toddlers and passed out snacks. I loved being there so much that I volunteered a few hours a few days a week over the summer as well.

I would go on to spend almost a decade of my adulthood working at a childcare center. Of course, I would also go on to serve my communities as a nurse. And I got my very first taste of nursing at the preschool in those pivotal middle school years too.

My parents sent my brother and me to YMCA summer camps in St. Louis, but the summer I turned twelve, I announced that I didn't want to go anymore. I didn't want to spend another summer in what seemed a lot like school, only with a pool and more field trips. My dad made it clear that I was not going to sit on the couch and watch TV all summer. He would set me up to volunteer at the Northwoods City Hall and the police department, mostly assisting with filing papers and answering phones, and this year I also signed up to become a candy striper at Normandy Osteopathic Hospital. At first, I found it boring. I wore a red-and-white-striped smock and went around filling patients' pitchers with ice water. I might read a book to a patient and generally checked in on people to make sure they didn't need anything. I did whatever the nurse or nurse's aide on duty asked me to do: hand me that book, or let me know when you see Dr. So-and-So.

As was the case at Ascension and most institutions I encountered, almost everyone with any power was white. The doctors and nurses were white; the people who performed tasks that required less professionalized training were Black. But one day on the hospital floor, I saw a Black nurse. She was pushing around her own cart, and I could tell that she was running things. And she was fly. She was poised and carried herself with a mix of class, elegance, and sass. Her short, brown and auburn highlighted hair was laid. She had gold rings on almost every finger. She was in charge. She wasn't taking orders from anyone else, it seemed. And the patients loved her. One day, while I was watching her chart, waiting for her to give me a task, I asked myself how I could become just like her. As had been the case with Ms. Whitfield, this Black nurse's very presence in the space commanded my full attention. I knew, "I want to do that." Nursing was my dream from that moment on.

While it was that encounter that made me aspire to become a nurse, both of my grandmothers worked in the field. Maybe they were not RNs, but they were nurses. I would see them in their white hats and dresses, the thick white stockings and sturdy white shoes. When I was a young child, I had often seen my grandmothers wearing their nurse's uniforms, getting off the bus, after a long day at work, or at church. I never really thought much about their clothing. I just knew that they both kept their uniforms spotless, a pristine white.

It never occurred to me to wonder what they spent their days doing. But in fact, the profession had deeper roots in our family. My father's aunt was a registered nurse who trained at Homer G. Phillips, a segregated public hospital that operated in St. Louis from the 1930s until the late 1970s. Black clinicians from all over the country traveled there for their clinicals and rotations. My mother also had an aunt who became one of the first Black RNs in St. Louis and received numerous awards and accolades. Their stories would have been fresh when I was thirteen, but it never dawned on me that I could walk in their shoes. I needed as many images of Black women in their power as I could find.

. . .

As I HIT THOSE ages of twelve, thirteen, fourteen, I discovered that I had entered a new world, both complex and unsettling. One day it just happened. My mom had taken me along to the grocery store for a shopping trip when an adult man looked at me. Then he whistled and winked. My mom noticed and sternly reprimanded him: "Leave my daughter alone." But I soon learned that she couldn't protect me from this new kind of unwanted attention. This started to happen more and more.

It was one thing to have boys at school think I was cute or make remarks to that effect. I was used to that. But it frightened and confused me to receive this kind of attention from people who were outside my school, people I didn't know and who were often way too old to be paying me any mind. I wondered, am I supposed to like being treated like this? I didn't. My instinct was to punch the men in the mouth for the way they approached and spoke to me. But the behavior became so commonplace, the expectation, as far as I could tell, was that I was to accept it.

Sometime later, I was with my friend Renee, walking around the city on our way to get some fried rice. We came upon a group of much older men, likely in their thirties, leaning against the back of a car. They started catcalling, whistling, and grabbing their crotches. "Hey, baby," they called after us. "Come over here!" We ignored them and kept walking, but they kept at it, their voices growing louder and louder. Finally, I called back, "I'm thirteen. You're way too old for us." One of the guys, still holding his crotch, responded, "You old enough to pee, you're old enough for me." A sudden fear rose up in me, and Renee and I took off running.

On another occasion around that time, I was walking home from North Oaks Plaza by myself. I'd had enough encounters with McGruff the Crime Dog, a bloodhound character that was often used in schools to teach crime awareness in the 1980s, and seen enough missing kids' photos on the side of milk cartons to know that I needed to keep my wits about me. But I was in my neighborhood, close to home, and I felt safe. I couldn't imagine that danger would be lurking here.

One of my strongest recollections from that time in my life is from that evening. It was my first experience of sexual harassment. A police car pulled up beside me and slowed down, but I didn't think much of it. Because my dad was in local government, he made sure the officers knew who his kids were. I figured it was someone who recognized me, and he was pulling up to say hello or to make sure I was okay. When I turned my head, he started making small talk. Where was I going? What was I doing? I kept walking, confused and unsure of what he wanted from me.

Out of the corner of my eye, I noticed one of his hands moving up and down in a repetitive motion. He kept talking and eventually asked me, "Don't you want some of this?" I focused on him then, in an innocent effort to see what he was offering. That's when I saw his erect penis in his hand as he massaged it back and forth. Other than changing a baby boy's diaper, I had never seen a penis, and I struggled to make sense of what I was looking at. I didn't know what to do. I was embarrassed. "How does this end?" I wondered to myself. "Don't you want to get in?" he asked. I told him I didn't and made up my mind to fight him if I needed to. If I ran, he might follow me. But I didn't see any other way out. "I'm a kid," I yelled at him, and then I bolted.

During my childhood, the Northwoods police came to our house once a week to drop off an envelope to my dad, documents related to his business as an elected official. They would watch our house periodically. When I was very young, I understood the police to be a source of protection. If I was walking to the store, they would drive beside me sometimes to make sure I got there okay. But this encounter subverted everything I believed. I became afraid that this officer would come to my door, show up at our home. What if I had to talk to him? Would I even recognize his face if I saw him again?

I considered telling my dad about this encounter, but I worried that he might be upset with me. Had I done something wrong? Maybe I'd provoked him in some way. Maybe my hairstyle was too grown. Maybe my earrings are too big. Is it the lip gloss? Is it the way I'm walking? People did say I walked with a switch, my hips swaying back and forth. My body was developing, and I wasn't looking as much like a little girl anymore. I wondered if my dad might feel angry that I was changing physically, but I didn't know how to stop those changes from happening, just as I didn't know how to stop the degrading responses I was getting to those changes. I didn't want to burden my dad. I didn't want him to be afraid for me. I also didn't want him to be upset with me. I didn't know what to do, so I didn't do anything at all.

Another time, while I was volunteering at city hall for the summer, someone who worked there commented on my makeup in a lewd manner that turned my stomach. "Boy, your lips look good in that lipstick," the grown man said. I had on mood lipstick, a fad at the time. It was more of a tinted lip gloss actually, but it was a huge deal to me that my parents allowed me to wear it because I was forbidden to wear makeup until I was sixteen. What could I say? Again,

I just darted away, which I had started to learn to do when I was made to feel scared or uncomfortable.

I told my dad I didn't want to go back to city hall. I didn't tell him what happened, just that I didn't want to be there anymore. By then, my friends and I were being initiated into the attacks that came to shape our teenage years and beyond. We were ogled, manhandled, and disrespected on the streets, at our workplaces, at sports events—ordinary places we should have been able to feel safe in. Instead, being sexualized, objectified, and propositioned became our new normal.

The love and encouragement that I received at home and at Ascension would influence me deeply in the years that followed. But so would the attention that I got from boys and men.

Chapter 2

FIRST FREE WILL BAPTIST Church was my home away from home as soon as my siblings and I were old enough to be dropped off and to attend on our own. My dad wanted us to go to church more regularly. But he often worked Sundays, and my mom was less interested in making the weekly commitment. Church wasn't a big part of my life until my siblings and I became more independent. Our paternal grandmother, her husband, and my two aunts attended First Free Will too. And it didn't take long for me to become part of the community of young people there.

I met Terrell on Easter Sunday when I was in the seventh grade. The ruffled layers around the bottom of my white dress bounced when I walked, and I wore white stockings, white gloves, and an Easter hat over my freshly styled hair. At Sunday school in the church basement, I noticed a boy around my age who kept looking at me and rolling his eyes. Another group of boys kept pointing in my direction, whispering and laughing, then running away when I looked their way.

I asked some girls in the group what was going on. The boy rolling his eyes was Terrell, they said, and he had a crush on me. The boys pointing and laughing were his friends, and they were both making fun of Terrell for his crush and trying to get my attention. It took another month or two for the two of us to start to talk. I didn't pay him any mind at first. But over the next few months, I realized I liked his dark brown skin. I noticed when he got his hair cut in a box and used a texturizer to stretch out his curls. I thought he was cute and told him I liked him back. He asked me to go out with him, and we ended up dating on and off for the next nine years.

First Free Will Baptist Church was where I met who I thought was my first love. It was also a community institution that held great importance to my family and to the families that I would grow close to in those years. The brick church with stained-glass windows and concrete front steps sat on a corner in what many called "a rough neighborhood" on St. Louis's west side. My dad's mom had grown up on the same street as Terrell's grandparents. It was his family church, too, and his whole extended family attended services there.

I too felt in my element in the sanctuary filled with cushioned burgundy pews and matching burgundy carpet or in the vestibule, where I performed my duties as an usher, handing out donation envelopes and the program for service. I was shushed by the church mothers as I gossiped with my friends in the pews. I gave Easter speeches in front of the congregation and sang as part of the youth choir. I listened to my cousin and the singing group he'd started sing "Center of My Joy," a song that moved me to tears. His mother, my aunt, had a beautiful voice, and she participated in one of the choirs as well.

On Sundays, I got to see my paternal grandmother dressed in her crisp white nurse's uniform. She was one of the nurses at church, and if someone was caught up in the spirit, she would fan them and make sure the area around them was clear enough to keep them safe. If someone fainted, she would bring them water, tend to them, and help them to a room behind the sanctuary where they could rest. She could also often be found in the kitchen in the church's basement, where she helped cook and serve special meals, whether it was a pastor's anniversary or a prayer breakfast. As her grandchild, I was afforded special privileges and could visit in the kitchen and get closer to the hot, fragrant meals as they cooked. Other kids had to keep their distance until it was time to get in line for a plate.

. . .

IT WAS SOON TIME for me to leave another of my homes away from home: Ascension. For high school, I knew I wanted to go to a school that had built a solid reputation in sports so that I could play volleyball and be a cheerleader at a competitive level. I chose to go to an all-girls Catholic school in suburban St. Louis. This school was in a Black neighborhood but continued to reflect the demographics of the neighborhood as it was before white flight took place, from the 1950s through the 1970s. In choosing that school, I became one of a few Black girls in the incoming freshman class. But I was giddy at the prospect of enrolling there.

As a younger student at Ascension, I'd been paired with an older student named Terri as part of the school's big sister/big brother program. I'd admired Terri, and she had gone on to this high school. I wanted to go, too. When representatives from the school visited Ascension to recruit, I noticed that there seemed to be a real sisterhood among the students. I was drawn to their camaraderie. And the school was known for its excellent academic program. To me, it was a place where I could excel at everything I wanted to do.

Thanks to my parents' willingness to sacrifice, I didn't have to think about the cost of my tuition as I prepared to move on to another private Catholic school. They never told me that certain schools were beyond what they could afford. I knew that they were budgeting strictly, and my siblings and I felt that sacrifice, too. While our peers wore name-brand clothes that I lusted after, we shopped at Walmart. Sometimes, my father would purchase us the most affordable name-brand shoes he could find. He'd take us to a Black-owned sports store in the city to buy us Converse. An aunt of mine, who was stationed in Korea at the time, sent me my first pair of Pumas. I wore the black-and-gold tennis shoes with pride.

To get into the high school I'd set my sights on, Blessed Trinity, I needed to pass an entrance exam. I remember that I didn't understand why it was necessary, if the school could look at my past grades and see how well I'd done. I remember thinking, "Would this one score define me?" But I thought of it as just another step in the application process, like turning in my application and writing an essay. I didn't study. I wasn't nervous about it. When the other hopeful applicants and I arrived to take the test, the school's proctors led us into the auditorium. I did what I came to do and thought nothing more of it.

A day or so later, the school contacted me to say that I needed to come back and take the test again. When I arrived, an administrator explained why. I looked up at him as he dispassionately said, "You had the top score on the test, which would make you the top incoming freshman. We don't believe you scored that high on your own." The school thought I had cheated. "You need to take the test again," they said. I was stunned, but I took the test again that day. They put me back in the same auditorium, but the seats all around me were empty. I was alone. And this time, the administrator told me I scored even higher. I didn't tell my parents what the administrator had said about why I needed to come back, because it didn't occur to me that there was anything amiss. I didn't realize until I was older how racist and wrong things had been at that school from the very beginning.

.   .   .

I WENT TO THE school eager to join in the sisterhood I'd witnessed. But from the start, icy glances and cold shoulders welcomed me instead. During orientation and other introductory events, people were friendly and readily extended greetings and a welcoming spirit. But on that first day of school, people I encountered in the hallways looked at me with disgust, they stared at me, and some even stood directly in my way, as if daring me to say something as I tried to make my way through a new environment. "Is this just typical freshman hazing?" I wondered. My homeroom teacher barely acknowledged my presence, except to call my name while taking attendance. Class after class and day after day, my classmates treated me as if I didn't exist or were in the way. One day, I opened my locker to find my books covered in shaving cream foam.

People had told me that high school would be hard, and I began to think that this is what they meant: that it would be lonely, that it would require that I get used to persistent coldness, that there wouldn't be any sense of belonging. Maybe I was just having a hard time adjusting. Maybe I wasn't cut out for high school, I thought. Maybe I needed to toughen up. I wondered each day what I could do to turn things around. Meanwhile, I grew more and more hurt and confused.

It didn't even enter my mind that racism could be a reason for the abuse. After all, this school recruited at a school with an all-Black student body. Of course I would be welcome there. There were only a few of us Black girls in the freshman class, although we weren't in the same classes, and the others seemed to be doing fine. Terri was a few grades ahead of me and loved it there. When I approached her and shared my concerns, she encouraged me to give the school more time. But in the hallways, people called me "nigger." I even had "nigger" written on my locker. The truth was that I experienced harassment and intimidation all day, most days. Eventually, I came to understand that race was at least a part of what was keeping me targeted and isolated.

In math class one day, my teacher was explaining a formula when he called, out of the blue, "Cori, you're so smart, but I bet you can't do this." I hadn't been talking or disruptive and was caught completely off guard. Why had he singled me out? On another occasion, he told me that my grades at Ascension had been good because the teaching there had been subpar and the standards lower. In another class, I witnessed a teacher change her tone completely as she turned her attention from other students to me, almost snarling as she did so. The same teacher accused me of not turning in work.

Soon after, however, while standing close to her desk, I saw the missing paper in question and pointed out to her that it was there on her desk. She'd written an F at the top. She picked up the paper and ripped it into pieces, refusing to explain why I had gotten no credit for the assignment. "You didn't turn it in. You're lying," she said as the class stared, watching our interaction.

I saw the pattern and started to make sense of it. People knew that I was number one in my freshman class based on my entrance exam, and they did not like it. They were threatened by the possibility that a Black girl could be smarter than the white girls, and they wanted to put me in my place, dampening the fire of my motivation and curiosity. My grades started to drop.

One of my classmates was a white girl with long blond hair who had homeroom with me. She would look at me with big doe eyes in a way that showed me that she saw what I was going through. When we had to pair up with a partner, she sometimes asked me to be hers. Just before Christmas, our homeroom class drew names for a Secret Santa gift exchange. I was nervous. Would whoever drew my name get me something? I bought my gift for the person whose name I had and arrived at homeroom anxious on the day of the exchange. The doe-eyed girl handed me a green-and-red Christmas stocking with a small teddy bear on it perfectly decorated with green and red tissue paper stuffed inside. As she handed it to me, she said out loud what her eyes had expressed: "I'm sorry."

She wasn't apologizing for anything she had done. Days earlier, she had been among the students who watched the teacher rip up my paper while denying that I ever turned it in. I didn't know if she had drawn my name initially, or if she took it after others had handed off the slip of paper that said "Cori" as if it were a hot potato. However it came to be, she warmed my heart that day. I felt that at least one person at that school cared about me. Inside her present were huge

Tootsie Rolls and an assortment of candy. She had taken great care in putting it together, and the gift was the envy of the classroom.

The worst attack that I remember came in my Hebrew studies class. My teacher was explaining to the class that Christians don't read the Old Testament literally, as they do the New Testament. I raised my hand, and after being called on, I said, "At my church we take the whole Bible literally. It's the Word of God." This could have been an opportunity for the teacher to facilitate a wide-ranging conversation about faith and doctrine. Instead, he shut me down. "That's not true," he said. We went back and forth for a while, me doing my best to defend the religious teachings I was learning in my church in a respectful manner. But he ended the exchange, telling me to leave his class and to not come back, not that day or ever again. I was crushed. At Ascension, I had never been sent out of class or to the principal's office. But here I was marked as a "bad" kid, a problem. I went to the principal's office after our encounter, where I didn't expect to receive empathy. They sent me home and made me wait in the hallway until my grandad picked me up. I didn't have a single adult at the school—not an administrator, guidance counselor, or teacher—whom I believed to be on my side.

My dad picked me up from school on his days off. At the start of the school year, I was determined to be optimistic when I climbed into his car. But my demeanor gave me away, as did my monosyllabic, reluctant responses when he asked what I'd done or learned. My dad became angry when I'd tell him about the abuse and discrimination, but, like me, he believed things would change for the better if I just hung in there. One day after school let out, I walked out the door to see my dad standing next to his car. My spirits lifted just at the sight of him. I was so happy to see somebody who loved me and cared about me. He looked at me, and in him I could see my own brokenness and hurt reflected.

"You're miserable, huh?" he said to me once we settled into the car. I acknowledged as much. "You don't ever have to come back here," my dad said to me then. I couldn't believe it. My dad lived by the rule that if you start something, you complete it. His word was his bond. But more than that, my dad was determined to get me out of an awful situation and determined to protect me. I never went back to that school after that day. I transferred after the first semester of my freshman year. And that's how I ended up at Cardinal Ritter.

. . .

Cardinal Ritter College Prep was another St. Louis Catholic high school that attracted students who excel in the classroom and in athletics, but its student body was coed and Black. The school employed powerful Black adults in leadership too. Being there was like being back at Ascension for me. I felt valued, appreciated, respected. I felt at home. I was reminded that it's okay to be Black and excellent.

These days the school is housed in a new, multimillion-dollar building. When I attended, it was housed in a different building where there were bars and graffiti on windows and bullet holes in the exterior walls. But the campus belied the greatness that the school fostered. Students were required to take leadership classes during all four years of high school, and my leadership teacher, Mr. Leon Henderson, influenced me greatly. The class he taught was Afrocentric. As I had with my dad when I was younger, with Mr. Henderson we learned about the civil rights movement, the Black Power movement, the origins of Kwanzaa, and Black leaders like Marcus Garvey, Angela Davis, Stokely Carmichael (Kwame Ture), and Huey P. Newton. We watched the documentary series *Eyes on the Prize*. We listened to the speeches of Dr. King and Malcolm X.

Unfortunately, returning to a nurturing environment could only do so much for me. Those months at my first high school had shattered my self-confidence and motivation. While there, I had learned and internalized that it was safer to hide that I was smart and that expressing my opinions and curiosity made me a target. Until high school, I had been an A student. At Cardinal Ritter, I was placed in all honors classes. But something in me, whatever it was that had given me my self-determined passion for learning, had died. Rather, it had been killed off in the first high school I had attended.

The challenges of early teen years just made things worse. Being "smart" as a kid earned me praise from adults and peers alike. But I was a teenager, and outside of the Cardinal Ritter community, it wasn't cool to be bookish and brainy. Instead of receiving attention for my intelligence, now I was noticed for the way that I looked.

Cardinal Ritter itself was a safe haven and a refuge, but the surrounding neighborhood sometimes offered me challenges. The street harassment I had experienced while on the cusp of my teen years persisted. One day after school let out, I walked with the other members of the cheerleading squad to a place to grab a box of fried rice to eat before practice. On the walk back to school, we came upon a group of guys who wouldn't leave us alone. "Hey, baby, what's your name? Can I talk to you? Can I have your phone number?" they called. We ignored them and kept walking, but they started shouting louder and louder, following us.

One kept yelling at me in particular: "Ain't you gonna stop? Talk to me! What's your name?" "I'm cool," I responded over my shoulder. "I got a boyfriend." He hurled a forty-ounce bottle through the air. Pain shot through me as it made contact with the back of my head. The only thing that saved me from being knocked out was the distance between me and the man who'd thrown it.

The world was a hostile place, but Terrell made me feel safe in it. I knew he wouldn't let anything happen to me. By the time we were in high school, Terrell had become a leader in the gang that he was involved in, and people began to fear his physical strength as age gifted him height and mass. This was the early 1990s, and gangs were a big part of life in St. Louis. Repping colors was part of the culture in our communities, as was the violence that accompanied it. Terrell had a natural authority and his voice mattered. Teenagers throughout the city knew him as someone who would not hesitate to knock someone out if that's what the situation called for.

My classmates knew Terrell too, either through the sports he played around the city or because I brought him around with me. They were afraid of him, and they never got to see the softer side of him that I knew. Terrell shied away from places where he might slip up, where he might let down his guard. He would agree to go to a school dance with me, and then he wouldn't show. Or he might show up and spend the evening in a car, having me come outside to talk to him. He was too cool to come as my date.

I was infatuated with Terrell, but I hadn't expected that this is what it would be like to have a boyfriend. My ideas about romance and relationships had been shaped by the white teen romantic comedies of the day: *The Breakfast Club, Sixteen Candles, Grease 2*, and *Ferris Bueller's Day Off*. I read the Sweet Valley High books and watched *The Wonder Years* on television. Pop culture taught me that my boyfriend would be the best athlete in the school. I'd cheerlead. He'd pick me up in his car. He'd try to get frisky with me, and I'd be coy but eventually give in. Terrell and I didn't go to the same school, and he spent a lot of time with his friends, more than the boys in the movies seemed to. We never went to the movies or even out to eat. We didn't walk down the street holding hands. We didn't wear matching outfits and take pictures of ourselves as a couple, as some of my friends did. During the week, I was busy with schoolwork and sports practice; we spent hours talking on the phone. I'd page him and he'd call me from wherever he was.

We saw each other every week on Sundays. His grandmother would cook, and dozens of friends and family congregated at her house after church. Terrell and I would sit on his grandmother's porch and just talk. Or we'd watch something together on TV. He was thoughtful, and I knew he cared about me. But in some ways, I had a more intimate relationship with Terrell's family. I'd become good friends with his cousin and god-sister, and I spent a lot of my time with them while I was over.

Terrell's mother was a minister in the church and sang in the choir. She was a kind, dark-skinned woman in her forties who wore only dresses and skirts and always had a Bible in her hand. Every week she went to the barber and beauty college for a discounted rate to keep her shoulder-length hair styled. Terrell's mother was a social worker by trade and worked with youth in children's homes and juvenile detention centers. She was devoted to the children that she worked with and the children in her community, and I also benefited from her patience and attention.

Terrell's mom stayed on me like white on rice. One day she walked up to me and handed me a journal and pen. "The Lord told me you're going to need these," she told me. "So write everything that happens. Write." After Sunday services, my friends and I would sometimes pile in her tan Nova and go off to another service somewhere else. She kept the radio on Hallelujah 1600 AM, the gospel station. She didn't mind the static in the reception and sang along loudly to her favorite songs.

At the end of one of these long Sundays at church, I was in that tan Nova as Terrell's mother pulled up in front of his grandmother's house. An ambulance was parked there, too. Terrell had been shot. He was okay, but it was a harrowing reminder that we were headed in different directions. He had stopped going to high school. He was living a fast, dangerous life, while at fifteen, I was looked at as the good church girl. When he needed me, I was available. When he couldn't be bothered, he didn't want me around.

From the time I was twelve, when we first started seeing each other, Terrell tried to pressure me. When we kissed, he would ask to go further. I said no. I wanted my first time to be special, not some hasty, sloppy decision made in the heat of the moment. I told Terrell that I wanted to wait until prom night, junior year. That way, he'd stop asking me and have a date to look forward to. My sophomore year, I found out Terrell had been cheating on me. His mother told me he had a baby on the way. When I confronted him, he confessed. He told me all about the other girl. She was older than I was. She had a job, her own car.

In part, I blamed myself. She must have known what he needed,

I thought. I didn't have what she had. I couldn't compete. I'd been so busy with volleyball and cheerleading practice. I'd been focused on my studies, on choir practice and usher rehearsal. Maybe if I had been around more, this wouldn't have happened. Besides, I'd kept saying no to sex, so I'd been the one to open the door to his infidelity, I told myself. The TV shows and movies I watched had told me that teenage boys were fiends for sex who lacked discipline and self-control. They left girls for not sleeping with them. At least Terrell hadn't broken up with me. I was special.

I was also humiliated. Our families knew each other. The whole church knew that Terrell and I were a couple. But they all told me not to worry about it. Terrell was just being a typical boy. "At the end of the day, you two are the couple," they said. "You two will end up married." We were growing up together, and these were growing pains, they said. "Hang in there," they told me, and I did. Terrell and I entered an agreement moving forward. Terrell was going to admit that he made a mistake, come to his senses, and be with his girlfriend—me. In the months and years that followed, I watched him be a father to someone else's child. I loved that baby and the baby loved me back. I would hold him and play with him. But the situation with Terrell didn't improve. It got worse.

We tried. Terrell put on a tuxedo and escorted me to my junior prom. We made love for the first time that night, and our relationship changed for good. I believed that I'd only ever be intimate with one person in my life, and I believed my first time would be with the person I would marry for life. I was going to stay committed and try to make it work. My connection to Terrell felt so much deeper than what I had felt with him before. But Terrell continued to keep up his connections with other girls and fathered more kids with them.

I felt alone. I couldn't talk to my family about his cheating and the strain it put on our relationship. I wanted to stay with Terrell and didn't want them to think badly of him. My friends weren't going to be able to offer me much support either. None of them had been in a relationship that had lasted so long or that had them so enmeshed in the lives of their boyfriend's family. Dealing with the situation the only way I knew how, I took Terrell back over and over again. I told myself that the two of us shared a beautiful love story and I had to take the good with the bad. Truth is I didn't really know what love was then. I confused attachment, attraction, control, and codependency with love. But, in any case, it was hard for me to break away.

The stress of my ups and downs with Terrell added to what became a downward spiral to my high school years. My parents didn't know what to do about my flagging work ethic or the Bs and Cs I started bringing home regularly. They couldn't figure out if this was a prolonged reaction to those difficult few months at my first high school or if I was being a rebellious teen. My grades slid. I was in trouble. My dad prohibited me from playing volleyball or going to cheer until my grades improved. That only made things worse. Extracurriculars helped me feel connected to my old self, to who I was, and motivated me. At one point, I won a writing contest, and the prize awarded the winner an opportunity to study at a local university for dual high school and college credit. I flaked and never followed through with the university. It wasn't that I was trying to fail. I just couldn't figure out how to be me anymore.

Parts of my old self still lived. I wanted to go to college. I wanted to pledge Delta Sigma Theta and become a registered nurse. I wanted to go to a historically Black college or university. My dad had talked to me about Howard University since I was little, and I fantasized about attending there. My peers and teachers at Cardinal Ritter held up HBCUs as the goal to aspire to, and *A Different World,* with Lisa Bonet's *Cosby Show* character off at the fictional Hillman College, was a pop cultural force at the time. I loved watching Whitley, Kimberly, Freddie, and Dwayne Wayne. They made college seem like a dream that was within reach for me. My junior year, I applied to five schools, Tuskegee and Prairie View A&M among them, and—despite what I felt were lackluster grades—I got into all five.

By senior year, I was ready to go, and to move on. I loved my friends and I loved Cardinal Ritter, but I was in need of a new chapter. When I was a young girl, I had imagined my senior year would be this perfect, giddy time, when I'd open fat envelopes bearing good news from all the schools I'd applied to. I imagined it would be like what I'd seen on television: I'd pick my future alma mater without a care in the world. I'd have the scholarships to help smooth the way. My family would kiss me with excitement. They'd take me shopping to prepare me for the big move to campus.

That wasn't how things unfolded. Instead, I fretted that I wasn't going to pass my classes and would graduate with a GPA below 3.0. Still, I managed to eke by. I matriculated at Tuskegee, which had a nursing program I liked and a Delta chapter on campus. I thought between whatever financial aid package the school would put together for me and a job, I could make it work. But, no. Things were not going to be so simple. We were shocked to find that even as a lower-middle-class family, my parents earned too much money for me to qualify for a substantial enough financial aid package.

I didn't acknowledge the predicament I was in until the last minute, a few weeks before I was supposed to arrive on campus. I wasn't going anywhere, and I didn't have a backup plan. I could've applied and gone to a community college, but I had my sights set on a four-year university, and I never pursued that option. I despaired.

I thought, briefly, that instead I might follow in the footsteps of a few of my other family members and join the military. I prepared an application and took the test to enlist in the U.S. Air Force, and I did well. A representative who was administering that day told me that with my score I could get any job in the force that I wanted. But I got nervous about the commitment and never completed the process. Instead, I was going to work low-wage jobs for the next ten years.

I often look back and think of the interlocking forces that derailed the early vision my family and I had held for my life. My experience at the first high school I went to had taught me there was a glass ceiling for ambitious, dark-skinned Black girls like me. Instead of being welcomed into a new and supportive learning environment,

I was met with racist, insecure adults and classmates who learned racial hatred at home. Those short months filled me with self-doubt so profound that it would take years to understand and undo it. It wasn't just me. Some kids are given the opportunity to fail and start over. It's an opportunity that should be afforded to all. It wasn't to me. Structural challenges held me back, too.

.   .   .

THE SUMMER AFTER I graduated, Terrell and I were a month into one of our dramatic breakups. Terrell had refused to take me to my senior prom, a fight ensued, and we parted ways, not for the first time. I was hurt, lonely, and still couldn't see my own self-worth. A little while later, I went away with other teenagers from my church to an annual youth conference. The attire we were expected to be in was pretty conservative, even the casual wear, but I wore the kinds of outfits I was drawn to in those days: coochie-cutter shorts and tight-fitting tops. I wanted to announce myself. We were expected to carry ourselves as holy Christian girls. I wanted an escape from Terrell's mind games and an escape from the guilt I carried for disappointing myself and my parents when I failed to get any college scholarships. So I made my first stop in that town a local liquor store and grabbed a couple of six-packs of Zimas, the clear malt liquor coolers that were popular in those days, for me and my friends. At the conference, I met a boy a few years older than me whom I was attracted to. During the course of our flirtation, he asked on the phone if he could come to my room to talk. I agreed. The request didn't strike me as strange. At previous youth conferences, the other girls and I had had boys in our rooms, and we'd gone to boys' rooms. We'd turn on music, dance, and play cards. But we all were there for the purpose of getting what we needed from the Lord, and we knew our chaperones were serious about making sure everything stayed innocent.

He never showed. Three hours later, my friend and I had already gone to bed when I heard a knock at the door. I looked out the peephole and was surprised to see him standing there. I'd thought he'd stood me up, but there he was, asking if he could come in and talk. I answered the door and quietly told him he could come in, imagining that we would talk and laugh, like we had done over the phone. He walked in, and we sat on the bed together quietly. Before I could figure out what was happening, he was on top of me, messing with my clothes and not saying anything at all. My friend, a younger girl from church, was a few feet away, fast asleep in the next bed. I couldn't make sense of it.

"What is happening?" I thought. I didn't know what to do. I was frozen in shock, lying there as his weight pressed down upon me. Terrell had been my one and only. When we were together, we kissed one another. But now, with this boy, there was no kissing. There was no discussion. I wanted him to stop, but I was too scared and confused to make a sound and wake my friend. Finally, he stood up and pulled up his clothes. He wouldn't look me in the face, in my eyes. He didn't look at me at all; he just left. I was confused, I was embarrassed, I was ashamed. I wondered what I'd done wrong. Our initial conversation earlier that day was light and funny; there were no sexual innuendos. The next day at the conference, I saw him again. He barely spoke to me and acted as if nothing had ever happened.

Today I understand that what I experienced then was sexual assault. At the time, I didn't think of it that way. I thought I had miscommunicated. I assumed he had taken advantage of a young church girl who didn't know what she was doing. If I had been more experienced, if I had been older or smarter, I would have understood why this older guy had wanted to come to my room by himself and what he expected. Instead, I was naive, and this person took something I could never get back. Even though we were split up at the time and he had cheated on me on numerous occasions, I felt as if I had let Terrell down.

I've since learned enough about sexual violence to see that what happened on that church trip was a violation. I never gave my consent. There was no enthusiastic "yes," and there was no reciprocity. But back then we didn't talk about consent. We didn't describe all the ways that rape can look. I suffered, and I blamed myself.

Six weeks later, just before I was scheduled to start at Tuskegee, I found out I was pregnant.

. . .

I CALLED TERRELL FROM my bedroom at my parent's house in our finished basement. I closed the door and dialed his number. He paused for what felt like many long minutes. "Well, I don't want any more kids," he said. Then he told me to get an abortion.

I tried to explain to Terrell that that wasn't what I wanted. But he started yelling and repeating himself. I hung up the phone, sat on the bed, and stared at the royal blue carpet as tears rolled down my face. I believed that he was going to celebrate me, that he would rush off to tell all his friends. I'd thought we would have to figure out how we were going to raise this child together. I was his long-term girlfriend, after all—the person he claimed he loved and wanted.

Terrell kept calling me back after we hung up. "You're gonna do it, right?" he shouted each time I picked up. My parents, already disappointed that my college and scholarship plans hadn't panned out as we'd hoped, would now have to hear this news. I felt I had already let them down, and I didn't know how to tell them something that I expected would make them lose even more faith in me. A few days after telling Terrell, I approached my mom—cautiously. I was terrified, and as I spoke, I couldn't bring myself to look her in the eye. When I finished, she said simply, "You have to decide what kind of life you want." She never stopped moving, never stopped straightening up the living room, as she had been before I'd come upstairs from the basement.

Soon, I came to understand that it had been my encounter at the youth conference that resulted in this pregnancy. I turned to friends, who suggested that I tell the guy from the church trip. "He'll understand," they said, well meaning but naive. He'd want to know and help take care of the baby, they advised. I contacted him through a friend who, after relaying the message, told me my rapist's response. He laughed and denied that the baby was his at all. I was lost.

On a September day in 1994, my mother drove me to a reproductive health clinic to terminate the pregnancy. When we arrived for my consultation, I was given myriad reasons why it was probably best for me not to carry my pregnancy to term: The ultrasound had shown that the baby would be underweight and was likely to have developmental problems, I was told. I would have to be on Medicaid. I would be unable to give the child a good start in life. My own life chances would deteriorate. I had imagined that the clinic would offer me a safe and supportive environment, but I felt judged.

In the room where I was told to wait prior to the procedure, I sat alongside half a dozen white girls who had just gone through the same consultation I had, but apparently had had a completely different experience from mine. They talked among themselves, chatting about how comfortable the clinic's staffers had made them feel. One of the girls talked about how she hadn't been able to talk to her mom about what was going on, and the clinic staff had felt like the empathetic friend she needed. Others discussed how much help they had making their decisions. They were advised about the benefits of adoption, told how loved their babies would be by the families who took them in. This had not been mentioned as an option to me. I was treated differently, and I couldn't believe it. Still, I moved forward with the procedure that day.

Later that day, I told Terrell about my abortion. "I can't believe you would kill our baby," he said, completely contradicting everything he told me before. But it was okay, he said, because he had gotten someone else pregnant in the meantime. What could have been a tender moment where I leaned on him for support became just another ugly "gotcha" that went straight through my heart. I was crushed. Terrell, my love since I was twelve years old, believed I had been pregnant with his child, and his first instinct was to lash out and try to hurt me more than I'd hurt him. As was becoming my habit, I blamed myself. I'd gotten myself into this mess, and now I was paying for it.

I sank into a deep depression that followed me for nearly a year. I was numb. Nothing made me happy; nothing made me sad. I didn't care what people thought of me. I spent entire days at home, on my parents' couch or in my room. I would have continued to despair if my dad hadn't intervened to help me find a job. I started working retail, at a local hardware store and at a Dollar General. That's when I met Nate.

It was a gloomy but warm fall day. I was walking home from the bus stop after work at the hardware store, when I made a stop for an errand at North Oaks Plaza, and there he was with two of his friends in the parking lot. He stopped me, asked me for my number, and told me he was a football player. Nate was six feet four inches, dark-brown-skinned with a box haircut. He was four years my senior, and his maturity appealed to me. Even though the idea of dating or another relationship was the last thing on my mind, I agreed to exchange numbers.

Over the next few days, we began talking over the phone. We went to our first date at the movies. We didn't share much chemistry. But I liked having someone to talk to and worried that my ongoing depression was getting between Terrell and me. Nate would often pick me up from work, and we spent hours at his house. He lived at his mother's home in the basement. It was fully finished, set up like an apartment without the kitchen, and with a private entrance off to the side of the house. We dated for a couple weeks. It was nice to feel wanted by someone again, and I let myself believe that if I tried hard enough, I might begin to feel something more for Nate the more time I spent with him.

One day, he picked me up from work as usual to go to the movies. Instead, he drove me back to his house. At the time, I carried a white marble switchblade knife in my bra and an orange box cutter in the back pocket of my pants. I was tired of the harassment and the hurt I received, and I decided that I was going to be ready to fight back. As we entered the home, we met Nate's mom sitting in the kitchen. "Hi," she said dryly, without ever looking up. We continued down to the basement, Nate pulling my arms toward his bedroom. This time, I told him no.

I broke free from his grip and walked away, ready to leave. Nate grabbed me from behind, squeezing me and pressing my arms together. I tried to break free, but my struggles only helped him to get me down on the floor. I went for my bra the moment I could wrest an arm free. But he had his full weight on top of me on the floor and grabbed my switchblade. He cut open my shirt and elbowed me in the face. I felt the burning to my face and nose but reached for my box cutter. "Bitch, you think I'm going to let you leave?"

I was confused. We had slept together once before, and I had been willing. Why was he now trying to force it? I cried out as I tried to squirm my other arm free. I pulled the box cutter from the back pocket of my jeans. He started to cut the middle of my bra off, and I took that opportunity to try to slash at him and get him off me. But it was to no avail. He put his elbow to my throat, pulled the box cutter from me, and cut my jeans and panties open. He slid one knee between my legs to separate them, but as he did so, I realized that most of his body weight had shifted to my lower body.

I hit him in the nose and kneed him in the face, finally breaking free. I jumped up from the floor and ran for the door. He caught me and picked me up, threw me over the pool table that sat in the middle of his basement living room, to the other side. I landed on the top of my head. I was dazed but got up running. "Help!" I screamed, praying his mom could hear me. I couldn't understand why she hadn't yet intervened.

I made it up the stairs and looked to my right. His mom was sitting in the kitchen, exactly where she had been when we came in. She never turned her head to look at me, and I kept moving. I ran into the street, and I kept running in the dark. It wasn't until a few minutes passed that I realized that I had no idea where I was. Then I realized I was almost naked. I was holding my clothes in my hands. I panicked. How was this safer, I wondered, and how do I make it home? Just then, Nate pulled up beside me.

Through the car window, he apologized and begged me to get in the car. Initially, I refused, but I caved eventually. "Please just take me home," I begged. "I won't tell if you just take me straight home." He agreed. I climbed into the car. He took his right hand and placed it on my thigh. He molested me the whole ride home, while I wept. When we pulled up in front of my home, I jumped out of the car and ran into the house, holding my shirt and bra in one hand, and panties and pants in the other.

What do I do now? I thought. It was an election year. If I went to the police station, this might make the news and cost my dad his reelection. So, I crept in, quickly went downstairs to my room, took a shower, and for years I never told a soul.

. . .

I WENT THROUGH THE motions, but I was a shell of my former self. I wanted to disappear. I no longer cared what I looked like. I started wearing baggy, dark clothing. I took care of my hair only just enough to not have to hear from my dad about how unkempt I looked. I'd do my bangs and hide the rest under a hat and hope he wouldn't notice or say something. I stopped believing that I'd live past the age of twenty-one. I was numb.

The things that used to make me happy no longer did. I didn't go shopping with my mom and Kelli, or even talk to them. I didn't want to see them. I was ashamed. I felt out of control. I didn't have a handle on what my future would be. I was emotionally and spiritually empty.

The next summer, I was standing in a hotel lobby, away on another youth trip with my church. I had pulled myself together enough to put on my old, sexy uniform: those coochie-cutter booty shorts and a midriff top. I wore big dolphin earrings, two on each side. An older man approached me and told me to come with him. In my haze, I started walking, following him out the door.

Terrell's mother, who was regularly one of our chaperones on our trip, stopped us. "How dare you?" she yelled. "This is a child!" As he scurried away, she turned to me and said, "You've got to get yourself together. Right now, you are like the walking dead." With those words, she broke me right open. It was as if I had lost my soul, and she saw me, really saw me. I knew I needed to get on a path of healing that would bring me back to myself. I just didn't know how.

I wrote down what happened in that hotel lobby in the journal Terrell's mother had given me. Something pivotal had just happened to me.

.   .   .

OVER THE NEXT FEW weeks, I started to feel as if I would be able to get my life on the right track again. I started with my love of medicine. I researched paramedic programs. I figured, why not start there, and apply to nursing school later? But the programs were more expensive than I had anticipated. Now what?

"Think positive, keep going," I told myself. I started looking for jobs in telemarketing and customer service, where I could earn a little more money. I looked for an opening that offered daytime hours so that my commute on the bus home wouldn't have to be at night. I was unsuccessful.

Out walking one day in the neighborhood, I met Justin. He walked up to me on the street. "How you doin'? You got a man? Damn you fine, can I get your number?" He was cute, so I agreed. We agreed to go on a date to a movie. He picked me up from my home and, like Nate, drove us directly into a residential neighborhood. "I need to run back home because I left my wallet," he said. I worried that we might be late to the movies, but I was pleasantly surprised that we just met and he didn't mind me knowing where he lived. "Okay, but I don't want to miss the beginning of the movie," I said. "We'll make it," he replied.

He pulled up on the street in front of the house, jumped out, and started to jog across the front lawn. But before he made it to the house, he turned his head back in my direction and said, "Get out the car and come in real quick. I want you to meet my mom." What part of the game is this? I wondered. I might not have wanted to meet his mom, but it was still a sweet gesture, I thought. I reluctantly yelled back, "Okay."

I entered a nice, ranch-style home. This was a middle-class neighborhood. I expected his mom to be somewhere near the front door in the living room. She wasn't. Justin called out to me to come down the hallway to the left. I could tell there were bedrooms and probably a bathroom in that direction. I thought maybe his mom was there, in her own bedroom. I walked down the hallway and saw her room to the right. It was empty. On the left side of the hall was Justin's room. Justin was having trouble finding his wallet, he said. "Let's go, we're going to be late," I said nervously.

He was rifling through things on his dresser when he looked up at me and yelled, "Sit down!" I sat. What is he about to do to me? How could this be happening again? I stopped carrying the knives after Nate used them against me. Justin walked over, pulled his pants down, pushed me back on the bed, and climbed on top of me. He began pulling up my long, sleeveless, brown and burgundy wrap dress, while I looked around for anything to grab. I was not about to let him rape me. "Stop! Get off me!" I shouted. But Justin just looked at me as if he didn't hear a word I said. At first, he stared at me with a blank gaze, but it quickly morphed into a mischievous grin.

The more I fought, hitting and pushing at him, the more force he used against me. And now he was angry. He twisted my arms; he choked my neck and hit me in the face. While I ached, exhausted, he seemed to only be gaining in strength. When he realized I was getting weaker, I was emotionally spent, he forced himself inside me. I cried out in fear and pain. "Stop! You're hurting me, get off me!" I screamed. My heart was going to beat out of my chest. "Do anything, just kick his ass," I thought. And then I saw them.

My keys were on the bed; they were about a foot out of my reach. I stopped fighting Justin, and I stopped crying. I lay there motionless. Once he let his guard down a little, I moved quickly. I grabbed my keys and keyed the left side of Justin's face like a scorned lover keying a car. He jumped back off me and cupped his face in his hands. I hurried off the bed, grabbed my purse, and headed for the door and turned to him. "Fuck you!" And I ran out of the house.

Again, I was assaulted. And this time too, I never told anyone what happened. I was too ashamed and believed it was my fault. My wrap dress showed off the curves of my hips. I had willingly entered Justin's car. I went inside his home. Years later, I learned that Justin went to prison for the statutory rape of a fifteen-year-old girl. Justin was an adult. Why didn't I speak up? When I learned that he went to prison and why, I thought I could have prevented that girl, and any possible victims, from harm. If only I had gone to the police. I was devastated.

But in the days after Justin assaulted me, I couldn't speak much. Just as I was about to get back on my track, I receded once more, enveloped again by numbness. I didn't eat or sleep and lost weight quickly. One day, I looked in the mirror and decided I was going to be tougher. I was not about to let some guy break me again. Slowly, I cleaned myself up.

Weeks and months went by, and at nineteen years old I started to be able to feel again, and I wanted to feel more. Once again, my dad threw me a lifeline. He didn't know what exactly was wrong, but he knew I was struggling. He offered to pay for me to go to Harris-Stowe State University, a local HBCU in St. Louis. He was willing to make an early withdrawal from his 401(k) fund, just so I would avoid taking on debt and get back on the path we'd dreamed of together years earlier.

I jumped eagerly at his offer. I knew some people from Cardinal Ritter who were studying there, and I figured it was a start. If I worked hard and found my footing, I could transfer to my dream school out-of-state, like Tuskegee University for a fresh start.

I had my doubts. I wondered if I was well enough to take on the responsibility of school. Still, I had to try.

· · ·

I WANTED TO TRY again with love, too. I had known Craig for years. He and Terrell were from the same neighborhood and moved in the same circle of friends. Craig was light-skinned and about five feet nine with curly hair and a light mustache. He was always laughing, showing off his pretty white teeth. Craig didn't judge me, and at that point in my life I craved the kind of unconditional kindness he offered. Craig treated me as if I were special. He had a calm, easy demeanor and worked hard to make me happy. If he noticed that I was blue, he cracked jokes. If I mentioned that I wanted a snack, he would run to the corner store to buy me my favorite bag of chips.

After a while, Craig made it clear that he saw me as more than a friend. We started dating, and soon I became pregnant again. It was the fall of 1995, right around the time my father offered to help me go to Harris-Stowe. After I learned the news, I wrestled with my decision for weeks, unsure what to do. Craig was excited to have the baby. But if I kept the child, I would have to leave my parents' house. My mom had told me as much in the past. Craig lived at home, too, and I knew I wouldn't be able to live with his family either. We couldn't afford a place on our own. Neither one of us was on any real career path.

I knew many girls who had had children as teenagers, and I'd watched them struggle. They'd thought that the father would be there. My friend Tiffany was a few years older than me and had twins with Terrell's cousin, who spent time with his kids but didn't contribute enough to really help her financially. She worked a full-time job to pay her rent and all the bills. She kept her kids well cared for and clothed in the latest trends. But I saw how hard she worked to keep it all together. One day I was over while she called company after company, trying to find a price she could afford for her car insurance. She was the first person, other than my parents, whom I got to see keep a strict budget. She had no other choice.

That January, a year and a half after I graduated from high school, I started at Harris-Stowe. I was still unsure of whether I might do right by a baby. But being back in school felt right to me. I could feel my self-confidence returning. The university didn't offer the nursing classes I wanted to take, but it did offer a program in childhood development. I opted to major in that, and minor in business, so that I could one day open a day care. Heartened and encouraged, I made the dean's list.

By the time I made up my mind to have an abortion, I was twelve weeks pregnant and up against the cutoff after which I wouldn't be able to have the procedure. Again, I told my mother, and again, she drove me to that same reproductive health clinic. What happened once we arrived haunts me to this day.

I remember the questions that flooded my mind in those minutes before the abortion: I was further along this time, and what if something goes wrong? What if I am never able to get pregnant again? What if God punishes me for terminating these two pregnancies?

I walked into the white-walled room where the procedure was due to take place. A doctor and the nurse assisting him were there already, waiting for me. They instructed me to climb onto the bed. I lay down, as I was told. But I had reservations. And I heard a voice in my head grow louder. Did I really want to go through with this? As the nurse standing nearby started to explain what was about to happen, I interrupted. "I don't want to do this," I said. But she continued. She described to me, in detail, what the doctor was doing. I watched him prepare what looked like a long straw connected to tubing.

Again, I told her, "I don't want to do this." She never responded.

She grabbed my hand as the doctor had instructed her to. She told me to look up at a mural of a stained-glass window that was on the room's ceiling. I wasn't confident enough in those moments before the procedure started to realize that they didn't have the power to do anything against my will. It didn't occur to me that the choice was mine, whether to leave or stay. I felt the doctor snake the long straw inside me, and then I heard the awful sounds as the vacuum sucked the fetus out of my body.

I hadn't heard such a sound with the first abortion, but I assumed it was because I had had that procedure earlier in the pregnancy, at nine weeks. I remember the intense pain and the feeling of helplessness in that moment. I was furious. That doctor ignored my pleas. I was just another person in his assembly line, just another little Black girl. I lay there, wanting to scream. But I couldn't find my voice. They showed me no compassion. No one asked if I needed to take some time to think about what was happening. When the sucking and cracking sounds ceased, I knew it was over. I got up off the table and walked out of the room.

In the recovery room, my body throbbed with pain. A nurse came over, took her shoe off, and, with my consent, pressed her foot against my stomach. Immediately, the throbbing in my abdomen was relieved. I learned that this was a common practice used for uterine pain relief. She then offered what I'm sure she thought were words of comfort. "You're going to be fine," she told me. "It's done now." I nodded. I convinced myself that despite my last-minute change of heart this was for the best.

I know that many supporters of reproductive rights will be outraged by my decision to share this story. Antichoice activists will no doubt use my traumatic experience to try to strip abortion providers of their ability to serve our communities. Still, I am sharing what happened that day because my experience—like those of many people who seek reproductive health care—was complicated. I was silenced, my concerns ignored, and it is not lost on me that I was a young Black woman restrained by white medical providers.

They should be held accountable, but their lack of judgment should not be used to prevent other people from having the opportunity to choose what they need for their bodies at any given time. People will still seek out abortions regardless of the restrictions states place on their ability to access care. And if I was subjected to that kind of mistreatment in a medical environment with trained professionals and governed by requirements, imagine what can happen when women terminate their pregnancies in unregulated environments. We open the door to even more atrocities.

. . .

I HADN'T TOLD CRAIG that I was going to the clinic that day. I kept my initial resolve to myself, knowing that he would try to persuade me to keep the baby. When I finally confessed to him, he was broken. He was angry with me for making the decision I'd made. I was angry with him too. If he'd led a different lifestyle, if he was able to support a family, maybe I could have made a different choice. Our frustration and hurt drove us apart. We parted ways.

About a year or so later, Craig and I reconnected, and we started to spend time with each other again. Craig offered me safety. He had never raised a hand to me, and he treated me with such gentleness and kindness.

One day, I had the foreboding sense that I needed to reach out to Craig to see him. We played phone tag, and when I was finally able to contact him, I asked to see him. He wasn't free, but I pressed, insistent that he let me come pick him up. He told me he'd call me later, after he ran an errand he couldn't get out of.

That was the last time I spoke with Craig. The next day, my friend Tiffany called me at work. "Are you sitting down?" Tiffany asked when I picked up. "He's gone, Cori," she said. "I'm so sorry. He's gone." "Who's gone?" I asked, bracing myself. Craig had been murdered the night before as he accompanied another friend of his on a run. He'd been sitting in a car when he saw his friend, having just emerged from a nearby house, shot dead. The killers noticed Craig, then told him to get out of the car, kneel on the ground, and put his hands behind his head. They shot him in the back of the head.

I dropped the phone, and it dangled from its spiral cord before springing back up. I slid down the wall and looked out over my students' toys, the miniature chairs that surrounded their tables. I'd known that I was supposed to be with him the night before. I knew he needed me. I had to pull myself together enough to get back to the children. It was time to take them outside, to help them on the slides and push them on the swings. But I could barely stand up. I couldn't figure out how I was going to finish out the workday. I just wanted to go be with my friends and mourn Craig's life.

Craig was twenty years old when he was killed. I was twenty-one. At that point, it felt as if my friends were losing their lives one by one. Lil D, Keith, Cornell, Man, Jay, T, Marquis, Demetrius, Trey, Keyvon, Mike D, Raheem, Pretty Boy, were all shot and killed. Micki and Michelle overdosed. Often, my friends were still breathing but had lost their freedom. Isaiah, Rashad, Demarcus, went to jail for marijuana-related crimes and other nonviolent offenses.

We spent our days conscious of where the police might show up and how they might perceive and harass us if we crossed paths. Craig didn't die at the hands of the state, but he died aware that as a young Black man tomorrow wasn't promised. He knew he could be the next one caught up in the carceral net. As a young woman, I worried about my friends and boyfriends and wanted to protect them, both from police and from the intracommunity violence that surrounded us.

When Craig was killed, I felt that I'd failed him. If I hadn't had the abortion, we would've moved in together. I could have had the baby and saved Craig's life.

Chapter 3

I NEVER FINISHED COLLEGE. After one semester at Harris-Stowe State University, I dropped out. I couldn't bear to see my dad coming out of his pocket to pay for the next semester. He would've done it and he wanted to. But I knew where he was pulling that money from, and it broke my heart. I wasn't going to endanger his retirement for my sake. Instead, I took a full-time job over the summer, and I never went back. I was nineteen years old then. I couldn't work as many hours as I needed to pay for school, so I decided that I would put school on hold until I could figure out another way.

I was at Holly's Hair and Nails getting my hair done when I met Daphne Rice. Daphne and I were around the same age, and like me Daphne knew what it meant to have parents who were visible and widely respected in the St. Louis community. Her mother and father were co-pastors of Victory Christian Outreach Church. We were both church girls, and both had our share of fun and wild times. But we also knew that as members of our respective families we were scrutinized by others in the community. We had reputations to protect and expectations to live up to. We became fast friends, and it was Daphne who told me that her mother, Pastor Doris, ran a preschool called Lighthouse. And Lighthouse was hiring.

I knew this was an opportunity to work a job I loved. I was confident. My dad used to lead workshops at which he would teach young people how to apply for jobs, how to look professional. From him, I learned how to dress properly for an interview. But I didn't want to come off too stuffy, either. I wore a black dress with puffy shoulders and a floral pattern and a thin black patent-leather belt. I matched it with a black sun hat and black jellybean sandals with a bit of a heel. Miss Shirley, the assistant director and a longtime employee, complimented my outfit during our interview. I left her small office hired, with a start date and a starting rate.

During my first couple years at Lighthouse Preschool, I spent my days with toddlers, two- and three-year-olds, who were bursting with energy and brimming with honesty and humor. I adored them. With them, I learned how to be loving and nurturing while also offering the structure and discipline that they needed. I learned that they craved direction and instruction and that they liked repetition.

I decorated the classroom with the alphabet, colors, numbers 0 to 20, shapes, vowel sounds, and animals. I created a song that would take us on a journey every morning naming all the things on our walls. After the first couple weeks with my new class, I was able to hand off the pointer daily to a different student to lead us. The song started with "Good morning to you. Good morning to you, to A-a-apple. B-b-bell." It ended with the alphabet and numbers in Spanish. The kids liked knowing what came next and what I expected of them. From "how we start our day" to "this is how we clean up," or "how we line up to come back inside from recess." They even liked learning "this is how we wash our hands."

Parents would come up to me when they arrived to pick their children up from the center and tell me they wished their kids listened as well at home as they did to me at school. They would tell me their kids would often tell them, "That's not how Ms. Cori does it." As I grew more comfortable, I never had a problem putting the children down for nap time, which can frustrate some people. I was happy to be able to offer these parents tips on how to put their children to bed.

I had a knack for working with young people, and I took enormous joy and pride in it. I stayed at Lighthouse for a decade. Between two locations in St. Louis County where I worked, we served more than 150 families, mostly Black. Over time, I took on new roles there. I taught pre-K, and then I became program coordinator. Eventually, I became assistant director. I maintained staff records and made sure we adhered to government regulations. I managed the ledger and coordinated all the programs we put on, including concerts and graduations. I was responsible for the day-to-day operations of Lighthouse, overseeing staffing, upkeep, hiring, parent needs, and more.

Over the ten years I ended up working at Lighthouse, I was never paid much above minimum wage, $4.25 at the time. I started at $5.35 an hour. If my supervisor determined that I deserved a merit raise in any given year, they would increase my salary by five or ten cents each year. When I took over hiring for the center, I saw first-hand how offering so little narrowed our applicant pool. I remember hearing one of the owners, who we called Pastor Doris or Mrs. Rice, talk about wanting to increase salaries but how difficult it was to do. Balancing "more affordable" out-of-pocket rates for parents and not enough of a reimbursement from the state was challenging. We didn't always get people who wanted to work with kids. And I would often have to turn down qualified and trained professionals because they wanted more than we could pay. People walked in with a master's degree asking for $15.00 an hour, but I could offer only $9.00.

When I was nineteen years old, I didn't mind earning that little. I had just moved out of my parents' home for the first time. My father was disappointed that I left school, even if I did it out of care for him. He was a firm man. And he felt that anyone who lived in his house needed to follow his rules. Fortunately, my friend Carla was looking for two roommates to live with her in a three-bedroom home with a finished basement. This arrangement sounded like heaven to me. I pictured three single young women beginning our adult lives in a girls' pad, and I jumped at the chance. My portion of the rent was around $300 a month.

I had a home. I had an income. I also had a new man, and he would soon become the center of my world. It wasn't exactly the life I had envisioned for myself when I was in high school, but it was finally beginning, and I felt ready. I was going to greet it.

.　　.　　.

I MET DEVON OUTSIDE my family's church. People were ambling through, finding their seats in time for the sermon. I liked to sit out front, on the church steps, with some of my friends from the congregation, and I settled into my usual place. I'd seen DeVon around the neighborhood before. He would drive past and smile at me or holler, "Hey, cutie!" at me from a distance. On this August Sunday, he stopped to talk to me.

There he was: five foot ten inches and slender with brown skin and loose curls cut into a box and tapered down to a fade. He was walking past the church, on his way to a nearby corner store. He stopped in front of my friends and me, pulled a wad of money from his pocket, and looked at me. "I'll give you this whole stack if you walk with me to the store," he said. I hesitated, and he gestured at the store and tried to put me at ease. "Your people could still see you." I remember thinking that if he was giving it, I was taking it.

I had by that point taken on more of what has been called a gold digger mentality with men. I felt as if all they do is hurt you. They lie and make you fall for them, I thought; then they add more lies and cheat on you. So why not get something tangible out of it and keep my heart to myself? At that moment, however, I refused his money. I didn't want him to think I was too eager, but I did go with him. I liked his pretty white teeth and thought he was charming. That's how we got started.

From the very beginning, I knew how DeVon made his money. He never exposed me to the drugs or the transactions. He kept that part of his life carefully tucked away, away from me. Instead, he quickly brought me into what I believed was the rest of it. He introduced me to his friends and family. His grandmother lived a couple blocks from the church. My parents had also grown up around there and had gone to school with DeVon's. Our families knew of each other.

DeVon's childhood had not been as stable as mine. He had been told that his father killed himself while in prison. His mother, who was tall and light-skinned with loose, wavy hair like her son, was addicted to drugs. DeVon and his older brother had grown up taking care of themselves and their mom. When DeVon and I met, his brother had recently gotten out of prison and was trying to get back on his feet. Now the three of them lived together not far from my parents' home.

DeVon and I had fun together, and I was happy. Here was a guy who had some money and was always willing to spend it. He would do unexpected things to make me feel special. One time, before taking me on a date, he showed up with two brand-new Dooney & Bourke purses, one for me and one for my sister. I loved the surprises. I loved that he was going to the mall with me on his mind and that he was able to guess my sizes and what I might like. He was always spot on. I never had to return anything because it didn't fit or because I didn't like it. DeVon might have been trying to buy my affection, but it was sweet, and I enjoyed the attention he paid me.

For four months, life was okay. I lived with my friends, but the girls' pad was falling apart. Nobody was cooking. Nobody was cleaning. Little spats would break out between us increasingly as the weeks went on. So, DeVon and I decided that we would live together. We hadn't been together half a year, and I moved into the house he shared with his mother and brother. Then, suddenly, everything came apart.

· · ·

DEVON WAS CLINGY FROM the very beginning. I loved that he always wanted to cuddle and hold me, and I'd come to accept that he wanted to be with me twenty-four hours a day. If I went to the manicurist, he wanted to come. If I went to get my hair done, he was there with me. I loved that he wanted to spend so much time together. But I slowly started to see that clinginess in a new light.

One day, we squabbled over something relatively small. Maybe I hadn't called him back as quickly as he'd thought I should. I don't remember exactly. What I do remember is that I'd been away from the house. When I came home, I walked into the basement bedroom we shared, and I froze. Before me was not the usual scene— some stray articles of clothing strewn on the chair, my jewelry neatly arranged on the dresser, a book on the nightstand. Instead, I was looking at the remains of a bonfire in the middle of the floor. I stepped closer and saw it was a pile of my burned belongings.

While I'd been at work, DeVon had gathered everything I had at his house—clothes, shoes, purses, books—and he had set them on fire. I blinked several times. I could not believe what I was seeing. The pile was half my height and as wide as a full-sized bed. Items were charred, melted together. Nothing was salvageable. I only had left what was on my back.

Later, when DeVon was gone and I had a moment to myself, I called my friend Daphne and told her what had happened. She coached me and gave me the courage to retaliate in my own small way. I went to where I knew he kept his stash of drug money, rolls of bills secured with rubber bands, and took a little from each roll. If he was going to take what was mine, I was going to take at least a little of his.

The following day, I wore DeVon's clothes to work. His apologies came gushing. He swore to me that he would replace everything, and he soon made good on that promise. The day after he burned everything, he picked me up from work with five new outfits in shopping bags. Every day he added more clothes, shoes, accessories, and more.

I was young, and I believed that he loved me. Others might see manipulation and abuse, but I saw someone who was crazy about me, someone who would do anything for me.

Soon, disturbing revelations presented themselves to me. I saw DeVon's name and number pop up on my phone and answered to hear a woman on the end ask if I was his girlfriend. I told her that yes, I was, and she proceeded to tell me that she was his baby's mama and she was due any day.

Due any day? I was standing in the dimly lit basement by the bed looking at all of our belongings mingled together, and I felt duped. How could I be in this type of relationship with someone whom I spent so much time with, who didn't bother to tell me someone was carrying his child? I confronted him. DeVon's response was matter of fact. I was irrational for being alarmed. "That's my baby mama. I'm not with her. I'm with you." But this woman was a part of our lives. I didn't know how to break away from the relationship, because I cared for him, but I was angry.

After about a month living with DeVon's family, I rented us an apartment where we could live together, build our relationship. My dad had also bought me a burgundy 1996 Mercury Tracer as a gift and to help me commute to and from work at Lighthouse. On the days I worked, I let DeVon drop me off and pick me up for lunch and then again at the end of the day to take me home. I discovered that he was also picking up the woman pregnant with his child when I found articles of another woman's clothing on my backseat. I confronted him about it. He said he had to take her and the baby to a doctor's appointment. That's when everything changed.

That day marked the first time that DeVon put his hands on me. When we made it home to the apartment, our argument took a turn. DeVon lunged at me. He hit me and choked me. I didn't understand what was happening. We were fighting the way two men would, but the imbalance in our strength was inescapable. I couldn't defend myself against him the way I wanted to. He brutalized me, and eventually he stormed out, leaving me bloody and shaken.

I tried to wrap my mind around what happened, but in my body I felt tremors and panic. I felt pain. Some parts of my body stung and burned; others throbbed. I wondered if I had even really been hit in all of the places where I hurt, but I couldn't concentrate on anything long enough to figure it out. I stood in our living room, which we hadn't gotten around to furnishing. A few hours later DeVon returned.

He was wearing a soft smile, holding dinner in his arms. He apologized, his eyes down. He spoke of all the things he wanted to buy me. I wanted to believe he was sorry, but mostly I wished he would leave. Every subsequent time that he laid his hands on me, he'd leave and come back repentant and loving. I lived that cyclical reality. I survived his attacks. I thought I was able to take some space for myself, and think independently, during the times when he left. And I reconnected with him, only to go through it all again and again.

DeVon and I lived on the second floor in a four-family flat. We had neighbors next to us and below us, and sometimes one would overhear us fighting and call the police. "I'm sorry, Cori, but I can't just keep letting this happen to you," the neighbor across from us shouted through the door one night after she'd called 911. "I can't keep listening to this," she said. DeVon was always gone by the time the police arrived, and I would tell them everything was fine. My bruises were visible, and my friends and others in my life would look at me, sometimes, in horror. But no one ever tried to get between us. Perhaps they thought that I couldn't be saved until I was ready to save myself.

One day, I arrived at work after an early morning attack that left me bloodied and in rags. I had been ironing my clothes, preparing to get dressed for the day. DeVon walked up to where I stood, grabbed the iron, and poured the water inside it onto my head. I had just gotten my hair done, and he was determined to ruin the style. I yelled and tried to get away from him. He escalated. He broke a bottle of my green fingernail polish and threw it at me, dousing my hair and clothes in it. Then he took a box cutter and came at me with it. He sliced at me, cutting my shirt and my stomach beneath it. He didn't stop. He continued to assault me. He pulled me into my car and drove me to work, insistent that I go.

And I went. Just like that in a ripped maroon, green, and off-white Polo shirt, his jean shorts, and some three-inch white heels that were closest to my front door. My hair and clothes were a green mess, my shirt bloodied. Once in the car, he began to pinch me. He pinched me over and over so hard that he pinched off my skin. At the time, my godmother, Lynn, worked at Lighthouse alongside me, and when I walked in, she looked at me and said, "Your life doesn't have to be like this." I couldn't hear the wisdom in her words.

I went on with my day and took care of my kids. My colleagues looked at me with pity but said nothing. DeVon paged. He called my cell. I listened to his voice messages and shuddered. "I'm going to kill myself if you leave me," he said. "I'm slicing myself right now." "Tell me you're not leaving me," he told me, over and over. When I got off work, he picked me up as usual. I watched him pull up to the curb and wait for me. It was as if he had never said those words. I got in the car. I looked at him as he drove, and I felt pity for him. I let him drive us home.

I didn't need DeVon for his money. I earned my own income. In fact, I covered the $360 a month that we needed for rent, as well as our bills, and car insurance. He put bread on our table and bought me whatever my heart could desire. Leaving DeVon didn't cross my mind, but it wasn't because he showered me with expensive jewelry every time he put his hand to my face. That wasn't why I stayed. I stayed because I didn't know how to leave.

Eventually, I gained the courage to break free. The police had come to our apartment that night to intervene in one of our fights. DeVon left and stayed out all night. The next day we talked and decided to split. He came to the apartment while I was at work and moved out all of his things. I thought it was the end. Finally. I had started seeing someone else casually. His name was Cain. We would frequent the local park together on Sunday afternoons. One day while we were together, gunshots rang out. Instead of ducking or running or yelling for me to move, Cain grabbed me and shielded me with his body. I was drawn to him from that moment, and our new relationship blossomed for a happy month.

I didn't know that DeVon had been stalking me. He started appearing at Lighthouse during my shift, at the park, or at the mall when I might be out shopping with Kelli. On one such occasion, he saw me with Cain. That day, he showed up at my apartment unannounced, angry after seeing me in the presence of another man.

We broke out into one of our vicious arguments. We were screaming, and we fought. We wrestled with each other, until he pushed me onto the floor. He put his hands around my neck, while I clawed at him. He gripped me tighter and tighter, choking me until I could barely breathe and my body went limp. The scene around us fogged in my sight.

I looked up at him then, and I saw foam dripping from the creases of his mouth, his eyes bulging. He appeared to me then as he was, clearly. I didn't see my life flashing before my eyes. I saw that there was no love between us anymore. He was a devil. It must have been minutes that he held me with my neck in his hands, pressing into my flesh. He was a devil. That's the last thought I remember having. Then I passed out.

When I came to, DeVon was gone. He had left me there to die. I was weak and terrified of being alone. A long time must have gone by. I brought myself up and called Cain, who I knew could protect me if need be, and I called my sister. I told them what was going on and begged them to come over. They did, and Cain brought a relative of his about my sister's age, Deonte. In my very bones, I knew that DeVon would finish me off. If he came back and found that I was alive, he was going to kill me.

When they arrived, we changed the locks to the apartment and waited inside, praying that we'd be safe. My sister tended to me. And, sure enough, a few hours later, we heard footsteps. DeVon was back. We could hear him struggling with the door, trying to get it open any way he could. We stayed silent, but Cain paced back and forth in anger. DeVon banged on the door and shouted. We stayed silent. He quieted down, and then a few minutes later a window smashed and then another. He was waging an assault with rocks he must have picked up off the front lawns that lined our street. We sat there, as panes of glass exploded around us like fireworks, shards flying in the air, and he screamed and screamed. "Come outside," he yelled. He said he was going to take the license plates off my car to make sure I couldn't leave him. I yelled back. I wasn't coming. This time, I wasn't going to come.

I walked over to a broken window and watched him as he knelt down and carefully unscrewed all the bolts attaching my plates to my car. Then he took them in his hands, walked over to his car, and drove away.

I told Cain and my sister that I had to go after DeVon to get my plates. But I couldn't go alone. He was trying to lure me away from people who knew him and his temper, I knew. Cain pleaded with me not to go, but I insisted. I wasn't going to let DeVon win like that. Cain stormed out in protest, upset that I would be putting myself in danger, but my sister and Cain's cousin accompanied me.

Whatever happened, I knew I needed to stay in control. I grabbed a Sharpie, and I scrawled "plates stolen" on a piece of paper and taped it in my car's window. Deonte, my sister, and I piled into my Mercury Tracer and drove to the house that DeVon shared with his mother and brother. We found him there.

DeVon was quietly sitting in his Cadillac DeVille, out on the street in front of the house. It was as if he knew I would arrive for him. I pulled up and yelled at DeVon to give me my plates. He yelled back at me to come get them. I worried that if I got out and went over to his car, he might try to snatch me inside. But shouting had gotten me nowhere. I was going to ask him for my plates back even without shouting if that was what it was going to take. I parked the car, left my sister and Deonte to sit there, and approached DeVon from his passenger's side. I figured that he wouldn't be able to grab me into the car as easily from there. I was wrong.

As I approached, DeVon wore an ugly, mischievous grin. He reached toward the passenger's window with the plates in his hand. When I was near, I reached to grab them, and suddenly he dropped the plates and took hold of my arm, firmly and viciously. Through the window, he yanked me as far inside his DeVille as he could, and then he drove off.

My torso dangled out of the open window, my body whipped along as he sped through the streets. He pulled me in farther, and once DeVon was able to get me fully inside his car, he pulled my torso and head into his lap. He held me there and punched me and punched me as he drove. I struggled. I screamed. I scrambled frantically trying to get myself out of the car any way I could, but I couldn't.

When we stopped at red lights, people in nearby cars heard my screams. I could see them turn their heads and see DeVon pummeling me. They turned away. They didn't want to get involved. DeVon kept at me as he drove at frantic speeds on residential roads and then on the highway. We were on a multilane thoroughfare when I realized I needed to risk death to save myself from whatever he intended to do with me. I opened the door the first chance I had and tucked my body into a ball to roll out. But DeVon grabbed my legs. And he held on tight.

I could make out that there was an older woman driving in the next lane. She heard my screams and looked over at me as I flung the door open. She could tell what I was about to do, and yet again she turned her head. DeVon put his foot on the gas and took off again. The door was open, and half of my body was flying, flailing out of the car as he gripped me. My blood streaked the car. I couldn't stop hollering. I couldn't get away from him. He raced on to the street where he would try to break my will to live, or at least my will to live without him.

DeVon made sure to park in a deserted place where no one could watch as he tortured me. He pushed me beneath the steering wheel, trapping me in the small space between his legs. He held me captive in that makeshift cage for hours. He bit me. Repeatedly and fiercely, he pulled whole chunks of meat from my body with his teeth. He pinched me, using his fingers to tear at my flesh and rip into my skin. He stomped, kicked, and punched my body. He choked me. He used his hands and his mouth to degrade me. "How could you do this to me? Who was that at your house?" DeVon demanded, yelling with an uncontrollable rage as he beat me into submission. "You don't really love me. You, my mama, how could you do this to me?"

In that moment, one of the most desperate of my entire life, while fighting with every inch of my body to survive, I reflected that it had always struck me as strange that he called me Mama. His own I knew was an addict. She hadn't shown him much nurturing throughout his young life. His father had been found dead years ago, in prison. DeVon had lived through more trauma than his nineteen years could hold, and here he was taking out his pain by inflicting it on me, his "mama."

For four hours, I screamed and cried. I was dizzy from pain and lack of oxygen. I prayed and prayed that someone might come to my rescue. Then I heard a voice in my head, clear as a bell. "Tell him you'll get back with him," the voice said. "Okay, okay," I eventually sputtered out, tears and blood crusting on my face. "We can get back together," I told him.

Then, like magic, it was over. He pulled me up from under the steering wheel, pushed me into the passenger's seat, and drove me back to his house, where my car was waiting for me.

·   ·   ·

MY SISTER AND DEONTE, just thirteen or fourteen at the time, were waiting there for me. They were too young to drive away themselves, and they didn't know what else to do but stay put. As we neared, before DeVon even brought his Cadillac to a full stop, I jumped out, and I started running.

That morning, I had started the day in a white shirt and shorts set. That set was now completely soaked through with my blood. DeVon peeled off as I climbed into my own car and what I felt was safety. I wasn't sure what to do. Should I go home? To the hospital? The three of us pulled onto I-70 eastbound. I breathed a small sigh of relief, still trembling, but it was too soon.

Someone rammed their car into ours from behind. It was DeVon. He must have parked nearby and patiently waited to follow. I kept driving and sped up, but he followed close behind, hitting us repeatedly—over and over. I switched lanes. DeVon did too. He rammed us from the side. He knocked us into the median, but still I kept driving. The whole time, my sister was screaming. She was looking out the passenger's side mirror and screaming. Deonte was cursing. He kept yelling instructions out to me as he watched DeVon's movements: "Go faster." "Swerve left." "Go."

But the faster I went, the more DeVon sped after me. I thought I had broken free, but here I was again, hours later, out of control, pursued by someone who wanted something from me that I couldn't quite name. I took an exit that I knew would lead me to a neighborhood where I felt safe, a place where I knew the guys likely to be outside, including Cain. I hoped they would have my back and do what they could to run DeVon off.

As we pulled onto a street I had in mind, DeVon rammed us again. I was driving the block in circles. The noise brought a crowd. About a dozen people ran out of their homes, screaming and cursing as he barreled toward us. Gunshots rang out behind us. I kept driving. I made it to the corner while DeVon, being shot at, finally stopped the car.

I made Kelli and Deonte get out of the car, and I told them to run, fast. DeVon wanted me, so if I was going to die, I didn't want them hurt too. I drove back in the other direction to lure DeVon away from them and give them time to make it to safety. I could see Cain and the neighborhood guys chasing DeVon's car on foot as he chased mine. He caught up with me yet again, pounded my car so hard with his that there were only three wheels left touching the ground.

I thought that I had reached my end. DeVon had caught me now, and my life was going to be over. But the guys kept running and kept shooting at DeVon's Cadillac, until, finally, he drove off—away from me, away from the neighborhood, and away from my sister and Deonte.

Cain walked over to where I sat in the idling car, and after determining that I was alive, if barely, he made it clear that he was upset. What had I brought to his home? Then he left. Kelli ran over to me. I was overjoyed that she was okay and unharmed. Tears streamed down my face.

By this time, a large crowd had gathered outside, and people walked up to me to see if I needed help. I remember viscerally the look that each one of them had in their eyes. "I can't believe she survived," they all seemed to be thinking.

They surrounded me, assessing the damage. Someone else I knew lived close by. I pulled myself out of the driver's seat, and I couldn't believe my eyes. The car that my dad bought me just six months prior was a wreck. It was nearly totaled. It was barely standing on the three remaining wheels, and the fourth was tilted up half a foot from the ground. The entire driver's side of the car was smashed. I could barely breathe.

I was standing bruised and bloody in front of people who watched my horror scene play out. They knew my secret. I was ashamed. I was ashamed I was in a situation where someone had so much control over me. I was ashamed at how weak I was and looked. I had to get away.

I stumbled toward my friend Kenyatta's sister's house. Kelli and I knocked on her door. She opened it, took one look at me, blood soaked and breathless, and said immediately, "I'm calling the ambulance."

In that brief moment, I was slightly comforted that she didn't slam the door in my face or ask me to tell her what happened. She chose to help. Eventually, I muttered out an explanation in between gasps. I don't remember what I told her, but the message got across. The moment the EMTs finished dressing my wounds and the police made a report, Kelli and I took a cab to the court building to file a restraining order against DeVon.

.   .   .

I WISH I COULD say that was the last time I saw DeVon. I wish I could say that I never heard from him again, that I never talked to him again. But I did.

DeVon and I separated for just a few days, but even then we were in contact. He called me day and night. If he couldn't reach me, he called Kelli.

When DeVon learned that he would be prosecuted and potentially do time for what he'd done to me, he started calling me with greater frequency. He told me he was going to kill himself. After many calls apologizing, he showed up at my apartment. I felt sorry for him. Tears streamed down his face, and he looked visibly afraid. I let him inside, and he stayed the night. The next morning, a detective contacted me, asking if I was going to press charges and testify against DeVon. I told him no. I refused.

Part of me was afraid of what would happen to me or my family if I did press charges. What if I agreed to testify, and he didn't go to jail right away? The other part of me couldn't stand the thought of being the reason that someone went to prison. I refused to participate in causing that type of harm to a person. Even after everything, I felt compassion for him. I knew him so well, and I knew that he himself suffered, even as he made me suffer. But my plans made little difference. The state was going to decide whether it was going to make a case against him, with or without me, the detective said.

DeVon asked and I agreed to go to the courthouse with him for his hearing. A few days later, as we walked toward the courtroom together, a man I hadn't seen before, in standard business attire, stopped us just before we could enter the room. He asked our names. DeVon gave his, and the man looked down at his list and motioned as if he were checking a box. When I said mine, the man's eyes grew big. He looked at me as if he were seeing a ghost. He turned pale as his white button-down shirt. I felt ashamed—naive and foolish in that moment. I felt as if I had let this perfect stranger down. He motioned to a detective who asked to speak with me separately. He was the first to ask why I was at the hearing if I wasn't going to press charges. I kept my mouth closed. Are you here with DeVon, he asked, did he force you to come? Are you afraid of him? The questions kept coming.

Meanwhile, I had received notice that I was being evicted from the apartment we used to share. My landlord cited property damage, noise disturbances, and the multiple calls to the police made by our neighbors. I packed up my belongings, and I moved back to my dad's house to try to move on with my life. The case proceeded, even without my testimony, but that would be the last I heard about it for a long time. DeVon would eventually go to prison for his crimes. But in the many months before then, I went back.

DeVon reached out. He called. He showed up at my job. He showed up at the mall while my sister and I were there. He promised he was going to change. He didn't try to hurt me. He just appeared wherever I happened to be, and he was sweet the way he had been when we first met. Kelli started calling him "the stalker." He helped out, carrying our groceries, buying us meals before going on his way. Eventually, he sweet-talked his way back to me. We got together again. We got another apartment. This time he found it, and he insisted on putting his name on the place. It was a little one-bedroom, one-bath apartment with an all-white kitchen in an old building located in the Central West End above an Italian restaurant. We lived on the third floor.

Our first night in our new place together, after we'd moved our things in, DeVon gestured at a low cabinet in the kitchen and told me to open it. I bent down to do so and saw a gun lying in it on its side. "That's for your father if you ever try to leave me," he said. And I believed him. I felt stupid. He'd been relentless, doing everything he possibly could to convince me that he'd changed and that our lives would be different. I also felt trapped.

I was scared of what he would do to me if he became upset, and I had no idea what might trigger him. I walked on eggshells. That gun in the cabinet wasn't the only gun in our home. At night, DeVon made us sleep with a gun in the space between our pillows. Our little bedroom was so small our bed had to be pushed against a wall to fit, and I slept flush against it. Each night, I lay there, trapped between that wall and DeVon's body.

If I climbed out of bed in the middle of the night to use the bathroom, I would come back to find him sitting on the edge of the bed, the gun in his hand, waiting for me, and ready to pounce in case I'd try and leave.

One day, we argued, and I did try to run. I ran out the back door of the apartment, I ran down the steps, and I ran across the parking lot in the back of our building. He was running behind me, but I had a good start ahead of him. I kept running straight, without looking back at him. Then I heard the pop-pop of gunfire. It didn't cross my mind that somebody could be shooting at me. It was only when I heard a bullet whiz past my ear, and then another, that I realized. Somehow unscathed, I figured I would make a sudden dart to my left down an alley heading to a nearby grocery. I had escaped, I thought. I won! I got away!

But my doubts crept back immediately. Had DeVon let me get away? I walked around the grocery store that day, and then the rest of the shopping center that enclosed it, trying to figure out whom to call. I was ashamed, and so many of my loved ones were already disappointed in me for getting involved with DeVon again. How could I call them for help now? And, most important, what would happen to my father if I left? A few hours later, I went back. I believed DeVon. I believed him when he said he was going to kill my dad, and I wasn't going to let that happen.

My father and I weren't in close contact at the time. He had been heartbroken that I decided to get back together with DeVon. From the moment I started dating him, my dad had told me, over and over, that DeVon and I weren't on the same level. "This man is going to dumb you down, Cori," he said. I hadn't listened then, but now I could see that he was right. I wasn't the same person I'd been before I met DeVon. I could barely articulate myself the same way. That vocabulary I'd been so proud of building as a child faded away. Then, beyond just the difference in our life trajectories, my father had knowledge and proof of DeVon's abuse. He couldn't understand why I would leave the safety of my family's home and go back to him after having barely escaped with my life so recently. He, like the rest of my family, feared for my life. They didn't want to see me hurt again, and I felt I couldn't endanger them by sharing what was happening with them or calling them for help.

DeVon made sure he was around to watch me, and the only time he allowed any distance between us was when I clocked in for work at Lighthouse. I was working long hours, and the strain of my life with DeVon was wearing on me. Now back with him, the violence he meted out to me was happening with an increasing frequency. The smallest thing would set him off.

One day, while we were sitting in his car listening to music in front of his grandmother's house, his friend came up to us by the passenger's side door. He popped his head in the car to say what's up and then left. But as soon as Dre walked away, a slap came so hard across my face I was dazed. My face was on fire, my nose bleeding. I wondered what prompted his anger. I cupped my face in my hands, hoping that another hit wasn't going to follow. I had smiled too hard at Dre, DeVon said, and I looked like a "ho." I didn't know what he was talking about. I was only being nice. DeVon lunged at me from the driver's seat and began to hit, bite, and pinch me.

I fought back as much as I could, but DeVon was stronger. I leaped and hurried out of the car, and I took off running down the street. I knew someone would be at my family church just up the street. It was Saturday morning, and people must have gathered for choir and usher rehearsals. If only I could make it inside the church doors, I thought, he wouldn't dare step inside. "Help me!" I shouted as I ran up to the side door to the church. Someone was standing there at the door, watching me as I ran toward him. He slowly shook his head and closed the curtain, locking the door behind him. I stopped running, shocked.

This was my church, and everyone here knew me. I was bleeding and screaming and they turned me away. Seconds later, DeVon was standing over my shoulder. He wasn't angry anymore. He was happy I didn't get away. A different time, I ran to the church for help again, and was turned away again. I decided I would never go back to my church for help again.

Every day, I felt exhaustion sink deep in my bones. Finally, I couldn't take it anymore. I couldn't keep going. I took a chance— I called my dad. When he answered, I couldn't speak. I didn't say a word. Silence grew between us as the minutes dragged. "Cori," he said finally. But I still couldn't speak. I was trying so hard not to cry. I knew that the moment I opened my mouth, sobs would rush out of me. But my dad knew. "Pack your stuff," he said. "Only take what you have to have." We made a plan for that upcoming weekend, and I had to quickly figure out how I was going to convince DeVon to let me be alone that day.

I went home and told DeVon that my dad would be over Saturday morning to have breakfast with us. "You two need to have a talk, hash some things out," I told him, knowing full well that DeVon would never go for that. He agreed. But on the morning of, sure enough, he made himself scarce. "I've got some runs to make. I'll be back," he said, before darting out of the house and hopping onto a city bus. I watched him leave; then I quickly gathered my clothes and a few other items I'd hidden around the apartment. I threw what I could in two trash bags, and then I tossed the bags over the railing the moment I saw my dad pull up in his black minivan, just as we'd planned. He threw the bags in the van while I ran down the steps.

Seconds away from my freedom, I kept thinking, "One foot in front of the other. Just keep going." When I got in the van, I shut the door and locked it, and I knew it was over. I wanted to cry, to sob in my dad's arms, but I didn't make a sound. My dad, one hand on the steering wheel, reached over and placed his other hand on my shoulder. "You're okay now, baby. Daddy's got you, you're okay," he said. Finally, my mind felt at peace. Daddy's got me.

That was how it ended. That was how I got away. DeVon didn't make good on his threat, though he continued to stalk and tail me. It took another man coming into my life for DeVon finally to leave me alone.

.   .   .

A YEAR AND A half after I met DeVon in front of my family's church, I met my future husband in the very same place. My life had started to look different. It was better. I recommitted myself to God, and I moved out of my dad's house into my own apartment. I was finally living independently. I spent much of my time when not working studying God's Word, learning about Jesus, listening to sermons from preachers like Juanita Bynum, T. D. Jakes, Sheryl Brady, and Clarence McClendon. I traded my Tupac, Eazy-E, and Master P No Limit CDs for gospel. Fred Hammond, Greg O'Quin, Yolanda Adams, Kirk Franklin, Walter Hawkins, John P. Kee, Tramaine Hawkins, Milton Brunson, Commissioned, Richard Smallwood, BeBe & CeCe Winans, Hezekiah Walker, and others streamed from my stereo speakers.

My friend Daphne helped prompt this transition. She'd listened to Juanita Bynum's *No More Sheets* sermon while at a hair salon one day and was moved by the way Bynum talked about sex, love, addiction. Bynum called for women to dig deep inside themselves to find their self-respect. Daphne recognized the significance that Bynum's words held for our lives and shared the tape with me. I too wanted to be and do better.

For years, Daphne's mom, our own pastor Doris, had been telling Daphne and me that the way we'd been living our lives was beneath what God wanted for us. "Dumb girl," she'd say to me, "you're just acting like some hussy out in the streets." There was humor, deep care, and concern in her words whenever she'd call Daphne and me "professional hussies." I felt that there had been some truth in her attempts to shame us into doing better and finding a better life for ourselves. I, for one, was finally ready to try something new.

I was going to church services every week with my dad. The youth conferences I attended as a teenager were usually coordinated with our nearby sister church, which was now sharing our building. The faith leader of those services rented space from our church to hold services. His nephew Hakim, who was my age, would come to hear his uncle preach, but he often arrived hours early. My church's services were before his uncle's. During service, Hakim tried everything he could to get my attention. I would look up to find him staring at me. He enlisted his cousin, whom I knew well, to introduce us. That same cousin told me that he'd never seen Hakim so interested in a woman before. Despite his persistent efforts to get my attention, I wasn't interested. But Hakim was relentless.

He asked around, and soon his other family members who were connected to the church were approaching me to advocate on his behalf. I was the reason he kept coming back to church, that he was turning his life around, they told me. I should give him a chance, they said, he was a good guy. Over time, I started to like the attention. But what I liked most about Hakim was the effect he had on DeVon.

One day, I was leaving service with Hakim when DeVon drove by the church. I saw him and watched as he looked at Hakim and me walking down the sidewalk together. My mind raced. How will DeVon react? I could see his expression through the front windshield as he came toward us. He was wearing that same mischievous grin I had grown so accustomed to. I pointed out the car to Hakim. DeVon was revving the car engine. He was coming closer, faster, and straight for us.

We ran across neighboring front yards to stay clear of DeVon's car. But he jumped the sidewalk. DeVon tried to run us over. But once it was clear I was safely out of the way in the grass by someone's porch, Hakim turned around and ran toward DeVon's car, shouting and threatening him. DeVon peeled off. He had been scared. Did I just witness the man who had terrorized me so many times drive off because he was afraid of another man on foot?

I saw Hakim in a new light. If Hakim could keep DeVon away, I thought, then he could help keep me safe and take care of me. After years of the pain and trauma that was inflicted on me by romantic partners—whether through cheating, verbal and physical abuse, or sexual assault—I desperately longed to feel safe. I badly wanted to believe that I could find a partner who would safeguard me from any threat that came my way. It didn't occur to me that my rescuer, the man who protected me from the violence of others, could also harm me. I stayed with Hakim.

·　　·　　·

HAKIM AND I WERE compatible enough. I looked past much of what I really wanted in a partner and tried to tell myself that I needed the stability and safety he offered me more. I wanted to settle down, but I didn't want to "shack up." I didn't want to be having casual sex with someone only for the relationship to fizzle out. And, from the start, Hakim was serious. He wanted me to meet his family and friends. He took me around, introducing me. I didn't think he was playing games or that there were other women hidden away somewhere. Hakim was looking for a committed relationship too, and I loved that about him.

We moved in together within a couple months after meeting. Neither one of us had a car. Mine had been totaled out by the insurance company after DeVon decimated it. We were commuting across town to see each other by bus or in cabs. I had just signed a new lease, and Hakim's was near its end, so we decided that he would come to live with me.

It was a relief to have another person around to help with the stresses of everyday life. I thought we were making progress, being mature. I needed to share my life with someone, or so I thought. I craved a peaceful, quiet life with shared responsibilities and mutual respect. And with Hakim, I thought I might finally find it.

But there were certain things I noticed once we moved in together that I didn't like. Hakim had a habit of raising his voice, cussing, and snapping his fingers loud and hard in my face to punctuate his demands when things didn't go his way. This happened during small disagreements over dinner. I decided to make light of it, to live with it, to see if the good would outweigh the bad.

After a few months of living together, however, I found that our life wasn't especially peaceful or respectful. I wondered if I was being sensitive. Perhaps I was too traumatized by my past. Hakim wanted us to be a family and I also wanted a family, the stability it offered. For the Fourth of July that year, Hakim and I visited Fair St. Louis, which until 1992 had been known as the VP, or the Veiled Prophet Parade and Ball.

As native St. Louisans, we knew the racist history of the Veiled Prophet. Since 1878, a veiled man in robes and gloves had been at the center of a celebration of the city's captains of industry. Looking eerily like a Klansman, the Veiled Prophet chooses a young woman to accompany him, a daughter from a local elite family. Each year, girls vied to be crowned the "Queen of Love and Beauty," giving the whole affair the air of a white supremacist debutante ball. Those at the center of the VP Fair have historically been white and powerful, and this is by design. The Fair dates back to 1877, when the city's ruling class crushed a workers' rebellion, a mass strike, that for a period of time brought together Black and white laborers who demanded fair pay and humane working conditions.

By the time Hakim and I were attending, some of the racist and classist sheen had faded away, and Fair St. Louis was an annual four-day celebration commemorating the holiday with food vendors, activities, concerts with big-name musical artists, an air show, and a majestic nightly fireworks display. The fair was held on the grounds surrounding the Gateway Arch. We were among thousands of other people, sitting on our blankets together, looking out over the Mississippi River as the sky lit up with fireworks bursting over the arch. A few in the shape of red hearts exploded over us, and I turned to Hakim to comment on how pretty they were and how strange it was to see hearts on the Fourth of July.

As I turned his way, I saw him sitting there, with his arm outstretched, an engagement ring in his hand. I didn't really hear what he was saying, but I got the gist. Surprised and giddy that he'd planned such a moment for us, I said, "Yes," just as the rapid, thunderous booms of the fireworks crescendoed into a finale. A crowd gathered around us on the banks of the Mississippi that evening and erupted in applause. People hugged us, congratulating us on our happy union. Hakim's friends high-fived him. Just a few weeks before my twenty-third birthday, I was engaged.

.   .   .

HAKIM AND I WERE eager, excited at the prospect of getting married, but our families were less so. Hakim had had a difficult upbringing. His parents spent bouts in and out of prison. And as a result, housing and food insecurity punctuated his childhood. His parents had needed help, an advocate, or humane policy—not prison. Periodically, Hakim lived out of vacant buildings. His family rifled through dumpsters behind restaurants in search of food. They dealt with the trauma that this instability caused the best they could. And they remained a tight-knit and loving family.

When I entered the picture, I was not welcomed with that same love. While in an argument once, Hakim remarked, disparagingly, that my family was like the one in *Leave It to Beaver.* His mother wanted to know, "How could you marry someone so bougie, so high seditty?" Meanwhile, my sister told me, as she had before, that I picked up stray dogs, that I was trying to rehabilitate men by dating them.

And my parents loathed Hakim. They met him for the first time two months after we started seeing each other. My dad was hosting a campaign event at our local bowling alley. His stature in politics and activism was growing. Around that time, my dad had been among the hundreds of protesters who linked arms across Interstate 70 and shut down the highway during morning rush hour, all in an effort to get more highway construction contracts and jobs for Black workers. He faced down the stopped traffic, was yelled at by commuters who couldn't abide him, and with the other demonstrators, he put his body on the line in the name of economic justice. He and more than 120 other protesters were arrested, including Rev. Al Sharpton and other local elected officials and civil rights leaders. It worked. They were able to get some Black St. Louisans employed.

That night at the bowling alley, the venue filled with his friends, family members, local elected officials, and supporters. I'll never forget what happened when Hakim arrived. I had been looking forward to introducing him to my parents for weeks. Finally, I was with someone whom they would approve of, I thought. I was standing just outside the room where the party was underway when I looked up and saw Hakim walking toward me. My excitement and eagerness quickly turned into panic. Hakim was wearing a thin, white tank undershirt with his chest out, a gray Members Only jacket left open, jeans, and Jordans. I was mortified.

Why would Hakim wear a tank when he knew he was going to

meet my parents for the first time? My head was spinning. But I put on a smile and prayed that no one would mind his clothing. They did. As I introduced Hakim, I could see the revulsion in the faces of my parents and their friends. I had done it again. I disappointed them. They exchanged pleasantries kindly and briefly, and they didn't meet again over the next few months. When my mom and dad found out about our engagement, they asked me, "Why would you marry a man who has kids and no real future?"

Hakim had five children. Four of them were with a woman he'd been living with in the years before we met, and one from another relationship he had before that. My parents might have been mortified, but I didn't think the kids were necessarily a bad thing. I liked kids, and we would still be able to build a new family of our own, I thought. And I was touched, and heartened, that over the weeks that we'd spent dating, Hakim changed.

When we became serious, Hakim took jobs working minimum wage at factories, warehouses, and restaurants. He stopped smoking weed when I asked him to do so. I was working on cleaning myself up, and Hakim was on a similar journey. We were trying to work it out as best we could, one day at a time. But I was firm. I knew that slipping backward could be a death sentence. I demanded that Hakim stop drinking, and I warned him that I wouldn't marry him unless he did. I myself had given up alcohol recently, after hitting rock bottom.

A few months earlier, just before I was about to turn twenty-two, DeVon was still stalking me, and I was sleeping on an air mattress in my friend Kenyatta's living room for a little while over the summer. Just to get to work at Lighthouse, I needed to catch three buses each way. My mom and sister left to visit family out of state for a while. I felt alone, and I turned to alcohol. So many of my friends and peers had, so why not me? I thought. I drank Crown Royal, E&J VSOP, Courvoisier, and Seagram's gin, no chaser needed.

For my birthday that year, my friend and co-worker Tina and

her husband, Mike, offered to take me out for a drink. We went to a local lounge in St. Louis that had some of the best fish and chicken wings around. I was recently liberated from my relationship with DeVon and felt I had finally figured out what freedom looked like. I wore a see-through all-red lace dress and five-inch red heels. Tina told the DJ it was my birthday, and our table filled with drinks. I danced for a while with men at least ten years my senior and then decided to take on the bounty of alcohol waiting for me back at our table.

After sharing several mixed drinks with Tina and Mike, I was drunk. I had never been drunk like this before, and my memory of what happened next is hazy. I remember hearing Tina announce that we should head home. Then in the parking lot, a man picked me up off the ground and carried me just a few feet to his car. Tina and Mike yelled and ran to him, grabbing me from his arms. They helped me safely into their own car and took me home. Mike helped me up the two flights of stairs to the apartment and then laid me down on the air mattress. The next morning, I woke up completely naked, my head throbbing and spinning. I realized someone had tried to kidnap me. That day, I resolved that I was done with alcohol.

I told Hakim early that I wasn't going to date someone who drank or smoked. He understood, and I wanted to give him a chance. He had been trying to quit, he told me. I reminded him later of how I felt, given that we were about to be wed. Though he gave up weed to be with me, I was still on the fence. Ultimately, I postponed the wedding. His aunt Diane had given me the idea. Her husband, the pastor who preached at our church, offered us marriage counseling sessions and help with coordinating our wedding. She was over one day to talk to me about our plans and she noticed the beer cans that littered our apartment. From the look of sadness and worry in my face, she gave me some sage advice. "You need a husband to take care of you and his family. Tell him you will postpone the wedding if he doesn't stop. See that he puts your family first."

I gave Hakim the ultimatum and told him the wedding was post-poned when he refused. But I played myself, really. I never canceled our venue or caterer. I never told my family, bridesmaids, or guests that we were putting off the date. I didn't even mention it to Kelli. A week went by, and Hakim came to me and pledged he was done drinking. He wanted the wedding. Deep down I was skeptical. I knew he was telling me what he felt. I knew also that this would be a hard process for him. So, I called Diane, told her the news, and we proceeded with the counseling her husband facilitated. Mostly he taught from the Bible and asked us questions. One day he said to Hakim, "If you go back to who you used to be, she's not going to love you anymore." I wondered why he would say such a thing.

Hakim and I were married on November 6, 1999, at my family's church. It was a beautiful day, sunny with a high of seventy-eight degrees. I had painstakingly agonized over our wedding, and all had gone according to plan. I took the smooth course of things as an omen, a sign that I was making the right decision by moving for-ward with my life with Hakim. My dad even offered to hire a pho-tographer for us. "Never be alone again, Cori," I told myself, "build a family."

As I dressed in one of the nurses' rooms of the church, I thought back to a call I had received from Terrell, a few days prior. "You don't have to do this," he had said. "All you have to do is say one word to let me know Cori, and we can get back together." I told Terrell no, that I wanted to do this. I needed him to know I was no longer under his thumb. I no longer had feelings for him, even though he had changed his life, and was no longer the person he was when we were together. He didn't try to stop me again. Another sign, I told myself.

I looked at myself in the mirror, wearing a white beaded lace ball gown. The dress itself was a miracle. Our budget for the wedding was quite low, and I planned to buy myself a $99 gown from a bridal shop, or catch one at a thrift store. About six weeks before the wed-ding, a prophetess from New York came to speak at our church. She called me out during the service that day and in front of the entire congregation announced that I needed to quit shacking up, get married, and get right with the Lord. I felt humiliated and ashamed. Was God that angry with me?

A couple weeks later Diane received a package in the mail from that prophetess. Inside was a cake knife and server set and a wedding dress. Aunt Diane told me that the prophetess found the dress at a thrift store and knew it was for me. The dress fit me perfectly. As I gazed in the mirror, I thought about my stylist's words as she draped my hair into a bow. "Today you are a gift," she said. My veil was white, as were my heels. Our wedding colors were ivory and gold. It was time.

As the doors of the sanctuary were opened by the ushers before me, I took my first look at how it all turned out. Tulle bows with ivory flowers brightened the ends of the benches; gold candelabras with ivory candles stretched across the front of the room. The flames from all the candles created the perfect lighting for romance. My eight bridesmaids wore gold satin floor-length dresses with sashes, hair in updos. The groomsmen wore ivory tuxedos with matching gold, ivory, and black bow ties and cummerbunds. There were junior bridesmaids, flower girls, and a ring bearer.

As I turned and looked up at my dad, I saw that his face was sad. My father was quite unsettled at the mere thought of my wedding. How he cried as he walked me down the aisle, gently pulling me toward the exit and away from where Hakim stood waiting. During the ceremony, the preacher asked, "Who gives this woman away?" My daddy didn't say a word. He held me tighter. My mother stood and offered her blessing instead. Hakim's mother had made her discontentment heard as she stumbled down the aisle. I was later informed that she might have had a drink or two beforehand.

I was determined to have a sober celebration and forbade any alcohol at our reception. But as the evening went on, I began to notice drinks appearing, here and there. I looked over, and Hakim's friends were drinking straight from bottles on the dance floor. I was livid. I had seen Hakim's people get drunk and fight enough times to know what was in store for us.

I went to find Hakim. He was sitting outside the venue talking to his cousin with an open bottle in his hand. "Let people enjoy the wedding," he said. "Chill." I would deal with him in private later. By the time we made it to our hotel room at the end of the night, Hakim had had plenty. He had sent his people out to buy him his drink. After I changed, I lay down ready to sleep, exhausted by the day's events. Hakim was at the table. "What are you doing?" I hissed. "I thought you weren't doing that anymore. No weed, no alcohol." His retort was simple: "Well, we're married now." I realized then that Hakim wasn't going to make good on his promises to me.

.   .   .

A FEW WEEKS LATER, on Thanksgiving, I felt unusually moody, emotional in a way that was new to me. It did not occur to me that I could be pregnant. After my second abortion, I'd been given the Depo-Provera shot, a long-acting, reversible form of birth control. The side effects came swiftly: I gained weight and suffered frequent migraines, and my skin felt as if it were burning. It made my periods so irregular that I bled only once a year. My friend Kenyatta said to me once about Depo-Provera, "Girl, it does everything but kill you." I was so miserable after receiving the shot I went to a clinic near my dad's house that accepted uninsured patients and saw an ob-gyn. The doctor told me I was sterile.

Sterile? How could this be? When I pressed him with questions, and asked him to explain this diagnosis to me, the doctor was short and callous with me. He treated me as if I were insignificant, a bother. I was devastated. I couldn't breathe. I felt as if the room were closing in on me, and time stood still. My heart wouldn't fully allow me to believe the doctor's words, but who was I to know better? He was the medical professional after all. Instead, I worried that I was doomed to a future without biological children as God's punishment for the pregnancies I'd terminated.

After my last abortion, I'd sometimes look at the children in my care at Lighthouse, or at my colleagues who were single parents and think, maybe I could have done it when I got pregnant with Craig's baby. Maybe I would have gotten the support I needed to raise a child well back then. But I tried not to let myself get bogged down in thinking about what might have been. Another day would come.

Two weeks after that emotional Thanksgiving and a short few weeks after my honeymoon with Hakim—a two-night stay at the Ballpark Hilton in St. Louis—I took a pregnancy test that came back positive. Another day had come, and we were going to keep the baby.

My first trimester was hard. I couldn't eat. My hair fell out, and my gums bled. I had hyperemesis gravidarum, severe nausea and vomiting. When I lay in our bed day and night, in the same apartment we lived in soon after we started dating, I felt as if I were on a small boat—being rocked by waves on the high seas. The entire room spun in one direction and my bed in the other. On top of that, I was a spitter. My mouth filled with saliva every few seconds. Every day my meal was a chocolate milkshake from the White Castle by our house. I was in and out of the hospital. Other women told me all of this would subside when I turned three months pregnant. Well, it didn't.

At around four months, I started to feel better. I was beginning to believe that I could do this. I could handle pregnancy, and I could bring this baby out into the world. I was finally able to nibble solid food. Unfortunately, the only solid foods that I could handle were well-chilled fruit cocktails and plain turkey sandwiches. The rest I regurgitated. Around five months in, I went to see my doctor for another routine prenatal visit. I was diligent and hadn't missed any. I sat on the examination table, waiting for the doctor to come in. It was your typical exam room, with a table and cabinets. I noticed a

poster on the wall directly in front of me. It featured a white pregnant woman looking down at her bulging belly, which she was holding in her hands. The words on the poster read "If you feel like
something is wrong, something is wrong. Tell your doctor."

I had been experiencing deep cramping for several weeks. When
I mentioned it on a prior visit to the doctor, I was told it was normal and to expect Braxton-Hicks contractions, a natural tightening
around the abdomen. Now, weeks later, something still felt wrong,
really wrong. When the doctor finally walked into the exam room, I
explained I was having severe pains. Although they were occasional,
the cramping was severe enough to stop me in my tracks. I couldn't
walk. She flicked her wrist at me, "Oh no, you're fine." I explained
that I felt that something was wrong, and I pointed to the poster on
the wall in front of me. "Your poster says if you feel like something
is wrong, something is wrong. Something is wrong!" She flicked her
wrist at me again and shook her head as she turned to walk toward
the door. "You're fine," she assured me. "Go home. I'll see you next
time."

Home was a new place now. Hakim and I had just moved into
our next home, which was in bad shape. It was unfinished, but
Hakim had insisted we live there. He dreamed of raising our child
in a proper single-family home rather than in an apartment. And
this was the best we could afford. Hakim agreed to help renovate
the home in exchange for a reduced cost of rent. But this house was
in no shape for tenants, and especially not for a young family. The
kitchen was missing drywall. The flooring didn't yet extend to the
walls or cover the floors in all the rooms. There was no heat. It was
a two-bedroom, one bath, but we slept on a mattress on the living
room floor next to a space heater.

I woke up on a Wednesday morning, a week from my last appointment, feeling pressure on my abdomen and cramping. I told Hakim
I was hurting. I couldn't even get myself up off the mattress, but
he wanted to have sex. Through it, I sobbed quietly. The pain was

sharp. Afterward, he helped me up off the mattress to go to the bathroom. I squatted over the toilet and clear fluid came pouring out of me. I called my doctor.

A nurse told me to sit down and drink four cups of water immediately and said that then I should be fine. I did as I was instructed, but the pain and pressure kept mounting. I had to go to the bathroom and again squatted. This time, you would've thought someone was pouring entire pitchers of water out of me, one after another. Hakim went about his day and left for work.

I called the hospital again, and they told me to come in. Then I called my mom, and she rushed over to pick me up. It was a twenty-five-minute drive to Prince of Peace Hospital where I received my prenatal care, and I felt every bump and pothole my beloved St. Louis streets had to offer. I tried holding myself up off the seat by the handle on the ceiling of the car to give my uterus a rest. When we finally arrived, I was quickly put into a single-patient room. And the doctors ran test after test. They entered my room a couple hours later with news that would change my life. "You're in preterm labor," they said.

I was only twenty-two weeks, and this couldn't be. "There is no chance the baby can survive a birth this early," they continued. As they spoke, I stopped listening. Their words sounded like nonsense to me. At church and while reading my Bible, I'd learned the difference between fact and truth. The fact was that I was in preterm labor, but the truth came flowing from my heart and out of my mouth for everyone to hear.

I started yelling, "But he was wounded for our transgressions, he was bruised for our iniquities: the chastisement of our peace was upon him; and with his stripes we are healed. Beloved, I wish above all things that thou mayest prosper and be in health, even as thy soul prospereth. I am the head and not the tail, above and not beneath. I am more than a conqueror. And my God shall supply all of my needs according to the riches of his glory in Christ Jesus;

but in everything by prayer and supplication with thanksgiving let your requests be made known to God. He shall not die but live and declare the works of the Lord!"

I was ready. "What now, doctors?" I said as I finished. They admitted me and administered medication to slow my contractions. The nurses were instructed to check my dilation once a shift. Two days later, on Friday morning, my mom, who stayed at my bedside every day, reported to the incoming nurse that the overnight nurse hadn't checked me the entire shift. That day shift nurse checked first thing and found that I was nine centimeters dilated. The baby was coming.

We called Hakim, who had been by my bedside earlier. He had decided to leave for work that morning, not believing that the baby would be born just yet. "I have to work," he said.

I was twenty-three weeks pregnant to the day, just past the half-way point in my pregnancy. As I awaited the nurse's return to my room to prepare for delivery, the contractions came harder and faster. I was tired of the pain. What was taking the nurse so long to return? I stood up on my bed, still a little loopy from the meds, and began yelling again, "Come get this baby out of me!"

Before the nurse returned, a priest came into my room. He introduced himself and said he was there for the birth, and he began to read from the Bible softly to himself. I, meantime, had bigger fish to fry. "Where is the nurse!" I called. It was too late for me to receive an epidural, and my pain was worsening. I was wheeled into the OR as the priest followed at my side.

"What are you doing?" I asked him. "Baby Noland is going to die. I am reading his last rites," he replied. "What the?" I responded loudly just in case anyone needed to hear it. "His name is NOT Baby Noland. He has a name. His name is Zion, and he's not going to die; he's going to live!" I screamed. I didn't need this priest to validate the truth, I realized, and I turned my gaze to the frenzy of movements happening around me. Everyone had their role to play. It was as if I were watching a musical, only there was no singing. The chief of neonatal surgery at Prince of Peace Hospital happened to be by the OR right at that moment. She was picking up something from the hospital that she had left behind earlier. As she was passing, she happened to see our case on the surgery schedule board, and she decided to scrub in with the team. Just in case my baby needed to be resuscitated, I found out later.

"Push!" yelled someone I couldn't see from behind the blue drape sheet. But I didn't know how to push. I felt the pain but couldn't feel the baby because he was so small. He was really early, and I hadn't had a chance to take any birthing classes. Plus, it was my first time. None of this was at all like what I had seen on television. "I don't know how!" I yelled back. "Tell me how!" A nurse came to my side and told me that I needed to push as if I were having a bowel movement. I understood. "PUSH!" several of the team said at once. I did, and Zion came out of me, like a football. He was just barely twenty-three weeks.

The issue around my son's gestational age was one of life or death. Hospitals weren't in the habit of even considering resuscitation for babies who were twenty-two weeks, because the child's lungs wouldn't have had time to develop properly. But at twenty-three weeks, a baby had much better odds of being able to survive and breathe on a ventilator. Zion was quickly handed over to the chief and her team. They intubated him. And it worked.

"He's breathing!" the chief said as she looked up at me with joy. Tears gushed down my face. My son weighed one pound, three ounces. His skin was a beautiful brown. He had a head full of sleek black hair. Later, when Kelli finally saw him, she took to calling him Jerry Lewis because of that hair. But beautiful Zion, my miracle, had a long way to go. His ears were still embedded in his head. His eyes were fused shut. His fingers were grains of rice. My baby could fit in the palm of my hand.

I was wheeled back to my room, and to my surprise I was greeted by my mom, my friend Carla, and Hakim. They had my aunt Patricia on the phone. Patricia had organized an international prayer chain, and hundreds of people were praying for Zion to live. The team wheeled Zion into the room in an incubator. That was the first time that his family met Zion. Hakim reached toward him tenderly, and Zion held on to his outstretched finger. But the moment was broken. Zion needed to be airlifted to the children's hospital about twenty minutes away in St. Louis.

I was not in the slightest prepared for giving birth when I did. The only piece I had ready for my son was his name. From the moment I first heard Lauryn Hill's song about becoming a mother, I knew that I would name my child Zion. "Now the joy of my world is in Zion / Now the joy of my world is in Zion," she sang. I wept out loud the first time I heard the song. It touched me to my soul. Zion conveyed the strength I knew my boy would need for all he'd go through.

For the first month of Zion's life, he was on a ventilator, fighting to just live. Hakim, my parents, and Kelli were at the children's hospital by his side around the clock. I had developed a fever after birth, and I wasn't able to be with him for the first three days. When I saw Zion after my discharge from Prince of Peace, he looked different. He was no longer in his incubator. Tubes and wires hung on his small body. His skin was shiny, translucent. I could see his blood vessels and his lungs. One of his ears began to show, and he was wearing eye protectors to shield his eyes from the bright lights that glared overhead.

Zion was jaundiced and had to be kept under the bilirubin light twenty-four hours a day. I watched his body move and jerk when he cried, but no sound escaped him. The endotracheal tube he needed to help him breathe muted his voice. Every moment was one of agony for me, spent in uncertainty about whether my child would be able to breathe the next minute, or the next.

We were told that if he survived the first three days of life, he would have a better chance of living. As the days passed, we made sure someone from our family was with Zion at every possible moment, together with me. My parents and sister came to the NICU every day after work and stayed until late at night. Hakim would often be there, every chance he could.

When I saw Zion after my discharge from Prince of Peace, he was no longer in his incubator. The staff placed him in an open bed with a covering like Saran wrap over him. Kelli took to sitting there and rubbing his feet over the plastic. Zion recognized her whenever she entered the room. He would stretch out his leg, lift his foot up toward her, reaching to be held and caressed. He would keep his foot up for as long as she would rub it. Zion responded to his dad's presence, too. If Zion's heart rate was up or his numbers were otherwise off in some way, he calmed when Hakim walked in the room. At the time, Hakim was working twelve-hour shifts and depended on the bus for transportation, which added another two hours to his already long day. But still he came to the hospital on his days off and whenever my parents offered to pick him up from his job and drive him over.

After four weeks, the doctors determined that Zion was finally stable enough to be held outside his covering. Finally, I was able to take my baby in my arms for the first time since he was born. Tubes, wires, I didn't care. I wanted to hold my baby. The nurse put him in my shirt so we could share skin-to-skin contact. He wiggled so much that I lost him inside my shirt for a couple seconds. The ET tube and wires weighed more than he did. Zion was also now strong enough for a heart surgery he needed for patent ductus arteriosus. The surgery closed the ductus arteriosus blood vessel. This vessel normally closes at birth, but Zion's hadn't yet because of his premature birth. Blood was flowing to his lungs instead of his body, which made breathing more difficult for him. I was scared, but also excited. I knew that once the surgery was over, it was only a matter of time before Zion could breathe on his own.

For four months, Zion grew in neonatal intensive care. Every day, I sat in the NICU pumping room and pumped breast milk into tiny thirty-milliliter bottles. The nurses froze the bottles so they could later be fed to Zion through his nasogastric feeding tube. Every day when I visited him, I couldn't stop looking at him. I could see when he was upset, even though the endotracheal tube kept any sound from coming out to reach me.

I watched the medical staff stick and probe Zion all day long. For the most part, they treated him very well, and I felt he was in good, secure hands. On a few occasions, I noticed when something was amiss and alerted the nurses. One day, I noticed his breathing, through the tube, seemed labored. His little chest wasn't rising and falling evenly with every breath. He looked as if he were suffocating. I told the nurse and she assured me he was fine, his numbers were fine. I asked her to get the doctor, but she told me it wasn't necessary. Zion's body started quivering. I yelled as loudly as I could, "I need some help, my son can't breathe!" Still nothing. I picked up a chair and slammed it against the nurse's desk. Then the doctors came running.

I pointed them to Zion, telling them he was in distress. They examined him and they agreed. His lung collapsed, and a team worked quickly to save him. The primary doctor thanked me for advocating for my child the way that I did. Oftentimes when I would talk with his medical team, they were surprised by how informed I was about Zion's medical history and the medications he was on. I was more surprised that they were surprised. Shouldn't I know about my baby boy's health and medical regimen? Shouldn't I be invested in his care?

I know that some saw me as this young, Black, low-income, Medicaid mother, as if being that were synonymous with being lazy and unintelligent. They didn't hesitate to let me know the limits of my rights as a parent. I was told that if I didn't pump breast milk, if I tried to have him formula fed, I could be charged with medical neglect. I'd meet the same fate if, following his discharge from the NICU, I put Zion in day care before he reached the age of one. "We will take him back," someone from the hospital told me. "In fact, we don't even have to release him to you. Because you haven't taken him home yet, technically, he is a ward of the state."

In the United States, Black women have higher rates of premature birth than women of any other race. This is true across class lines. A middle-class Black woman is much more likely to give birth prematurely than a lower-class white woman. The reason for that is not the access to care that a birthing person enjoys but simple racism on the part of health-care providers. Those biases against Black mothers and families don't stop once a baby is born. They continue in the NICU.

When Zion was finally allowed to leave the NICU, he was still on a heart monitor. A feeding tube snaked down from his nostril to his stomach. It was possible that he would need to be put back on oxygen again. He was a four-month-old who weighed six pounds, five pounds more than he weighed at birth. I worried and fretted about how he would survive in our new home, and soon my worst fears were realized.

Late one night, when the three of us were sleeping in our shared room, Hakim and I woke to the sound of several somethings running through the walls of the house. I imagined rats, raccoons, or possums gnawing their way through our things. I could tell that whatever it was, there was a pack of them. I jumped up, pulled Zion from his crib, just beside us, and stood clutching him on our bed. I dialed my mother and asked her to come pick us up. She came.

Hakim thought I was overreacting. "I'll deal with it in the morning," he snapped. He was making $12 an hour and trying to support a family on his own, as I wasn't working at the time. He was adamant that our family stay together, that we live together. But in that moment, I wasn't having it. It wasn't safe for our baby to be in that house. He was welcome to stay if he wanted, I told him, but I was taking our child and getting out of there. When my mom arrived, I jumped down from the bed, ran through the house toward the front door with Zion in my arms, intent on reaching the safety of her car. Hakim stayed put that night and for a couple days after; then he packed up our things, deposited them in storage, and moved into my parents' house with Zion and me. We stayed there, with them, for several months.

By that time, I was well into another pregnancy. I'd had Zion in April, and by July, I found out I was pregnant again. I was nervous about having another baby prematurely, but at the same time I was thrilled. The idea that our kids would be close in age reminded me of how close my brother and I had been when we were growing up. Those were happy memories. So far, my only experience of pregnancy was marked by illness and pain. I didn't know what it was like to enjoy a healthy pregnancy and a full-term birth. I wanted to find out, and I was determined to make sure this time was different.

I went back to the doctor who delivered Zion. She apologized profusely to me for not trusting me when I'd told her something was wrong. "You were right," she said. She apologized to me, and she offered to mark me high-risk and to monitor my pregnancy closely. She begged me to give her another chance. So I did.

She put me in the high-risk category, and I trusted her commitment to make sure that my baby and I were safe. Each week, she gave me an ultrasound, alternating between abdominal and vaginal. At sixteen weeks, or four months, I went for a vaginal ultrasound at the hospital. While there, I was seen by the doctor who was on duty that day. I was in preterm labor, he told me, and the fetus wouldn't survive. I wouldn't believe him, but he was adamant. "Just go home and let it abort," he said.

My sister, Kelli, was with me at the hospital that day. She had accompanied me to make sure I wasn't alone while Hakim was working. I asked this physician to call my personal doctor. He wouldn't. I demanded that he call my doctor, and he refused. Zion, who was with me that day, began to cry and I turned to care for him. Kelli took a turn to try to change his mind, again to no avail. We yelled for help. No one came. When the doctor finally left the room, we sat with the news for a moment. Then we exploded with rage and frustration.

Kelli picked up a chair and threw it down the long hallway by where we stood. Nurses came running to us. We explained what was happening. One of them immediately went to call my doctor, who instructed them to put me on a stretcher and admit me right away. The next morning, my doctor arrived and performed a cerclage placement on me, a procedure that keeps a woman's cervix closed, holding the fetus safely inside. Thanks to that surgery, I was able to carry my baby to thirty-six weeks.

At thirty-three weeks, I started having contractions. I consulted with my doctor again, and she advised me that my cerclage would undoubtedly hold the baby until the forty-week mark. I disagreed. I knew, inside me, that my baby would come out of me the moment those stitches were removed. But my doctor assured me that couldn't happen. My cerclage was scheduled to be removed at thirty-six weeks, the recommended time. I was scheduled to come to my doctor's office for the routine procedure. "It will be fine," she told me, when I tried to suggest it be performed in an exam room instead.

When my doctor cut through the cerclage stitch, she was instantly showered with amniotic fluid. My water broke and sprayed her office, reaching the walls and bookshelves. "That never happens," she said as she motioned to shake some of my fluids off. My baby girl was born that day. She was seven pounds thirteen ounces, four weeks early, but beautiful and healthy. We named her Angel, because that's what she was.

.   .   .

I WAS TWENTY-FOUR YEARS old with two children born just eleven months apart. I had worked on and off for short stints since becoming pregnant with Zion, but I wasn't able to spend long hours or days at Lighthouse. My pregnancy was too difficult, and later the demands of having a newborn in the NICU were even more so. Once Zion came home, I was told that day care could be harmful to his health. His immune system wasn't strong enough to fight all the germs he would be exposed to from other kids. He would not be able to go to day care until he was at least a year old. When Angel was four weeks old, Zion turned one, old enough to go to day care, and I returned to work. Hakim was out of a job and no longer working by then, and I had no other choice.

Our growing family sorely needed an income. My parents helped us out as much as they could, but we couldn't abuse their kindness and stay in their home forever. Hakim's inability to provide for the children and me confirmed all of their fears about him. On top of that, Hakim and my father got into frequent clashes. After one particularly nasty disagreement, Hakim announced that we were leaving. I wasn't ready, but I had to decide whether I was going to stay with my husband. I wasn't sure what the consequences of staying put might be. I was afraid to say no to him and face his anger, afraid that my husband might leave and not come back. "He'll take care of us," I told myself as we readied to go. "We won't be living on the street or anything," I thought. Hakim didn't have a plan, and I could not have been more wrong.

·   ·   ·

WE LEARNED HOW TO attract as little attention as possible. We parked on a street in a residential neighborhood, in a space between two homes, never directly in front of one. That would be too suspicious. We never stayed in the same place all night. I got maybe an hour or two of sleep a night, just enough to avoid being incoherent. Angel was two months old, and Zion was almost as small as his sister. They were both on formula.

I couldn't produce enough milk for them by then. I mixed their bottles in the bathrooms of fast-food restaurants, after asking the cashier for a cup of water. I learned that McDonald's had the most accessible bathroom. It never required a key. That is where I would get cleaned up for work every morning. Some nights, a friend or a relative might take us in. I would spend a couple hours ironing clothes to last us for the week or more. But people usually weren't willing to open their doors for long to a family of four, especially when there were babies in tow. Even if we could find a place to sleep for a night, we often had to be gone by dawn when others in the household got up and moving.

No one at my job knew that I was unhoused, living out of our 1996 Ford Explorer, and I put on a brave face every day. The days spent in the car were warm, but the nights were cool at first. Cool turned to cold as the days went by. We kept our clothes and necessities in trash bags in the backseat. We let the backseat down, smashing the clothes underneath, and that back area of the SUV was where we stood up the two playpens for the babies to sleep. I spent most of those nights watching them sleep, turning the car on and off to keep warm but being cognizant of running the gas out too quickly.

Are the babies warm enough? Where can I use the bathroom? How and what can we eat? Will the police catch us and take our kids away from us? Will we be carjacked? Will someone take us in for the night? The questions swirled through my mind every night. I wanted to go back home to my parents', but would Hakim stop me from leaving with the kids? If I tried to leave, would things turn violent? I knew that Hakim loved the kids and me, but he was struggling with navigating how to be a husband and full-time dad.

After months of living in the car, we managed to stay at a hotel for an extended period, and then we finally found more secure housing again. But even then, things didn't improve between Hakim and me. Our relationship was strained. I no longer trusted that he could keep me safe. I lost respect for him, but I held on. I had married him, after all. I figured that I must have been the problem. Perhaps I was expecting too much from him.

I cooked, cleaned, washed bottles, packed the diaper bag, bathed the kids, transported them to and from day care. On weekends, I took the kids grocery shopping with me, because Hakim wouldn't stay home with them. They had to come with me because I was their mom, he said. I didn't push. I thought to myself that I did not want my kids around anyone who did not want them around. I did the ironing for the whole family, including every outfit Hakim planned to wear for the upcoming week. He'd be angry whenever I forgot what he'd worn recently, and when I accidentally prepared the same jeans for him two weeks in a row.

Sometimes, there were long stretches when Hakim was out of work. He started working in transportation as a chauffeur, courier, and transporter, but nothing was ever stable. He would leave the house in the morning, but where he went or what he did with his day was a mystery to me. Many days, he wouldn't get up in the morning. I would get myself ready, then wake the kids and get them cleaned up, dressed, fed, and off to day care before heading to work. When we'd return home, Hakim was often still in bed, eleven hours later. Then, and only then, would he jump up, dress, and leave within the hour.

Hakim was cheating. I called him one day after he had left home for the evening. He answered, and I could hear a woman in the background. When I asked who she was, he told me she was giving him what he needed. I put on a strong face and told him that he'd better keep her. But, inside, I was heartbroken. I was crushed. I'd accepted all the criticism from those who said I was making a mistake marrying this man. I had disappointed my parents. I had lived in a car with my kids. I'd dealt with his vices.

Once I learned of his infidelity, I stopped sleeping with him. A couple weeks later, Hakim and I got into an argument over our son. I wanted to leave. I tried to go get Zion so he, Angel, and I could leave. But Hakim blocked my way, and we broke out fighting. The struggle escalated. That was when I knew: There's no way we were going to stay together. I had dealt with everything I could as best as I could until that point.

We mutually decided to split. Hakim left that same day. A week went by before he came back. He had no place else to go. We agreed to be roommates until he could find permanent housing or until I left. That turned out to be a bad idea. Another week later, after we left church, he started shouting about what we would eat for dinner as we drove home. A new fight erupted, the worst I'd seen yet. That was on a Sunday. The next day, I went to work, and I saw myself in my friend Daphne's eyes. My friend held me while we cried. Later, she helped me pack her trunk with as many of our belongings as possible, and she told me not to worry about the rest. We'd be back to get it.

This time, I moved out with the kids and back in with my parents. I stopped by the house the following Wednesday to pick up more clothes for the rest of the week and to pick up the mail. I told Hakim I would be back on Sunday for more. That Sunday, I went to church looking for guidance. Afterward, I approached the two co-pastors. They had been married a long time, and I wanted their advice. The husband's advice was simple: Leave him. But his wife told me not to. As the wife, I had a duty to stay, she said. I was confused. I turned to God. "I don't know what to do," I said in prayer. "I need You to give me a sign."

After leaving church that day, I buckled Zion and Angel into their car seats and drove to our old home, praying that God would show me what I needed to do. Once again, I was picking up the mail and a few more clothes for us for the week ahead. We walked in the side door off the kitchen. Zion and Angel took off in front of me to find a woman's clothes strewn about the place and a purse on the kitchen table. Dishes and my favorite candles lay broken and scattered about the floor. I told the kids to stay back, away from the shattered glass. I walked down the hallway into what had been my bedroom to find Hakim in bed with a woman. She was lying on my sheets, my clothes and purses in the room around her.

Rage and humiliation washed over me. I wanted to scream at the injustice of it. I wanted to fight them. I was brimming with rage. I kicked the woman out and told Hakim that I wasn't going to pay the rent anymore. I packed my kids into the back of my car and drove to a Burger King. I called my mom while sitting at a quiet corner table with tears in my eyes. I worried about how my kids would be affected by all that had happened. I told my mom everything and asked for her advice. "I won't tell you what to do," she said. "But you have to decide: If he never changes, would you still respect him as a husband? Could you still be a wife to him? If not, don't stay. If you can, then stay." I had worried about what my parents would say and think of my getting a divorce. Her words liberated me. I had two toddlers, and Hakim and I had been married only three years. I was twenty-six years old. I knew the answer to her question was a firm no. There was no coming back from the disrespect he had shown me.

I filed for divorce. I contacted Legal Aid because I did not know where else to turn. They accepted me into a program that helped people leave marriages. It was exactly what I needed. They provided me with an attorney who worked on my case for free. If not for them, I don't know how I would have managed to complete my divorce from Hakim. I couldn't have afforded it. And during the almost yearlong process, I finally saw myself and my patterns clearly for the first time.

I saw how I'd ended up married. When I met Hakim, I had come out of an abusive relationship. I'd tried to drink my problems away, tried to sex my problems away, tried to see where I fit in. I didn't know how to find myself. What I did know was that my own decision making often led me astray, and I didn't know how to fix that. When Hakim came along, I felt that he cared for me, but I was even more certain that I needed an out. I wanted to feel safe. I wanted someone to keep me from making bad decisions. I was so hopeful that if I was married, there'd be no more decisions for me to make. There would be no more mistakes that I could make. I wouldn't risk being raped anymore. I wouldn't risk becoming pregnant by somebody I didn't love or wasn't serious with. I wouldn't risk giving my heart to somebody who would beat me. I would finally be free from those problems that I so badly wanted to be free from, I thought. If only I were married.

I was also tired of being a disappointment to my father. I wanted to make him proud and to be the daughter he had wanted me to be. I wanted to have my life and a relationship with him. I thought that being married would help me get my life on track and help me be the person my parents believed I could be. But my marriage to Hakim didn't bring me any of that. When the divorce was finalized, I felt a weight lift off me. It was official. I was the one who carried my family, and that clarity provided me with a new sense of confidence.

I know that some people will see the string of abusive relationships I've been in as evidence of repeated failure on my part. Society tries to paint women, especially Black women, who go through what I went through in my teens and twenties as stupid, ignorant, bad, lazy. Of course, we're not.

Too few have asked what caused us to end up in these situations in the first place. What were the traumas that we faced before we suffered violence from our partners? For me, the cycle began with the rupture that my sense of self endured when I entered high school. My teachers and peers at that predominantly white school undermined my identity with insults and cruelty. It broke me.

It's not entirely accurate to say I spent those subsequent teen years trying to find who I was. I thought I knew who I was: a nobody with nothing to contribute. I didn't believe I'd live to be older than twenty-one. When I was growing up, the culture was focused on the many young Black men who were dying and on gang wars. This is something we often still hear of Black boys, that their sense of what's possible is so stunted they don't expect to make it far into adulthood. It's true of us Black women, too; it's just not something we feel we're allowed to talk about. We are so accustomed to putting the needs of others first. We're expected to be strong. When things go wrong, when someone hurts you, you move on. We don't have time for that kind of talk, and even if we did, who would care enough to listen?

We are silenced by others, and we are silenced by our own shame. We're taught that abuse happens to people who are weak, to women who bring the abuse on themselves. When it happens to us, we can be slow to recognize the signs and aren't sure how to respond once we do. Shame is just one part of the emotional and psychological effects of abuse.

DeVon left me for dead, kidnapped me, tortured me, shot at me. For decades, I have been living with the trauma I experienced at his hands. When somebody raises their voice in my presence, I shrink and shut down. It took me a long time to understand what it means to be triggered into a recollection of the horrors I've survived. I shudder at the memories of how he manipulated me, how he would threaten to hurt himself as a way to get me to care more about his pain than the pain he was inflicting on me. Too many of us are living through this kind of abuse right now.

It is crucial that we give individuals the skills they need to form healthy relationships. To support healthy families and communities, we need to create an antiracist society. We need reparations, distributed both as cash and as resources that can help serve Black and Indigenous students and students of color. We need to close the racial wage gap and the gender pay gap. We need to pay a living wage. During my years at Lighthouse, minimum wage was not enough. No one who is educating children should go to work worried that her electricity is going to be cut off at home.

We need access to quality health care. No one should have to live through prenatal, birth, and postpartum experiences like the ones I endured. The men in my life have presented real challenges. But so has the pressure of living in a hateful society. I wish my young adulthood and my children's early years could have taken place in a different America, a better America. That's the structural change I've been working to bring about.

Part Two

Chapter 4

AFTER FINALIZING MY DIVORCE, I moved our family to a little apartment in Overland, Missouri, a city in St. Louis County. It was a cute two-bedroom with big picture windows. One look at all the natural light filling the space, and I knew we had finally found our home. Zion was three years old, and Angel was two.

The three of us lived paycheck to paycheck, and my income barely covered the childcare I needed to keep working. I was not receiving any help from Hakim, but I didn't allow that to weigh me down. It was just our little family, and I felt safe and happy.

I no longer had to carry the burden of another person who was not pulling his weight. I no longer had to wonder whether Hakim would insist I cook for him when I got home from a long day at work, or if he might help get the kids ready for school that day. I knew all the household tasks were mine alone to bear. There were no fewer responsibilities, but I felt at peace. My frustration and disappointment melted away. Although I couldn't afford the fresh produce that I wanted to be able to provide, my family did not spend a single day hungry. And I learned to be creative with my plating. I used canned veggies like green beans or carrots and canned mandarin oranges or fruit cocktails to make my kids colorful, and more nutritious, plates of food.

At that point, I had been working at Lighthouse for nearly a decade. As the assistant director, I earned $9 an hour. Pastor Doris, whom I reported to, had become so much more than a supervisor or a boss. She was the co-pastor at my church; she was my spiritual mother too. When I asked for a raise, she was sympathetic but firm. "I can't afford to pay you more," she told me. Instead, she offered me another job. She had just launched a new catering company, and she could pay me $10.50 an hour to be the office manager. I jumped at the opportunity. But after about six months on the job, managing the company's day-to-day operations, which included an after-school hot meal program in St. Louis, I knew that something needed to change. I was still struggling to keep up with my bills. I wanted security—a career, a piece of paper that no one could take from me.

My finances were a house of cards. The instability made it impossible for me to relax. Any issue threatened to derail my budget entirely: a blown-out tire, a day off work because one of the kids was sick. If I managed to get $60 in my savings account, I celebrated a rare and fleeting victory. Every month I sorted out which bill I could push off until the next. One month, I called to make arrangements with the gas and electric company. The next, I tried to adjust the due date on my car note or car insurance premium. On the Mondays before a Friday payday, I borrowed $40 from my mother to get me through the few days before I received my biweekly check. I used that money to fill my gas tank so I could make it to and from work and day care to pick up my kids. Whatever was left would have to get me through the rest of the week. My mind churned with a mix of worry, anxiety, and shame. The choices I made had brought us here, or so I thought to myself.

Pastor Doris empathized with my situation and challenged me one day, too. She herself was a nurse and encouraged me to go to nursing school. If I wanted to apply, she would write me a letter of recommendation. I remembered that Black nurse from when I worked as a candy striper, how capable and in control she'd seemed as I'd watched her make her rounds. I dreamed of becoming a nurse for years, but Hakim forbade it. I had too much to take care of at home to pursue a degree and I couldn't work long hours away from the family, he said. But finally, I was free from him. I could make my decision on my own. I told Pastor Doris "yes," understanding that meant I was quitting my job, and leaving a company I had come to love for nearly ten years. She swiftly wrote me a recommendation letter for my application to Lutheran School of Nursing in south St. Louis.

I applied in April 2005 and was notified in May of my acceptance for the incoming August class. That was unusual. Pastor Doris had connections at Lutheran, and I suspected that her endorsement of my application paved my way. I was going to enroll having no college degree and no license or certificate in nursing, and I was going to become an RN. I just needed to figure out how I was going to pay for it.

I knew that I was going to have to work, at least part-time. Hakim didn't pay me child support. And I would have to take out student loans. There was no way around it. I applied for a Pell Grant and decided I would move back in with my dad, which would also help make the transition possible. Unfortunately, it also meant that I was going to be evicted. Again.

It didn't make sense to get evicted because of a positive development in my life, but here I was, out of my apartment and thousands of dollars. I had gone to the property management company with my happy news: I'd been accepted to nursing school, and I needed to be freed from my lease. I figured my landlords would congratulate me, but instead of letting me out of the lease, they said I was responsible for paying the half year of rent remaining. There was no way I could pay it. I was about to quit my job in order to attend school full-time. Was I supposed to turn down this opportunity in the hopes I would get accepted quickly again in a year? No.

I packed most of our things into trash bags and moved out. That was when the property management company started eviction proceedings, allowing it to then sue me for the remainder of my lease amount. An eviction notice was placed by the sheriff's department on the front door of the apartment I had just vacated, and I was summoned to court. I sat in the courtroom for hours listening to the stories of others who had been evicted. It felt inappropriate to me, as if I were invading their privacy. This is something that should be handled discreetly, I thought. When my name was finally called, I wanted to be able to explain my situation to the judge. My chance never came. There was no discussion with the judge. My attorney, whom I'd met just an hour before, spoke to the judge while I stood there. She let me know how much I owed, and tacked on a couple thousand dollars in fees. I didn't understand. If I didn't have the money to be able to stay in my apartment, how could I pay more to not live in the space?

Years back, I had been evicted from the apartment I'd shared with DeVon. But I decided that another blemish on my credit was going to be necessary if I was to begin my career, a career I believed would save me from having to struggle so much to make ends meet. Maybe, I thought, when I could afford the court costs and attorney fees, I would try to fight it. For now, I would take the eviction, and I would go to school.

My excitement for school would not be dampened. I was giddy. It marked a fresh beginning for me. In the fall of 2005, I took anatomy and physiology, bioethics, and psychology, all of which I needed before I could begin the nursing program. I felt like my old self, an inquisitive girl who devoured books. It felt good to be back in a classroom learning new things. I wasn't at all nervous about whether I could do the work, but I was a little anxious because of how much older I was than my classmates. I was twenty-nine, sitting alongside people who came straight out of high school and college. Some of them already worked as licensed practical nurses, nursing assistants, or patient care techs, but I kept up.

Once the RN program got underway, the pace was relentless. I spent hours a day in class. We began by learning what our roles were as nurses; then we were introduced to basic skills. I loved the practical component, learning how to make a hospital bed, how to take blood pressure manually, listening and differentiating between different heart and lung sounds, counting respirations and heart rate. We were often assigned dozens of chapters to read overnight. The material was dense and complex, covering disease symptoms and treatments. We were often quizzed on the previous night's reading and assigned another huge chunk of text for the following day. While I was still trying to learn one thing, we'd be on to the next. I tried to sit in the front of the class to make sure I stayed engaged. If I let myself get distracted, my mind wandered as I worried about bills, what my kids needed, how to schedule study time, or what to cook for dinner. I snacked on chips, pretzels, and cookies in class to help me focus, and then quickly switched to caramel rice cakes and cucumbers with vinaigrette dressing once my strategy for concentration added more pounds than I'd expected.

Beyond the classroom, we had to take part in clinical rotations, which took me to places where I might work once I got my license. It was in these settings that I learned what it means to provide care. During clinicals, our teacher assigned each student a patient. I might get Joseph Smith, a fifty-nine-year-old white male with a history of heart disease who had been admitted for chest pains. I'd leave class and go to the hospital where this patient had been admitted and get his chart so I'd be ready to take care of him the next day. By the time I had what I needed, it might be six in the evening. I'd go home, feed and bathe my kids. I'd work on my homework for the night once I got them in bed.

On the nights before I had to visit patients, I'd be up until the wee hours of the morning, studying to better understand the diseases I'd be treating and medications I'd be administering. It wasn't unusual for me to be assigned someone who was prescribed dozens of drugs, and I needed to know how each interacted with the others. I'd sleep for an hour or so before waking to get to the clinical site by 6:00 a.m. for a twelve-hour shift. The day started with a huddle. Our instructor drilled us, making sure we were prepared. Then we'd meet whichever nurse we were paired with for the day. If we were at a hospital, we'd join in rounds and sometimes be asked questions in front of the doctors.

The pace was grueling, but I was proud to put on the scrubs that marked me as a nursing student. And I was proud that my kids could see me in that uniform. It was proof that I was on a track to change my life for the better. I had focus. And, most of all, I loved my patients.

For a few weeks, I worked in a children's rehabilitation hospital where I was assigned to a one-year-old Black girl. Tanya had been born with a condition that left her unable to move much of her body. She couldn't stand or walk. I administered her medications and helped exercise her limbs, moving her arms and legs against gravity so they wouldn't become stiff and she wouldn't develop circulation problems. The limitations of her body never dampened her spirits. Tanya had a huge personality. She would smile at me and nod yes or no depending on what I was offering and what she was asking for. In the weeks that I tended to her, I met her parents only once. I learned that their visits weren't frequent. They told me all about their many complaints about their daughter's care and the hospital. It was hard to listen to. Their daughter was such a sweet soul. I took the best care of Tanya that I could.

I also worked briefly on the psychiatric floor of a hospital in south St. Louis. My patient there was a twenty-three-year-old Black man named David who was often visited by voices no one else could hear. On the day we met, I sat down with David to complete my assessment. As I asked David questions to better understand his needs, he began to feverishly scribble on a piece of paper. As he wrote, he responded aloud to the voices he heard. He believed he had an esoteric understanding of numbers and told me what insights he'd gleaned about my past and future from their hidden meanings. When he finished writing, he pushed the paper toward me, proud. The paper was covered in a script I couldn't read. His hallucinations grew more intense, and the staff intervened to have him take a break from our assessment.

The next time I met David, he told me the voices had instructed him not to mess with me. "God has her," he said he'd been told. I knew from his medical records that David had been violent in the past, but I was not afraid of him. I knew that some of his caregivers were too frightened of him to offer the quality, compassionate care he deserved. That wasn't going to be me, I decided. During my time on that ward, I wanted to show him that he was valued and loved. I wanted to bring that commitment to care to all my patients.

For my rotations, I also visited an Alcoholics Anonymous meeting at a community center. I spent time on a geriatric floor, and I worked in a surgical unit. At each placement, I learned that most patients put up with nursing students at best. They knew we wouldn't be with them for long; we were people who were learning new skills. We completed regular nursing tasks like administering medications, placing an IV, even changing a bedpan or walking them to the restroom. I wanted to do so much more for the people I worked with. And I'd learned that confidence was everything.

Confidence was what made my patients trust us to provide them with care. If I was nervous before drawing a patient's blood or administering an injection, my patient would also be nervous. If I was confident before a procedure, the patient would relax. Patients could feel my energy. And so I resolved to bring a sense of self-assuredness to my work.

For two years, I exhausted myself with coursework and training. There were many times when I asked myself whether I would make it, whether I could manage to actually complete the program, given how much I had on my plate. My classmates were my support system. They kept me going. We studied together and encouraged each other. We told each other that we could make it through, just as the class ahead of us had. Yolanda, who lived in St. Louis County with her husband and children, was always there for me. She'd check in with me, to ask what I needed and how she could help. For Jeff, medicine was the family business. He worked at Holy Cross Hospital, where his mother was a nurse. While we were in school, Jeff's mother was head of the outpatient surgery clinic and told Jeff they were hiring. That's how I got a job working part-time as a unit secretary and patient care technician at that clinic.

My parents' help made it all possible for me, too. They had divorced a couple years before I applied to nursing school and were now living separately. Living with my dad provided Zion and Angel with another adult to care for them. On the nights I got home late, he would cook them dinner. If the kids and I got home before him, he would shoo me off and finish making the meal. He took care of the laundry or whatever other task I'd been engaged in. On the mornings when I left before sunrise, he would get them up and out to school. If I needed to work through the night and the kids woke up, my dad would wake up with them and get them back in bed. "You just study," he'd tell me. "Let me worry about these kids."

On the weekends, my dad took Zion and Angel along to whatever community event he'd planned to attend that day, just as he'd done with my siblings and me when we were young. Or he might take them out to the movies, a restaurant, or the Northwoods City Hall playground, all so they could enjoy the day while I hit the books. If my dad needed to work on the weekend, or happened to be away, my mom was right there to help out as well. The kids loved spending time with her and enjoyed a routine at her home as well.

My children were preschool age and coming into their personalities. Zion was quiet around people he didn't know. He idolized my dad and wanted to wear suits to school, because that's what he always saw his Pa-Pa wearing. Zion was particular about his appearance and liked his clothes and shoes to be clean and his hair to be freshly cut. I never forced gender norms on my kids, but Zion loved superheroes, wrestling, and trucks. Angel, on the other hand, loved sequins, unicorns, rainbows, and satin, especially if that satin was pink or purple. She would use Zion's wrestling figurines as husbands for her Bratz dolls. Where her brother was shy in new settings, Angel was a social butterfly, and she was fearless.

I got to know my children in the time I spent getting them ready for day care in the morning, on our evening drives home, and at our family dinners. I made it a point to eat our evening meals together, even when life was busy. Every two months or so, I'd get a weeklong break from school. I'd take Zion and Angel out of day care for some of that time. Those precious days I spent entirely with them, without feeling rushed or distracted by my cares. I would have loved to take them on a trip out of town, or even spend a day at a Chuck E. Cheese with them, but there was no way I could afford it.

I yearned to spend more time with my kids, but I knew I couldn't stray from the path I had chosen, and I never doubted that I'd made the right choice. I was attracted to science, and I was good at it. I earned several awards for academics in nursing within my first year. And I knew becoming a nurse was going to change my life. When I fantasized about where I would work after I graduated, I imagined myself at a pediatric clinic.

When Zion was in the NICU for the first four months of his life, many of those days were touch and go. Several times the doctors alerted me that Zion might have a brain bleed which could lead to paralysis or even death. If I had gone home to sleep after being encouraged to do so by the medical team, I would receive calls telling me to rush back to the hospital because it was not certain that he would make it through the night. The nurses were very attentive to him. One miscalculated dosage or the use of the wrong syringe could've proven disastrous, or fatal. I learned that nurses help save lives, and I felt that knowledge gave me a head start.

Our instructors encouraged us to work in a hospital on a medical-surgical floor for at least a year after graduation. The idea was that this would be the best way to gain invaluable experience and build a strong foundation for a great nursing career. I took that guidance to heart. I knew the fast pace of a hospital would prepare me no matter where I would ultimately practice.

Some people told me they thought I would be a natural in a labor and delivery unit. To them it seemed like an obvious choice for me. But the truth is that I struggled in that rotation. I helped and watched women give birth to healthy, full-term babies, and the whole time I was painfully aware that I had not been so fortunate. The conditions surrounding my own pregnancies had been too stressful. I wasn't able to adjust to giving a fundal massage, and I didn't feel comfortable applying pressure to a woman's abdomen after birth, to help the uterus shrink back to its pre-pregnancy size. Being coached to apply that pressure took me back to the clinic where a staffer had shoved down on my stomach after my abortion. I was triggered. I just couldn't do it. It was too much.

.   .   .

AFTER I GRADUATED, I took a job working on the transplant floor at Holy Cross Hospital, a level 1 trauma center in the heart of the city. Many of the patients there were recovering from strokes, traffic collisions, or gunshot wounds. While working there, I learned that my colleagues in the emergency room often found gunshot victims on the asphalt just outside the ER's front doors. The wounded had been pushed from cars and left there, sometimes near death. One day when I pulled up to work, I saw blood pooling near an entrance, evidence of what my colleagues had described.

I wanted to be a surgical nurse. I had my sights set on working in the operating room, but needed to have more experience first, so I took a job in the transplant unit. In my new job, we took care of people before and after they received new organs—often kidneys, livers, or pancreases. Whenever they got the call that it was time for their surgery, we would prepare them. After an hour or so recovering from the operating room, they'd come back to us.

My first weeks on the job, I was determined to understand exactly what I was doing, so I took my time. I didn't want my nervous rushing to put patients in harm's way, so I moved slowly and deliberately, and slower than some of the senior nurses would've liked. My caution made me a target of hazing and teasing. Another nurse might ask me to do something, but not mention an important piece of equipment that I'd need, sending me on a wild-goose chase. All the while, she'd just sit there behind the nurse's desk, laughing with the others.

One day, more than a dozen doctors, nurses, therapists, surgeons, and students were milling about as I approached the nurse's desk, where clinicians on the floor gathered when they weren't tending to patients. Upon seeing me, the charge nurse on duty yelled out, "Here comes Cori." She had a derogatory, exasperated tone. I heard her call me stupid and slow. I had to do something about this disrespect, to show them that I wasn't going to stand for it, and I knew I had to do it publicly. That day, I let the charge nurse have it and made sure everyone within earshot heard what I said just as well as they'd heard her come for me. She didn't say one word and that was the end of that.

After about a year on the job, I hit my stride. All the training, the studying, everything I'd learned on the floor, just clicked. I felt like the nurse I'd set out to be. My supervisor evidently felt the same way and promoted me to weekend charge nurse, even though I had the least seniority of most of the other nurses on our floor. In addition to taking care of patients, I now also cared for the nurses during the shifts that I was working, was an advocate for my staff, and managed administrative issues.

When nursing students came to our floor for their rotations, I treated them the way I would have wanted to be treated when I was in their shoes. The Black girls in those classes gravitated to me. They'd pull me aside and thank me. "I want to be just like you," they'd say. I made sure to pay special attention to their questions and concerns. I knew some of them were belittled by their classmates, excluded, or treated as if they weren't qualified to be there and weren't smart enough to stay there and graduate. I knew this not only because they told me but also because I'd faced similar problems while I was in nursing school. I would give them tips and show them things other people didn't take the time to show them. I tried to do for them what I wished more people had done for me when I was a student.

One day, I noticed an older Black nurse-practitioner working on our floor. She looked familiar, and I walked up to her. I quickly realized who she was and where I knew her from. Her style and confidence struck me, just as they had back when I was a candy striper. It was the nurse who had inspired me all those years ago. She was still fly. "That was you!" I said. "You were the reason I went into nursing." It was meaningful to be able to thank her.

My sense of fulfillment by my new career was tempered by the exhaustion brought on by the long days. At the end of my twelve-hour shifts, I took off the stethoscope I'd worn all day. I emptied my scrubs shirt pockets of scissors, Band-Aids, gauze, IV tubing labels, pens, and my daily patient assignment sheet, putting everything in its proper place. I got in my car and lost myself in gospel music as I drove to pick my kids up from school.

We had moved out of my dad's home soon after I got the job at Holy Cross Hospital. We were once again living in an apartment of our own. Before I even crossed the threshold, walking in the door, I took off my Dansko nursing shoes. I always bought the thick-soled clogs in iridescent, shiny styles and wore them over bright, colorful socks. That was my signature. It was a way to show some individuality despite the drab navy-blue hospital-mandated scrubs that my colleagues and I wore daily. I thought the flashes of color might bring some light and joy to my patients and us staff. But because of all the fluids and waste that I encountered at work, I never let the soles of my shoes touch my floors at home. My clothes immediately went in a bag in the laundry hamper. I fed Zion and Angel and tucked them in for the night, and then I took a couple hours for myself. I would sit in my bedroom, turn up my music, and zone out.

I might read my Bible or watch TV. I needed to calm down and rest my mind a little before I went to sleep myself.

Our lives had become much better, easier, since I started working full-time as a nurse. I had good, inexpensive health insurance for myself and the kids. I could take sick days when I needed to and vacation days once I put in enough hours to earn them. I was no longer pleading to make $10 an hour. Instead, I started off making $19.50 an hour, and I received more when I put in overtime and worked into the nights or on weekends. A year after starting there, I was making $32 an hour as the weekend charge nurse. With more money, I was able to buy fresh fruits and vegetables. Finally, our cabinets and refrigerator shelves were free from all the canned foods, hot dogs, ramen noodles, and pastas that we had relied on when times were harder.

As a single mom, when I was struggling to make ends meet, I found it nearly impossible to regularly purchase fresh and healthy food for my young family. But we needed more of those foods, rather than the more affordable canned and processed foods, which have added sodium, sugar, and preservatives. It's not lost on me why children and families living in poverty, so often Black and brown, are more likely to be overweight or have diabetes, high blood pressure, and heart disease. Structural racism and inequity create so many barriers—time, distance, money—that put healthy eating out of reach for us, particularly for those of us who live in neighborhoods considered food deserts. Farmers markets and quality groceries are rarer in lower-income neighborhoods. Often these have an overabundance of fast-food chain restaurants instead, in a phenomenon called food apartheid.

Now, on top of being able to buy them nutritious meals, I was finally able to clothe Zion and Angel in new outfits and buy them new shoes. I didn't have to rely on our local thrift stores as much anymore, even though we continued to shop there. If the kids wanted to go to McDonald's, or someplace else to eat, I was able to take them. I didn't have to say no to them anymore. I wanted to help them feel like carefree kids. I no longer fell asleep each night wondering whether we'd get some utility turned off the next day. I now had student loans to pay back, but many of my old burdens eased.

Money was still tight. When I switched to working weekends after my promotion, childcare became even more expensive. I worked twelve-hour shifts on Saturdays and Sundays, and there were some days when the demands of the job kept me at the hospital for as long as sixteen hours. Zion and Angel's day care charged higher rates after 6:00 p.m. and for weekends. So, my dad stepped in again to help lighten my load. The kids went home with him Fridays after school and stayed with him through Sunday evenings. A few doors down from us in our apartment complex lived a wonderful couple with three children. My kids became quick friends with theirs, and all five of them spent hours playing together on weekdays after homework. The mother, who stayed at home while her husband worked, kindly offered to watch my kids during my weekday shifts at the hospital, and I paid her a daily rate. That helped too.

I was still balancing household bills, and I was digging myself out from the hole I'd gotten into while I was married. Because of how our divorce played out, I ended up with some of Hakim's unpaid bills as dings on my credit. I needed to settle a massive unpaid gas bill before I could get our gas turned on at our new home. On top of that, after a yearlong grace period following graduation, I was responsible for paying back the loans I'd taken out to go to nursing school. These alone were a huge burden at $500 a month. When I needed to, I took out payday loans. No matter how much I tried to avoid it, sometimes it became necessary. Payday loans are predatory, and the worry of taking out a new loan to pay for an existing one weighed on me. I had a stable job and was able to be on a payment plan. But with interest rates of 400 percent, payday loans hurt hard.

One day, I pulled in to the parking lot of a payday loan place. I turned my car off and went to open the door and step out. I paused. I glanced at my kids in the backseat. My mind darted from question to question: Why do I have to come here and do this again? Where can single parents get real help? What are our elected officials doing to help ease our load? Sure, sometimes a politician paid lip service to helping those on the furthest margins of society. But substantive change felt far away. And I knew that as soon as a person makes pennies over minimum wage, the help dries up.

We still had shutoffs. Our gas or electric would be turned off because I hadn't paid a bill in full. The bills were getting higher and higher each year. Payment arrangements were not accepted, or still too expensive for me to manage. But I believed that if I kept going in my new profession, life would eventually get better. Someday, I could start to build a savings account, or savings for the kids' college tuition. Over time, I could pay off old bills of mine and Hakim's and rescue my credit score. I would be able to get lower interest rates on car loans, lower premiums on car insurance, and maybe I could even begin to save money for a house.

The question that tied me in knots was *how* I was going to keep going, given the demands of my job at the hospital. We were often short-staffed in the transplant unit. I knew that without the right people in place, I wasn't going to be able to properly take care of my patients. I also couldn't take care of my colleagues who looked to me as charge nurse for leadership and protection. The pace was relentless. I might not find time to use the bathroom even once during my long shifts, until I clocked out for the day. Other days, the bathroom was where I'd go to cry, hoping to release some of the overwhelming stress through my tears.

On one of the days that we were understaffed, a nurse from a different floor was with us. She came to me at around three in the afternoon. "I don't know if you heard, but I'm leaving early," she said. She told me that she had completed her duties and that the administrator who sent her to work on our floor told her that as long as she had carried out the doctor's orders, she could leave, and the rest of us could monitor her patient for the next four hours until shift change. The patient in question had been in our unit multiple times. We all knew Margie. She was an older Black woman who had gone into the operating room for a procedure related to kidney failure, and now she was convalescing.

I realized the nurse meant she was ready to leave at that very moment, and so I asked her to give me a report on the patient. Once in the patient's room, she pointed me to the IV tubing and medications being administered. Margie appeared to be sleeping comfortably in bed. The nurse left for the day, and I went back in. The patient was still sleeping peacefully, covered in two or three folded blankets. The nurse had tucked her in well. I checked her tubing, the equipment. Then I gently pulled back her covers for what we call the head-to-toe assessment, to make sure she was in all right physical condition. Beneath the blankets the bed looked as if it were full of red jelly.

The patient was bleeding out, and as the plasma separated, the blood coagulated. I had never seen anything like that. I put on gloves and yelled for help, moving blood out of the way to try to find where she was bleeding from. She was still breathing and still had a pulse. I dashed into the hallway because it was closer than the phone and yelled to the residents nearby for help. This wasn't something I would typically do. We never wanted to alarm other patients or their family members. But at that moment, it didn't matter. I needed to get her help and fast.

I ran back into the room and assured the woman that she would be okay and asked her to answer some questions for me. What was her name? Where was she? What was today's date? I wanted to assess her level of consciousness after all of the blood loss. I also asked if she was in pain. She mumbled responses, but she kept her eyes closed. She couldn't manage to put a full sentence together. I assured Margie that she would be okay.

The doctors on duty came running and took over, calling in the attending surgeon. They started trying to close her wound right there in her bed. I took orders from them as we worked to save her life until she was transported to the operating room. After many hours of surgery, the team was successful. She made it. I was told later that someone had likely nicked her artery, resulting in the bloody scene I discovered when I checked on her.

I was Margie's nurse a week or two later, on the day of her discharge. She was sitting up and walking around. I was overjoyed. She was finally going home. Her son was helping her prepare for her discharge. He gently put her shoes on her feet and took instructions about which of her personal items to place in which bags. Her son had left the room for a while, while she awaited the final discharge papers from the doctor.

I walked in to find Margie sitting up to the side of the bed, bedside table pulled up in front of her, eating lunch with her back to the door. Even from that angle, I could tell she was in distress. When I walked up, closer to her, I saw that she was choking. I stood her up and performed the Heimlich maneuver. As I held her up, I could feel her starting to go limp. Thrust one, two, three, four . . . Nothing happened. She was larger than me, and I wasn't sure how long I could support her weight while trying to clear her airway. I got to thrust five and the piece of food, finally, flew out of her mouth. Twenty minutes later, her son walked in the door and took her by the arm, and together they went home.

High-stakes and high-stress moments like these were part of the job. Nagging ethical and moral issues tore at me. In transplantation, the racial disparities in access and treatment were glaring. We didn't just care for patients before or after they were operated on. Our transplant team would treat patients in the early stages of being diagnosed with kidney, liver, or pancreatic disease. Every patient in our Transplant Center received an advocate from our team who would explain the process and the lifestyle changes they'd need to make to receive a transplant. But not all patients could get, stay on, or move up a list for a new organ equally.

A lot of my Black patients just didn't have the stability they needed. To receive a new kidney or liver, a patient would be told to quit drinking if a drinker, stop smoking if a smoker, lose weight based on BMI (Body Mass Index), and keep up with all medical appointments. But a lack of reliable transportation, a lack of a strong support system, financial instability, hectic home lives, or depression stemming from disease, trauma, or addiction often got in the way of Black patients receiving a new, healthy organ as easily as white and wealthier patients could. Structural racism was at play.

· · ·

THERE WEREN'T MANY PEOPLE I could talk to about what I saw and experienced at work. I put in a good word for a nurse friend of mine, who then got a job on my floor. She worked nights and I worked days, and in those moments of overlap we had before I left for the evening, we liked to talk. I would let her know what was going on. She understood the pressures we faced at the hospital, being chronically understaffed. I didn't have many people in my life who did.

After about three years on the job, those bathroom breaks when I would let out my tears and frustration were becoming more and more frequent. One day, at around eleven in the morning, I was hit by the overwhelming feeling that every one of my days was the same. Every day, I came into work. And every day I fought just to make it through the day. While on my lunch break that day, I called my doctor's office to ask if they could prescribe me Xanax. I had never taken an antianxiety drug or an antidepressant before. When I realized what I was doing, I hung up the phone. "If I have to have Xanax to be able to work, I shouldn't do this," I told myself. Plus, I couldn't take a sedative and then work a shift under the influence. I quit my job that same day.

I took a break from nursing for four months, but I didn't stay away from my chosen career for long. I went back to work as soon as I could. In nursing, a job application can take quite some time. Hospitals are thorough. They run background checks, registry checks, and personality assessments. They make candidates fill out questionnaires, take tests, and submit all of their credentials before they are offered a job. In some cases, it can take six months or longer. Finding a new job took me three months. In the meantime, I worked for a home health company, tending to elders and people with chronic illness.

I would see four or five clients a day. Some were newly admitted to the health company. I'd meet them, learn what their needs were, and work with their medical team to come up with a nursing plan for their care, based on a physician's orders. Others were already clients, and I'd tend to them.

One of my clients was an older white woman who had advanced diabetes and had been diagnosed "severely obese." She struggled to be mobile, and she spent much of her day sitting on the seat of her walker so she wouldn't have to move from the couch to a standing position in order to go into the kitchen or bathroom. At night, she often urinated in her bed because of how difficult it was for her to get up. Given how extreme her mobility issues were, this woman needed to have a nurse with her around the clock. But she hadn't qualified for that benefit, and she didn't want it, either.

She was a cantankerous lady who would often swat at me or hit my hand if I touched her food or medicine. She wanted independence. I was with her for an hour, three times a week, and she didn't like a moment of it. She wasn't able to cook for herself, so she kept a freezer stacked with frozen dinners. I knew that processed foods were especially harmful to her. She was diabetic. But I could also understand why the meat, two side dishes, and dessert her prepared meals included were desirable to her. At least these were full dinners, not cups of ramen noodles or cans of Chef Boyardee. And preparing them was easy. All she needed to do was pull a box from the freezer and pop it into the microwave. After she ate, there was no cleanup, no pots or pans or dishes to stand to wash.

She loved her crossword puzzles, *Jeopardy!*, her two cats, whose dander triggered my asthma routinely, and her cinnamon rolls. Pastries were like friends for her. She kept Bundt cakes, Danish, cookies, and brownies out on her kitchen table so she could grab one easily when she needed a snack. That way, she wouldn't have to stand to rummage through her cabinets. The sugar put her at ease. Whenever I needed to help her change out of soiled clothing or give her an injection, she became extremely anxious. Afterward, she would take a pastry and have a bite, and immediately I could see her calm.

I worried about her diet. I knew her swollen legs were a sign that the sodium in her food was making her retain extra fluids in her body. I'd urge her to drink water instead of juice. I also knew the problem was bigger than her own decision making. There was only so much lecturing about nutrition that I could do, when her kitchen needed to be stocked with what she could afford. Some of these items she received from food pantries. She didn't have the money to adapt her home and make it safer to accommodate her limited mobility. She reused the needle for her insulin because she couldn't afford to buy new ones as often as she should have. She often skipped checking her blood sugar levels, because the strips she needed to monitor herself were expensive too. She didn't want to hear me say, "I need to take your food from you." This was her comfort. Plus, a nursing assistant who came to straighten up her apartment and bathe her sometimes threw her food away. If I did too, what could I provide her with instead?

Another one of my patients' homes was infested with roaches. He had a peripherally inserted central catheter and two diabetic wounds that needed proper, ongoing care. I would prepare a sterile field before changing his dressing. But cockroaches fell from the ceiling onto us. I'd try to knock them off without breaking my sterile field. It was a challenge. The roaches crawled across my client's arm while I was cleaning his wounds. The bugs would drop down onto my shirt, climb up my pant leg. I would be mortified. My visits were billed to be less than an hour, but the unsanitary conditions made the job take much longer than it should have.

I was kept on a tight schedule, and it was easy for me to get thrown off by unexpected delays. I often didn't know what I was walking into. I'm allergic to pet dander, so I wasn't assigned to homes with pets, and eventually my patient with two beloved cats was reassigned to another nurse. But sometimes patients didn't disclose that they lived with a cat or dog, and I'd arrive and be unable to stay. That kind of mishap would cut into my earnings for the day. A few times, I did stay. Particularly when I didn't want to just bail on the client. But I paid for it later with an asthma attack.

I didn't always feel safe, either. I never knew who else might be behind the door I was walking through. One patient, a paraplegic, invited more and more of his friends to his home during my visits. They used much of the time to make sexual advances toward me, while I had my back turned to them cleaning my client's sacral pressure wounds. It was uncomfortable, and I refused to return there. I also didn't know who might be waiting for me once I walked back outside. People in my regulars' neighborhoods saw my comings and goings. They knew when to expect me. They would say things like "Hey, Nurse, what you got in that bag for me? Let me get that bag!" They thought I might be carrying items of value: medication, equipment, and the like. If I ever got into trouble, I knew not to expect help from my employer. There was one number to call, and if that number was busy, I had nowhere else to turn in an emergency.

The home health company paid less than I made when I was working at the hospital, but still, it was a better job than most of the ones I had previously in my life. But I couldn't keep this up. It brought too much disappointment. I knew I wasn't able to give my patients the care they needed to be truly healthy. I was horrified to leave the home of my client with the roach infestation. I didn't want him to be alone in that environment. I worried that I would leave someone's home and something awful would happen to them in my absence.

In my hospital job, I stayed with my patients for long stretches of time. And when my shift ended, I knew they would be safe in someone else's care. In this position, I felt I was merely putting a

Band-Aid on my clients' problems and hoping they would be okay in the interim, until I returned. Sure, I could call the clients' doctors, ask that they write orders for additional services. But even if the doctor agreed that there was a need, that didn't mean an insurance company would agree to pay for more care. And clients didn't always want to invite more intrusion into their lives.

Working in home health care also brought too much financial uncertainty. Sometimes, my hours would be cut unexpectedly, and I needed a more consistent paycheck. After a few months, I took a part-time job at Holy Cross Hospital's Student Health Center, hoping a full-time position would open up. I would work as a clinical nurse caring for the students who attended the school. It would have to do for now.

In 2013, a year and a half after leaving the hospital, I was still looking for a full-time job. Finally, I found one advertised online that seemed right up my alley. A community mental health agency on St. Louis's south side was looking for an RN case manager to work with clients living with debilitating and chronic health issues.

St. Louis is deeply unequal when it comes to health outcomes, and the burden of this inequity falls hardest on our Black community. Low-income Black residents are far more likely to be uninsured or underinsured. They are more likely to lack regular access to primary care services, to be unhoused or housing insecure, to have lower life expectancy, and to suffer from chronic illnesses like heart disease, late-stage cancers, and diabetes—all of which can be deadly. In St. Louis, Black women are twice as likely to die during pregnancy or childbirth as white women, and Black children make up the vast majority of children suffering from lead poisoning. The opioid crisis also accounted for the highest rates of drug overdose deaths among Black people in Missouri.

I wanted to be able to address these disparities, to help close the racial health gap I had witnessed after having spent so many years in the field, and I wanted to eliminate the inequities that plagued my community. The position at New Day Behavioral Center seemed perfect. I took the job.

Four weeks in, I could not believe what I was seeing. Prescriptions were written incorrectly. Medications were administered improperly. I tried to do what I could to fix the problems. I began auditing client charts, checking for prescription errors. I saw everything from incorrectly written names and birth dates, to drugs listed without strength or dosage forms documented, to missing quantities of pills or refills. Conversely, there were prescriptions for controlled substances written out with eleven, even twenty-two refills. Many of the prescriptions were illegible.

I took copies of the prescriptions with errors in them to the prescribing doctors and alerted them to the issues. I notified them that scripts must be written properly for the nurses to follow. I gave each doctor a template—a sample script—to follow. Every prescription with an error was fixed by the doctor before the client left the clinic. The medicine cabinets and refrigerator were filled with expired medications still in use, so I ordered new ones. I properly disposed of the expired drugs and implemented a logging system. Quickly, my boss promoted me, and I took over managing the clinic.

What I'd learned back in nursing school about how well hospital work prepared people with a professional foundation proved to be correct. As exhausting as those years had been, my job at the hospital had given me rigor and expertise I could take with me anywhere. But at the hospital, my work had been focused on acute care. I was meeting immediate and pressing needs. At the clinic, I started seeing nursing in a new way. Our focus was on preventative care and putting our clients on a path toward wellness. Keeping them on that path despite all the roadblocks was a challenge.

I had clients who were actively hallucinating. I had clients who had to come in every month for a shot just to stay stable. I had children come in who were desperate to go to school but were prohibited from entering a classroom until they received their prescribed medicine. If a child's Medicaid had lapsed, and a parent couldn't afford their ADHD medication, for example, the child would not be welcomed back to school. Often, parents couldn't pay out of pocket. Medicaid might determine that the child was too young for a particular controlled drug, like medication for depression or anxiety. Either the child would not receive his medication, or it could take months of documentation on our part to receive approval, during which time the child would be unable to attend school.

Every day, I witnessed how pharmaceutical companies make being poor so expensive. Our access to money determines our ability to get the prescriptions we need, and it's not right. Why should American families have to choose between putting food on the table and getting their children the treatment they need? This is why today I advocate for Medicaid expansion and Medicare for All. At the clinic, I got to learn firsthand that our system is broken.

We worked with entire families. We took care of the younger child, the older child, the parent, and the grandparent, all of whom had confronted the same types of traumas, whether from witnessing domestic violence, living on the street, witnessing a murder, being victims of sexual violence, or suffering from addiction. When I wasn't trying to heal the addiction, abuse, or neglect that had haunted a family across generations, I was seeing how those same issues wreaked havoc on entire segments of society. My clients were often unhoused or transient, and some were victims of human trafficking. I understood how badly they needed care and how critical community care is. For as long as I can remember, I have been drawn to working with people who need more help than others. I understand those who need somebody to recognize their dignity and humanity, because I've so often needed that myself.

One day, a Black client in his thirties who suffered from auditory and visual hallucinations, and who had been to the clinic a few times over the course of a year, popped into my office. "Nurse," he said to me, "I'm going to kill my five family members. I'm going to kill them." I looked up at him. I needed to know how far he had gotten in putting together a plan. I asked what he was going to do. How he was going to kill them. He wasn't sure. "I'm not going to do it today," he told me. "When you do get ready to do it, come and let me know," I said. "Come to my office and just let me know."

A few months later, he did just that. I was at my desk in my office, in the clinic. It was a small room. The walls were painted blue, and on them I had hung pictures of my kids and certificates of achievement. He poked his head around my office door. He looked me straight in the eyes, and he said, "Nurse, I'm going to kill all five of my family members today." Then he took off running. Just before his figure disappeared again past my door, I noticed he carried a gun.

I jumped out of my chair and chased him down two hallways, down several flights of stairs, and out the back door, calling his name the whole time. It was a lively clinic, and no one thought it too strange to see the nurse chasing a client. Maybe he didn't want his injection, they must have thought. He didn't stop, but he yelled back to me to leave him alone. He ran out the two front doors and down the street toward a bus that was stopped and waiting for passengers to board. When I got within what I assumed was earshot, I started screaming, praying it was loud enough for the bus driver to hear me. "Don't let him on the bus!" I called. "If he has money, he can get on the bus," the bus driver yelled back. As I got closer, I tried to tell her that he had a gun. But she was determined to let him board.

Then she must have noticed the man's words were garbled, his body twitching, his arms flailing. She kept the door closed, preventing him from getting on board. I approached as he stood there looking at the bus, motioning frantically to the driver to open the door. She pulled the bus away from the curb and drove off. He turned to me and said, "Aw, Nurse," shaking his head like someone who is going to be late for work because they didn't make it in time to catch the bus. He gave me a look as if to say, "You care about me this much?" He was no longer yelling. He dropped his arms. And the two of us stood there and talked. I persuaded him to come back with me to the clinic.

We walked together, slowly, taking in the beautiful sun, warm weather, and the sounds of the busy street. I asked him why he wanted to hurt his family. The voices told him today was the day, he said. He told me he no longer wanted to hurt them, and he never did. He received the help that he needed.

I went home that evening as I always did. I kissed and hugged Zion and Angel and cooked them both dinner, as if it were any other ordinary day. And, for me, it was. The truth is that I hadn't been afraid. It might seem like too big a risk to chase after someone who was carrying a gun and had already threatened to use it. But my skin had grown thick from my years nursing. I'd seen patients be angry and resistant, and sometimes even violent, sometimes toward me. Now and then I would see one of our patients on the news when they took their own life or hurt others. I couldn't let that happen. It was our job to help people get well, to save lives. What if the patient encountered the police while experiencing a mental health crisis? Mental illness deserves to be treated by professionals, just as physical illness is. And all people living with a mental health condition deserve to be treated with dignity, compassion, respect, and mercy.

That day, I knew it was my job to do everything in my power to help that man. He'd taken the step to come and tell me what he planned to do. It was my job to make sure it didn't happen. I just wanted to help him. He deserved that. Everyone deserves that chance, no matter who they are or what their circumstances may be.

In these years, the lessons I learned from my clients deepened my understanding of humanity and how I could best be of service. So too did the work I was doing to deepen my faith in the Lord, and my desire to share His Word with others, a journey that would soon lead me down a new path.

Chapter 5

I GREW UP IN the church. Starting from when I was about twelve years old, and through my adolescence, I sang in our church youth choir, and I ushered on the youth usher board. I went to vacation Bible school each year, where for a full week youth from the community were invited to learn about the Bible together. Parents from the neighborhood sent their children each day, happy to have their kids in the church's care and take a break from childcare themselves. Full, hot meals were served, and I heard, a couple times, from some of the other kids that what they ate at vacation Bible school was more than what they had at home. The church was there to help meet the needs of our community.

As a teen, I saw how the church could make a difference. After making the confession before my church that I had accepted Jesus Christ as my Lord and Savior, I was baptized at twelve. My church practiced water immersion baptism, believing that one must be old enough to know right from wrong and make the decision to be baptized for themselves. I took a short class to make sure I understood what I was agreeing to and how I was expected to live honoring Christ with my life.

Our church's baptismal pool was in a room behind the pulpit and up a flight of steps high enough for the entire congregation to witness the baptisms through a clear glass that made up part of the wall.

On the back wall was a painted scene of white angels and cherubim flying against an azure sky, around gentle clouds. It was what some might imagine heaven looked like. I stood, draped in a white baptismal robe, in the pool, water up to my shoulders, in front of everyone I knew—my friends, my church friends, and Terrell, whom I had recently started dating.

The bishop gave a short speech; I responded in agreement as he moved my head back and forth with his hands as he delivered his words. Oh, how heavy his hand was on my head! I wanted to move but my hands were crisscrossed across my chest, and the water was too deep. Next thing I knew, I heard, "I baptize thee in the name of the Father, and of the Son, and of the Holy Spirit." I was underwater, lots of water. When I came up, the witnesses were praising God, clapping their hands, and crying, "Hallelujah." I knew from that moment I was a part of something bigger. But, even though I was connected to the rhythms and community of church since childhood, it would take almost another decade for me to know Jesus in my heart.

The moment I knew that I was saved came in my early twenties. I was trying to escape DeVon's abuse. I had left him, but his threats against my father controlled my life. At the time, I knew DeVon was stalking me, and I didn't want to give him any reason to track me to my father's house. To safeguard my dad, I went to live with my best friend from high school, Kenyatta, who knew about my situation. She agreed to let me stay with her temporarily. I thought I'd be safe with her, at least for a while.

I was working at Lighthouse Preschool at the time, and my commute from my friend's home to work was unbearable. I met the bus every morning at 6:00 and arrived by 9:00, ready to start my day. On the way home, my scheduled bus was due mere minutes after we closed, and if I missed it, I would have to wait for the next. One day, DeVon had been harassing me. He was repeatedly dialing my Sprint PCS phone, which I was proud to have at the time and liked to show off. It was black with an earpiece that would slide up to answer calls and down to end them. At the time, calls were still charged by the minute. DeVon would call all throughout my shift, and there was no way, even on my lunch break, that I was going to rack up minutes just to hear him cry, beg, or verbally assault me.

I was glad to just go home that day, and when I finally made it there and opened the door, the smell of chicken roasting in the oven welcomed me. But I wasn't hungry, and the warmth didn't lift my spirits. Instead, I was exhausted. I ached deep in my bones. I trudged to my friend's empty living room, where I slept on an air mattress that I'd brought. I sank onto it. An immense pain pulsed through my head, it radiated to my fingers, covering seemingly every inch of my body.

Outside the windows, the summer sun was fading. As the intensity of my headache grew, the room went dark around me. I heard the footsteps of my friend's two-year-old daughter, my goddaughter Imani, quietly walking into the living room toward where I lay. I opened my eyes to look at her, but I couldn't see. Something was wrong. I told her, "Tell Mommy to call 911." Then I felt myself go limp. I heard her little feet running first across the carpeted living room and then on the linoleum kitchen toward the back bedroom.

Imani hadn't gone to get help. Instead, she found a thermometer, which she tossed at me before giggling and running out of the room. My arm felt like a lead weight as I went to pick up the thermometer and bring it to my mouth. The red LED light read 105.9. Alarmed, I dropped it. I was too immobilized by the pain to even raise myself from bed. So I just lay there.

I told myself that I was okay with dying. I was tired. My life felt heavy, and hard. Then, suddenly, I heard a voice. "But you know Jesus," it said, and I was transported. More specifically, it was as if I were transported across the room, from where I could see my own limp body on the air mattress. "What's Jesus got to do with this?" I asked.

Until that point, Jesus, God, the Holy Ghost, was an idea to me. He was imponderable, an elusive being that I believed existed, but certainly not one that had ever directly communicated with me. Or so I thought. "Just call His name," the voice said. I struggled with my doubts. Where was Jesus when I was abused? Still, I never questioned the voice I was hearing, and I thought, What could it hurt? Reluctantly and flatly, I said, "Jesus." As soon as I did, my consciousness reentered my body. That same disembodied voice commanded me again, this time with force. "Say Jesus!" it said.

With more confidence, I repeated Jesus's name. The pain left my body, and I was thrust up to a standing position. The unnatural darkness that had filled the room was gone, and the retreating light of dusk returned. The voice that had brought me healing spoke again: "Turn on the radio." I flipped on the radio clock that I kept right next to my bed and found the gospel station we liked to listen to at Lighthouse. "I Told the Storm" by Greg O'Quin filled the air. *I command you to move today, / Because of faith, I have a brand-new day, / The sun will shine—and I will be okay.*

I saw myself reflected in those words. "Okay, God," I said aloud. "I surrender." At that moment, with my fever raging, I decided to change my life. I was going to live for God. And I lived. That next Sunday, I went back to the church I'd grown up in, and I started attending regularly again.

One day after service, I was walking to the car with my dad when one of the mothers of the church, an elder and wife of one of the deacons, walked up to us. "I had a dream about you," she said. "One of you is going to preach." My dad and I looked at each other, amused. "It's you," he teased. "No, it's you," I shot back. It didn't occur to me that it could be me. It was me, of course. But I wouldn't know until many years later.

·   ·   ·

ONE NIGHT, IN THE weeks after I realized we were headed toward divorce, I sat on my bed crying. The pain of our situation had engulfed me, and I was praying. I was trying to figure out what had happened in my life to bring me here. What went wrong? Here I was with two small children, facing the end of my marriage. While I prayed, I had left the television on in the background. Pastor Juanita Bynum was preaching on TBN, the Christian television network. I opened my eyes, and I listened. I don't remember exactly what she said that day, but I felt, deep within me, that she was speaking about me and my situation. I picked up my Bible and it fell open, out of my hands, to the first book of Jeremiah, to a passage spoken over me by preachers and church mothers many times: "Then the word of the Lord came unto me, saying, Before I formed thee in the belly I knew thee; and before thou camest forth out of the womb I sanctified thee, and I ordained thee a prophet unto the nations." Tears filled my eyes, and I kept reading down to the nineteenth verse. Next, I landed on the fourth chapter of Luke.

"The Spirit of the Lord is upon me," I read, "because he hath anointed me to preach the gospel to the poor; he hath sent me to heal the brokenhearted, to preach deliverance to the captives, and recovering of sight to the blind, to set at liberty them that are bruised, to preach the acceptable year of the Lord" (Luke 4:18–19).

In the midst of my tears, I was overwhelmed with unspeakable joy and peace. I began to feel strength in my heart where I had been weak, courage where I was afraid. I was hearing the Lord speak, I could feel His presence, and He was letting me know that I was called to become a pastor. I realized that God cared about me. He was paying attention to me, and to my situation, and He had plans for my life that filled me with both joy and awe. But I was also astounded. A flurry of questions filled my mind. My self-doubt nagged at me. How can I possibly preach to other people? I didn't attend seminary. Why me? Who would listen to me? How and when will this happen? I knew ultimately it would be in God's time and that I needed to be ready.

I started attending a new church. A friend introduced me to the pastor there, and after some discussion about God's call on my life he placed me in classes he offered for those he was training, mentoring in the ministry. Everyone seemed to be at a different stage in their journey. Unlike so many others at the time, this pastor believed that women could preach God's Word, and he treated us the same as the men in training. I took his classes while I was completing nursing school and getting my career in order.

When I gained initials behind my name, when I graduated, I knew I had finally found a path to stability that no one could take from me. I was on the right track professionally and financially. I started to see myself differently. I saw myself progressing, and I saw someone with a future, someone who was no longer a disappointment to my family. But I wasn't completely satisfied. It felt to me that something was still missing in my life. I needed to be closer to God, walking in my true purpose and serving others in new ways.

Because of all the things I'd gone through in my life up to this point and the intensity of my job at the hospital, I craved a deeper relationship with the Lord. A pastor I got to know, who led a church in north St. Louis County that I'd been attending, told me about an evening revival happening at a local church for the next several weeks. The revival was to be led by a pastor who was visiting from Rhode Island and known as the Apostle. Soon, I was going every night.

.   .   .

IT TOOK SOMEONE FROM outside St. Louis's spiritual community to take me under his wing and guide me on my path. In most of the churches I attended locally over the course of my adulthood, I kept running into the same problems. I was a young, unmarried woman with children. I didn't always feel welcome at some churches. Some women felt that I was there to steal their men. They brought their complaints to the pastor. But I didn't go to church to find a man. I wanted only the Lord.

Some married women in the congregation, if they happened to spot their husbands talking to me, would interrupt our conversations and grab them away. At one church, some of the women told me they didn't like the way that I shouted when I was filled with the Holy Ghost. The way that my body moved was lascivious, they said. They worried that when I bent over, I was performing. I was trying to entice their husbands. They didn't believe that I was having genuine religious experiences, as other congregants freely did. And so these women would scurry toward me and hold up cloths to shield me so their husbands' innocent eyes would be spared. One of the elder mothers in leadership even called me a harlot during Bible study.

It was ridiculous. It also helped me understand why I was often one of the only single women in the congregations of the churches I attended. Any others usually came as part of a larger family unit. But I was a single woman who came on my own, and more than that I was an outsider. So I was seen as a threat.

It wasn't just the women. I hadn't been treated much better by the men in church leadership. Pastors would call on me to host guest preachers when they came to town. I was to help the guests, orient them to the church and serve them water or meals when the occasion called for it. These men—more often married than not—would inevitably make advances. We might be in the pastor's study or preparing to walk into the sanctuary where they were due to begin preaching. Oftentimes the guest pastors would comment on the size of my butt or my hips or on the shape of my lips.

I had looked to these men of God as people whom I might be able to learn from, and I felt violated and devastated by the vile things they'd say. I didn't know what to do. These men were often friends of the church's pastor, so I couldn't expect them to be held accountable. Had my own pastors told these visitors that it was okay to treat me this way? Were they spreading the word that I was unmarried and so sexually available? Local preachers too would hit on me during church services or right after, during those moments in the sanctuary when everyone gathered and talked. A few times, this happened while my children stood next to me.

It was refreshing to meet Apostle Tim, this preacher from out of state who had seemingly no ungodly agendas. He was a devoted husband and a father whose ministry touched churches around the globe. When I started going to the revival services that he led, Apostle Tim treated me like a human being and showed me respect. His wife was a kind woman, and I was drawn to her presence too. With them, I felt the Lord was leading me on a new journey.

During each of Apostle Tim's services, I could feel the very presence of the Lord in the room. It was as if Apostle Tim were speaking directly to me, building me up in my faith, laying a groundwork in me spiritually, brick by brick, that I didn't know was possible. The gospel he preached was filled with love as I had never seen before. People in the audience wept. They said when they walked in the door in pain, the pain disappeared. People who had difficulty walking ran around the room, just by hearing the gospel preached. How was this happening? I wondered. I watched it happen, and I thought of a passage from Corinthians that read, "Now you are the body of Christ, and each of you is a member of it. And in the church God has appointed first of all apostles, second prophets, third teachers, then workers of miracles, and those with gifts of healing, helping, administration, and various tongues." I knew Jesus was a healer; I knew Peter, Paul, and others like Philip were healers. But these were figures from the Bible. At the revival, my eyes were opened, and I learned that what the Bible teaches about healing still applies today.

There have always been Christians who believe in healing through faith, and this is particularly true in Black churches. The practices that have developed in this country are not so different from the rituals of divine healing and prophecy that we see in Santeria in Cuba, Vodou in Haiti, and Candomblé in Brazil. They all share an origin, their roots, in Ifa, the West African system of faith that many enslaved people carried with them during the Middle Passage.

Healing miracles were a central part of the ministry. There was no shame or deception involved. It was simply what was taught and what we believed.

One evening, during the revival, I was called up to the front. Apostle Tim would pray individual prayers and sometimes laid his hands on those who came up to the front of the church for prayer. When he got to me, he touched my stomach with two fingers, paused, and yelled, "Fire!" Apostle Tim then moved his hand back and quickly toward me, as if he planned to hit me. In truth, he barely touched me, but upon contact with his hand, I hit the floor.

The Holy Spirit consumed me, and I lay there on the floor as if in a hypertonic state for the next three hours. During that time, my body burned. It was not painful. Rather, it was as if a cleansing were taking place inside me. Something amazing was happening. Emotional scars were healed; burdens were lifted. I felt an unimaginable, unspeakable joy.

The next evening, Apostle Tim opened his service with a song. I prayed quietly, telling the Lord over and over that I gave myself to Him. As soon as I heard Apostle Tim's words amplified through the microphone, I felt a heavy but peaceful weight on me, and I fell prostrate on the floor just as I had the night before. I was knocked out again, this time for more than four hours. The Apostle told me that during those periods of what looked like unconsciousness, God filled me with His healing anointing.

Each time I was filled by the presence of the Lord, I felt stronger, more confident. I came back to myself knowing that I had a purpose. I didn't know exactly what that purpose was, but I knew that I mattered. I knew I was to keep walking and keep trusting.

My transformation wasn't just happening while I was at church. My private spiritual walk deepened, too. I was fasting from certain foods, even foregoing whole meals, for ritual purposes, for days, weeks on end. I listened only to gospel music and watched television shows that were spiritual, uplifting. I attended every evening revival service there was, and even invited friends. Zion and Angel were used to these services by now and brought their books and toys. I spent most of my time, after the kids were asleep and before they awoke in the mornings, reading, studying, and meditating on God's Word. It was my food and my air.

The meaning of scripture revealed itself to me in new ways. I often turned to the stories of David and Esther. David was the warrior who had the courage to fight a giant and win. He lacked Goliath's strength, but he knocked the giant down with one small, smooth stone to the head. David knew his purpose and carried inside him the wit and the wisdom of the Lord. He used what he had in his toolbox and emerged victorious. David wasn't perfect, but God still used him in mighty ways. Other people didn't see David's potential for greatness, but God could.

I, too, wasn't perfect. I had made bad decisions and done ugly things. I turned on my family to date first DeVon and then Hakim. I disrespected the church by showing up in coochie-cutter shorts, in a drunken state, even though I was supposed to be setting an example to the younger girls at the church. After my abortion, I showed them what it was like to be a cold, heartless vixen. I had been wrong.

Studying the story of David kept me from dropping my head in shame when I thought about the things I'd done in the past. I might not have gone to Tuskegee as I'd wanted to. I didn't join the air force as I had set out to do. But all was not lost. God could still use me. It was time to take my eyes off what I didn't have and where I'd stumbled, because God still had a plan for me.

The story of Esther had a special meaning for me as a woman who felt called to ministry. In the Bible, a powerful Persian king chose Esther to be his queen, turning away all the other women clamoring to take their place at his side. Esther didn't have a special upbringing. No one felt she was someone a king would pay attention to. And yet the king did. God put Esther in a position to stop her husband's chief adviser from ordering the genocide of her people, the Jewish people. She stepped out on that God-given mission and saved her people's lives.

Like Esther, I was a woman who didn't have any markings of greatness. I wanted to become a pastor because I was called to it, but I didn't come from a preacher's family. I didn't have the support of the city's powerful religious leaders. Still, I knew that I had to press forward.

Because I attended those nightly services so often, I got to know Apostle Tim, and I came to think of him as my spiritual father. Hundreds of people came to the revival services and sought out opportunities for more in-depth learning from him. The two he chose to take under his wing were LaShonda, a woman I had met at the revival and had grown close to, and me.

Apostle Tim told us that we were children of the king. He believed we should be treated like royalty because we were children of God, and he wanted to teach us how to carry ourselves with confidence and self-respect. One day, as Apostle Tim, LaShonda, and I were finishing a meal together at Red Lobster after church, he asked us to take him to whichever mall in the area had the most high-end shops. He dressed in expensive suits, and so I wasn't surprised to hear that he wanted to shop someplace that could cater to his refined tastes.

When we pulled into the parking lot at the Plaza Frontenac mall, I changed out of the heels I'd had on and slipped on a comfortable pair of flat shoes. But Apostle Tim wouldn't have it. "Oh no, put your heels back on," he said. "I want to show you something." As we walked from store to store, the staff gravitated to him and served him with deference and respect. Everywhere we went, Apostle Tim was treated as if he were a person of great importance, like royalty. In a store that sold luxury watches, the private security guard standing sentry moved out of the way as we entered, and a salesperson rushed to bring us glasses of champagne. I was taken aback. I was used to being ignored in places like this or else watched closely, as if the people on staff were worried I might steal something. Apostle Tim modeled for LaShonda and me how we should expect to be treated.

In the summer of 2011, I went to a conference that Apostle Tim's ministry was hosting in Rhode Island. The weeklong event was called Power School of Miracles, and it drew people from all over the world. I was struck by the racial, ethnic, and cultural diversity of those who gathered for Apostle Tim's teachings. We all believed we had a gift and had been called to be a conduit of God's healing. At the conference, we attended services several times a day, all of which were opportunities to build up our faith, courage, and knowledge of the Word and to surrender fully to the Lord. We learned how our words have power, how to lay hands upon someone in need of healing, and how to let the power of God move through us to the intended recipient.

After one of the services, when everyone was sent on break, Apostle Tim took LaShonda and me aside. He encouraged my dreams of leading my own church one day, and told us about a four-month pastoral internship program he offered there in Rhode Island. I would be able to take more ministry classes and work for the ministry while learning from Apostle Tim. This was a special opportunity, and I desperately wanted to take part, but I had a full-time job and kids to take care of. I didn't see how it could be possible.

When I returned home and got back to the hospital's transplant unit, where I had been working, I didn't see how continuing there was possible either. With Apostle Tim's help, I had gained a clearer understanding. I saw clearly that devoting so many hours of my life to a job that left me depleted—tired and worn out—was not the answer. This was not going to be my path to fulfillment. There had to be more. The phone call to my doctor's office in search of a Xanax prescription woke me up. It was time. I was going to take up my calling.

I left my nursing job and prepared for my family to move to Rhode Island for a few months. It was going to be an eighteen-hour drive, and I got as far as loading up the car. But when I came out to the car the day we were going to get on the road, I saw I had a busted tire. I'd budgeted so carefully to make the internship possible, and I didn't have any extra money with which to fix the tire and also fill up my gas tank to get us there. I had to put my dream on hold.

Apostle Tim wouldn't let me give up. Instead, I worked with

him by phone occasionally and took on reading assignments and spiritual tasks that he gave me. I was unemployed then, for a brief period, and searching for a new job. I had plenty of time to pray and read the Bible. I spent hours on research, learning about the histories, places, and cultures referenced in the Bible.

As I learned how to apply God's Word to my life in new ways, I better understood the power that was already residing in me. It was there, waiting for me to acknowledge it, to use it. I had the confidence to heal others with God's power just as I'd been healed and as I'd witnessed. One day, as I sat in an afternoon prayer service back in St. Louis, I noticed a toddler lying across the lap of an older woman. I was struck by her and watched her.

Unlike what would be typical of most children her age, she didn't try to get down to play. She lay quietly, resting on the woman. We finished praying, and as the room began to empty out, I heard the woman explain to someone that this girl was her granddaughter. Her daughter was in the hospital, and so she was taking care of the girl for a while. The child had had a bleed in her brain, shortly after she was born, and so couldn't walk. She had never taken a step in her life.

I viscerally remembered every time the doctors told me they suspected Zion had a brain bleed when he was a newborn, and I slowly walked up to the woman. "Do you mind if I take her for a moment?" I asked her. She agreed, eyeing me with a look, watching guardedly what I might do. I carried the child from the prayer room in the back of the church out into the sanctuary. My friend LaShonda was with me. I put the child down at the end of the aisle between two rows of pews at the back of the church. I held one of her hands while LaShonda held the other, and we stood her up. "Walk," I said gently to the three-year-old girl, "you will walk." And this girl took her first step. Then another, and another. She walked.

Her grandmother walked into the sanctuary just in time to see the child take about two dozen steps. She screamed, and then she kept screaming. When she caught her breath, she looked at me in wonder and said, "Praise God." She grabbed her granddaughter and walked with her out of the church and down the parking lot to the car. After they left, I never saw them again.

LaShonda and I had believed the impossible was possible. We stepped out on faith and saw God's healing power without any big names or titles; we saw it in people who love Jesus and love humanity. I thought of the book of Matthew, which read in part: "And Jesus said unto them, Because of your unbelief: for verily I say unto you, If ye have faith as a grain of mustard seed, ye shall say unto this mountain, Remove hence to yonder place; and it shall remove; and nothing shall be impossible unto you."

I was itching to take what I'd learned and share it with other people. I was itching to take it out to the streets of St. Louis. I felt blessed to have found Apostle Tim's service, but I couldn't expect everybody to just walk through the church doors, or to even know what was available to them inside. LaShonda and I wanted to take the message and the healing to where people were. We wanted to help anyone and everyone we encountered, if they had a need. We wanted to share meals with those who were unhoused. We wanted to bring healing to those who were sick, and connect them with resources, whether that was affordable housing, medical care, or jobs. We wanted to help make people whole and help them stay well. But how could I expect them to get to the church?

For a few months in 2011, LaShonda and I, along with two musicians from the church where the revival had been held, went out and prayed for people around our community. We would go to a park near a shelter for the unhoused and to other places around St. Louis where we thought we could find people who would accept our prayers. If we saw someone on the street who was limping, or who had some other kind of visible ailment, we would walk up to them and ask if we could pray for healing for them.

We saw some healings happen right there on the street. One woman whom we met had several visible tumors on her torso. She was due to have surgery but lacked health insurance and was living in a park. One of the tumors was particularly painful for her. I laid hands on her and prayed, and I felt that my hand was no longer touching a tumor. It shrank along with the others on her body. The four of us, LaShonda and I and the musicians, wore matching light blue T-shirts whenever we went out to pray. After a while, people came to recognize us. People would wave as they saw us approaching.

Once we were walking in the northern part of the city where fast-food restaurants, a gas station, and a bank crowded a busy intersection. We were on our way to a White Castle when, just ahead of us, I spotted a woman whose appearance was disheveled, whose clothing was soiled, tattered, and worn. She stomped the ground and moved with exaggerated force, but aimlessly. My companions and I glanced at each other and approached her. But as we drew nearer, she spoke before we could. "No," she said, addressing us with conviction. "I know what you want, and you can't heal me. I'm keeping my demons." Then she turned around, and she ran away from us.

Despite her withdrawal, I felt reassured, encouraged. She didn't want to be touched by our healing power, but she could feel it and trusted that it was real. Being recognized in that way convinced me that we were on the right path.

My connection to Apostle Tim and to Pastor LB, the local pastor who hosted the revival and who knew about and supported our street outreach, gave us legitimacy. Several months later, at the church with the cream-and-green-colored decor, I was ordained by the pastor who first told me about Apostle Tim's revival. He was a man of prayer and integrity who helped all those who petitioned him, no questions asked. I witnessed him doing so. I had grown close to him by attending his daily prayer services, and he showed delight in my development. He encouraged me to go and shepherd, as I had been called to do.

I had been introduced to bishops, evangelists, teachers, and ministers who were a part of Apostle Tim's circle, and they all cheered me on. Receiving their excitement and enthusiasm after I was ordained made me believe that I could pastor a congregation, even as a young, single woman. It was time to start my own church.

It was going to be a serious undertaking. I was a lone parent trying to stay afloat financially, and I knew I would be footing the bill should I start a church. Any rent, utilities, advertising, or outreach I wanted, I would have to pay for up front. That was a risk, and it made me apprehensive. But I was going to trust God. I wasn't alone. My local pastor and the Apostle urged me on. They believed in me and wanted to see me succeed. I wasn't going to be a youth pastor or an associate minister this time, like I had been for other ministries before. Instead, I would be the pastor, the visionary. I would be the one leading and preaching, the one building the church, pulling in congregants, and setting the tone. I would be the shepherd of a flock.

.   .   .

IN 2012, I FOUNDED Remnant Church Ministries. The remnant is the true church. It's made up of people who are set aside for God's holy purpose, those who overcome calamity and catastrophe to fulfill His will and return unto Him. Many people feel, as I had, that they have no purpose. They feel they can't do great things because they've made mistakes in their past. I wanted my church to be an open door to everyone, a place where redemption and purpose were for all.

I began by holding Saturday morning services in my home with a group of about fifteen to twenty people. At that time, Zion was fourteen and Angel thirteen. We had upgraded to a three-bedroom ranch home with a large finished basement in Hazelwood, a suburb of St. Louis. With us was a pet fish we'd named Blue. Friends I'd made at the revival and through my street ministry brought their families over to our home each week. We sat on the big tan and brown couches in our open-concept living room. We dragged in every chair from our dining room and breakfast nook. Together, we sang along to the gospel music on our worship playlist. Someone would read the scripture, and another congregant would lead the prayer. We'd collect a small offering, even though sometimes none came in. And then I would preach.

Those who gathered believed in the type of ministry I was creating. Like me, they were tired of worshipping in places that did not believe in the ministry of healing and miracles. We all believed in instantaneous, miraculous healing. We believed that there are people alive today who are anointed with the gift to heal the same way Jesus, Peter, Paul, and others were. In my ministry, I taught that it was important to love people as they are. I taught that through faith, love, and acceptance, healing and miracles are possible. I taught others to tap into their God-given healing gifts. My children and my nieces learned how to pray and lay hands on those who needed healing. It became second nature to them. Unlike other churches, I established that my ministry would primarily live in the streets. As LaShonda and I had wanted, we would meet people where they are. Yes, we'd meet in my living room for the time being. We'd come together indoors to encourage each other and build our faith. But we'd spend the bulk of our time outside exercising our faith out in the community.

Other people thought I had no business leading a ministry as a single woman, but those who stepped out with me on faith in those early days had no issue with my marital status. They believed that God had anointed me, and they stuck with me. It would have been nice to have a husband or a partner by my side as I led the congregation. I was doing it alone because I needed to answer my call. And I wanted to create a safe space for women, where they could come and worship without worrying that the preacher might make sexual advances.

I knew many women who stopped attending church because they'd been harassed or sexually assaulted there. Some felt ashamed because the preacher was married, and the women felt the unwanted attention was their fault. I knew what it was like to be hit on repeatedly and relentlessly, deceived, and lied to by a married pastor. There were single pastors and ministers who did the same. But not in my church. Mine was going to be one of the few congregations where that wasn't the case.

Our ministry didn't stick to the traditional hierarchies found in many churches. Women could preach the sermon. Women could wear pants during service. Our unhoused community members could walk in the door just the way they were. There was no dress code that they needed to meet to be welcomed. Children and young people also played an active role. We allowed children to speak before the congregation and read scriptures aloud. My son, Zion, preached his first message as a young boy. And bringing our ministry onto the streets continued to be a central part of our work. We went all over the city of St. Louis and St. Louis County to spread the Word of God and share Christ's love.

The very thing that made us unique—the close attention we paid to youth and the unhoused—also came with its challenges. I held services in my home because we didn't have money to move into a building. And I personally paid Remnant Church Ministries' expenses. Eventually, we received a donation from one of Apostle Tim's friends and decided that we would rent out half of a hotel banquet room at the Courtyard Marriott, by St. Louis Lambert International Airport, for our weekly Sunday service. Finally, we were in a formal space dedicated to church, rather than at what sometimes felt like an intimate Bible study in my home.

Early Sunday mornings, one or two parishioners and I would drive to the hotel. Maybe that was a week we could afford to hire a musician, and so we'd pull that person's drum set or keyboard from the trunk of my car before making our way inside. Walking through the lobby, we'd pass people we knew we would never see again, people who were staying overnight before returning to the airport and continuing on their way to someplace else. From the ground floor, we'd make our way one level down to the banquet rooms, decorated in dated brown carpets and ostentatious chandeliers. We'd lug the lectern to the right place and set up our chairs. One parishioner, an elder woman, had decided to take on hospitality. She'd neatly arrange the back table with water pitchers and the fruits or pastries we offered as breakfast snacks to accompany the hotel's carafes of coffee.

The effort it took to set up and break down the space was worth it. We had grown to about thirty members, and it felt as if we had momentum. Standing up there at the lectern, looking at those who came every week, I could feel that we were at the beginning of something important. Some of these people had become my good friends. And we were a ministry that would continue to grow and transform people's lives. Among the ministry were pastors who would preach and teach as well. Every Sunday, I couldn't wait to see people arrive, people who were invested in building up the church and cultivating their relationship with God. Some folks read scripture; some volunteered to hand out flyers in the community as part of an outreach program. People were eager to become more involved in the ministry.

We'd been there several months when I decided we were ready for a more permanent home. While we'd done the best we could with the banquet room, it felt temporary. Not having to set up and break down every week would be a welcome change. Because tithes and offerings still didn't cover the bills, I suspected that I would have to continue to carry the church financially. By then, I was working at the community health clinic, and I had steady income once again. I could make it work. But, still, money was tight. After searching for a long time, I found a space we could share with another ministry, dividing up the rent and the utility bills. It was going to be perfect— just what we were looking for.

The day that I was supposed to sign the lease, I arrived at the church, and I could tell something had changed dramatically since my previous conversation with the landlord. The bills, which included rent, water, gas, electricity, and trash removal, were doubled. He told me that the other church that had been renting the building had moved out. I would be responsible for the bills, entirely on my own, even though my access to the building would remain limited to three hours on Sundays and two hours on Wednesdays for Bible study. I begged the landlord to lower the monthly payment to what we had agreed, but he wasn't willing. Devastated, I had no choice but to abandon the plan. I informed my members that week. Some felt let down and stopped attending. We had been so close, and our hopes had been high. I questioned my mission again. It seemed as if we were starting to get on our feet, but our finances were a persistent challenge. I needed to figure out what our next steps were going to be, and in the meantime I returned to holding services in my home.

.　　.　　.

THE MORNING OF SATURDAY, August 9, 2014, our congregation had gathered in my living room, as usual. After everyone said their goodbyes, the kids and I went out to buy groceries and get lunch. I checked social media a few times, as was my habit, and noticed one photograph kept appearing in my feeds. In it, I saw a Black teenager lying prone on the ground, lifeless, with his arms down by his side. I could tell he was on a street in a residential area. He was just lying there; I couldn't tell that he was shot, because there wasn't blood in the photo that I could see, but you could tell by the way he lay on his stomach that he was lifeless.

I didn't pay much attention to it. I didn't read any of the commentary that accompanied the photo in people's posts, and I had no idea that this was a photo of someone from our own community in St. Louis. That night, I went out on a date. We were out to dinner, seated together on a restaurant patio enjoying a piece of chocolate cake between us for dessert. At some point, during a lull in our conversation, I picked up my phone and started scrolling again. That photograph. There it was again.

By 2014, I had followed the highly publicized killings of Trayvon Martin, Oscar Grant, Aiyana Stanley-Jones, and others. At times, I felt numb from the trauma of witnessing the broadcast of mutilated and degraded Black bodies on social media and television, lives tragically ended by police or vigilantes. "Why am I seeing this picture again? What happened?" I thought to myself.

I read that it was a photograph of an eighteen-year-old boy who had been killed by police at Canfield Green Apartments in Ferguson, a municipality in the northern part of the county, just six minutes from where I lived. His body had lain on the street for four hours and thirty-two minutes. It was left uncovered for most of that time.

At the end of my date, I went home. I lay in bed, and I watched video footage of what was unfolding: Michael Brown Jr.'s family members and neighbors had been out, keeping vigil at the place where their boy was killed, for hours. Nearly a hundred other people had gathered there with them. They demanded answers. As more and more people heard the news, residents of Ferguson and the surrounding areas filled the streets near where his body had been left, exposed to the heat of the late summer day. Our community was heartbroken and outraged. And so was I. I fell asleep watching the news.

Part Three

Chapter 6

WHEN I WOKE UP on Sunday morning, I called around to see if anyone wanted to head over to the protest. I found little interest. One of my friends said he'd go with me but later said he'd decided it was too dangerous to take me. Instead, he went on his own. Later that day, he called me with news of what he saw. "It's people looting. It's people throwing rocks at glass windows and breaking into stores," he said. "There's so much going on, gunshots ringing out. You don't need to be out here."

I decided to go on my own. I didn't get out of my car, but I drove around and took it all in. The police blockades. People running up and down the street. The dark, chaotic streets and the air filled with anger, tension, and uncertainty. I couldn't understand what was happening. But I could tell the police were on edge. I wasn't sure what they might do. Because I was alone, I didn't think it was safe for me to stay. I didn't know anyone there. I decided to leave.

Although it was once a majority-white area, white flight had led it to become a predominantly Black city of about twenty-one thousand. At the time of Michael Brown Jr.'s killing, it had a nearly all-white police force; out of fifty-three commissioned officers, only four were Black. Ferguson sits close to St. Louis city limits and throughout my life it has been part of my community. It was where I sometimes did my grocery shopping. On those streets where the protests were now brewing were many businesses that I patronized: the salon where I got my hair done, the shop where I got my nails done, the restaurant where I got my barbecue, and another where I got my soul food. I'd once looked at renting a place at Canfield Green Apartments, a series of three-story buildings covered in brick and yellow siding, the same complex where Michael Brown had been fatally shot. I grew up not far from Ferguson and was often there with my family, or seeing friends, as a child.

That Sunday, as the protests swelled with thousands of people, the police positioned tanks and what looked like other military-grade vehicles in the parking lot of the old Northland Shopping Center. This mall, where in my younger years my parents bought me my shoes for Easter services, was now law enforcement's command center in the area. It was where we picked up our take-out fried rice and where we frequented the local Sears and JCPenney. By the time Michael Brown was killed, a lot of those stores were gone, lost to disinvestment and white flight.

On Monday, I went to work at the community mental health agency and called my supervisor. What was happening in Ferguson mattered to me. I said, "I'm letting you know that I'm going to be out there. The people need help, and we need to do something." For years now, I'd been going into the streets to pray with people and do my best to meet their material needs. Now I held a position of influence within one of the city's mental health agencies, and it was time to take our expertise and resources to a community that was suffering. Later that same day, I got a call from my boss: "We decided to put together a mobile response team," she told me, and I was going to be a part of it.

Every weekday from eight in the morning until five in the evening, a medical doctor, therapists, a caseworker, and a nurse from our company were going to be in Ferguson, on the ground and administering services. We didn't know for how many days we would be out there, but we knew that we would stay for as long as was needed. We joined forces with Better Family Life, a local Black community development organization where my father worked. I was to be the nurse on the team. My first night out protesting, I went with my friend and colleague Jihad Khayyam. Jihad worked for Better Family Life Inc. with my dad. They had been colleagues for fifteen years. Jihad had looked after Angel and Zion at the organization's after-school program and was determined to make Angel, who had a talent for chess, into a phenomenon. I'd heard about Jihad for years from my dad and children, and we finally got to know each other when we began working together at Canfield Green. During the day, we'd talk about wanting to deepen our involvement in the community and address the issues surrounding Michael Brown Jr.'s death alongside the masses of people in the streets.

The next day, we drove to where Michael Brown had been gunned down and pitched a tent to shield our table from the sun. Flanking us on both sides of the street were the Canfield Green Apartments. It was a typical St. Louis August day, upwards of ninety-five degrees. The air was heavy with humidity. The intense heat had driven the residents of Canfield Green onto the building's wooden balconies and external staircases. The ongoing protests had brought out thousands and partially shut down nearby West Florissant Avenue. Buses and cabs avoided the area as unpredictable police lines popped up, stopping traffic. People from the neighborhood had to cross these lines just to get to the grocery store.

At Canfield Green, residents had limited access to nearby essentials, which changed their day-to-day lives drastically. Our job was to bring them what they needed. I posted our tent's location to Facebook and announced that we were accepting donations: food, formula, diapers, toilet paper, and other household items. People started showing up immediately. Soon, the one table that we'd brought with us was overflowing. By the end of the week, we had already expanded our operation. We had three tents, several tables filled with supplies, and another table where we performed medical triage and checked blood pressure for those who needed it.

I was nursing supervisor at the clinic at that time. In that role,

I oversaw the medical aspects of the organization's adult and children's mental health clinics and residential care facilities. I managed our team at Canfield Green, I was the primary contact for our partnership with Better Family Life, and I coordinated with staff within other departments at our organization to make sure that we had what we needed on the ground.

All day long, people came over to talk with us. One mother needed Pull-Ups. I'd chat with her about her children's weight and age, checking to make sure we had the right size. We learned that many neighbors needed what we were offering, but weren't willing to come outside to our tent. We started knocking on doors. One man had a wound that needed to be cleaned and dressed, but he told us he was too afraid to come outside for help. He couldn't get the picture of Mike Brown Jr.'s body out of his head. He couldn't bring himself to go to where he lay. And he wasn't the only one. People were traumatized. They didn't want to leave their apartments. So we came to them.

The doctor and I went door-to-door together and did prenatal checkups, monitored blood sugar, and bandaged surgical wounds. We asked people what they needed, then went back to our tents to pack bags with toothpaste, soap, and toilet paper and deliver them to people's doors. As the days went by, and the protests continued, I got to know the community in Canfield Green. I started asking the kids questions. "What did you eat today?" I would ask. "Nothing," I would hear. "What did you have for dinner last night?" Some hadn't eaten then either. It wasn't that they didn't have food at this point. These kids had no desire to eat.

"How did you sleep?" I asked. They found it hard to fall asleep and stay asleep. They were deep in grief. One little boy told me he was never going to school again. "Because the police got Mike Mike," he said when I asked why. "I don't want to go to school. I don't want the police to get me like Mike Mike." This boy, and so many others, had known Michael Brown. And now they were stunned and terrified by how the police had ended his life. That child felt as if even leaving the complex to learn could make him the next Black boy lying on the street. Dead.

At our tents, elders came to us sick from tear-gas inhalation. This was strange because the protests were over on West Florissant, not close enough for the chemical fumes to waft over to Canfield Green and be potent enough to make people ill. So how were people getting sick so far away? "In the middle of the night, the police come over here and fire tear gas," people told us.

.   .   .

My time as part of that mobile response team expanded my understanding of the public health impacts of policing and violence. Police violence is a leading cause of premature death for young Black boys in this country, and it is fully preventable. When our community's lives, livelihoods, and peace are threatened by the conditions of a lethal environment—be those toxic air or contaminated water or racist policing—we need public health solutions. We need to transform our approach to public safety so that it centers keeping us safe, keeping us alive.

For five weeks, we worked on the ground in Ferguson every single weekday. I often think back on the person I was then, dressed in my scrubs and knocking on doors, driven by my desire to serve God and my community. I didn't know it then, but this was going to be another moment that forever altered my life. It was my road to Damascus. Before then, and even at the beginning of that stretch of late summer weeks, I hadn't thought of myself as an organizer or activist. While police brutality affected me, I didn't know that I could be part of how to change it.

.   .   .

I understand why Michael Brown Jr.'s death at the hands of police woke up America in the summer of 2014. It woke me up, too.

Before then, I knew that police racially profile, that they stop and harass Black drivers and pedestrians. I'd grown up watching them do it to my friends. I'd thought racist and antagonistic cops were just an unfortunate and inconvenient fact of life. But when an officer of the law killed a Black teenager and it seemed he would just get off and be held no more accountable for a murder than he might be for harassment, that was different.

It might be hard to remember, but before Michael Brown was killed, there was not a lot of regular mainstream media talk about police murder. When someone died at the hands of the police, there wasn't typically a call for mass movement. There was no national outcry. A death would be dealt with as an isolated incident, a family tragedy, maybe something the local community unites over, to grieve together. People didn't, time after time, express their outrage and their grief on the streets.

I remember hearing about organizing to end police violence and save Black lives after Oscar Grant was killed by Bay Area transit police in 2009, and when Trayvon Martin was killed by George Zimmerman in 2012. These were tragic and critical moments when not enough of us had yet woken up and realized that state and vigilante murder of Black people could be eradicated in our lifetime, that we have the power to bring about the change our lives depended on. In the days following Michael Brown Jr.'s killing, I decided to not only help in my professional capacity as a nurse but also join the growing protests. Because of that decision, I got to see what made the Ferguson uprising a pivot point in the centuries-long struggle for Black liberation in this country. I was, however, hopeful. I went into the streets in my capacity as a nurse, and I sought accountability for Mike Brown Jr.'s death. "Any day now, justice will be served," I thought. That's what I believed. The police had demonized Mike Brown, and the officer who killed him was still on the streets. We weren't demanding much. We wanted Darren Wilson, the cop who killed Mike Brown, to be arrested, and we wanted to see Mike Brown vindicated.

Not long after we started protesting, we would be targeted by police, treated as if we were the ones doing harm just by demanding justice. Police tried to control and stop us. The Ferguson uprising would last for more than four hundred days and upend political complacency in this country and across the world, bringing racial and social justice to the forefront of public conversations. I would learn that I had to try to anticipate what would come next and that I needed to show up and offer the skills I had to meet the moment.

I had no idea that I would soon meet longtime friends. I had no idea some of those friends would die while doing the work of justice in the coming months and years. I had no idea that the world would change the way it did, and the way it continues to. And I had no idea that I was stepping onto a path that would eventually lead me to run for office.

.   .   .

DURING THE DAY, PROTESTERS gathered mostly on West Florissant Avenue, especially near its intersection with Ferguson Avenue. There sat Ferguson Market & Liquor at Ferguson Avenue, the convenience store Michael Brown Jr. was reported to have left minutes before former Ferguson police officer Darren Wilson shot him. The nearby blocks were the center of the protest action in those early days. About a mile from the convenience store were the Canfield Green Apartments, where we were stationed. The tenor near our mobile response unit was more mournful, more muted. People had set up flowers, candles, and teddy bears to create a memorial at the side of the street where his body had lain, just feet away from our tent. That memorial became a destination for activists, mourners, journalists, and people from all over the community and the world. They would come to take pictures, pray, or drop off resources for us to distribute.

After my shift ended at five o'clock, I'd go home, cook dinner for my kids, and check their homework. Then, at around seven o'clock,

I'd head back out. I never knew how long I'd be in the streets, but after a night or two, I came to expect I'd be out until at least two in the morning.

In those early days, cars were still able to drive on West Florissant. Thousands of protesters crowded onto the sidewalks on either side of the street, seething, grieving, and demanding answers. There were no coordinated chants yet. People simply yelled and asked aloud who the police would choose to kill with impunity next. The collective hurt was palpable. Some people prayed, and clergy from different faiths came out to issue an ecumenical call for healing. A creative few among us banged out rhythms on trash can lids and buckets. But the primary soundtrack to the sweltering nights was the loud music booming from the car stereos of people driving past. Some passengers sat on top of cars and trucks as they drove by. For the most part, these weren't casual passersby. These were people protesting in their own way, drawn to that stretch of Ferguson for the same reasons we pedestrians were.

As the long summer dusk turned to darkness, even more people came to the streets. Jihad and I were both in our late thirties, older than many of the protesters who would stay out as night fell. I loved to see so many young Black people with their fists raised, voicing their frustration with a system that has never been designed for us, or worked for us. I was proud as I watched them grab that moment for themselves, and I didn't take issue with their modes of expression, as some older participants did. Some went around admonishing protesters, telling them, "Don't sit on top of cars" or "Don't yell at the police." In my mind, these people were perhaps young, but they still deserved to be heard. They had the right to express their pain and confusion however they saw fit. The real issue at hand was police behavior, and we needed to stay focused on that.

After a few nights, the police decided to become more aggressive in their efforts to disperse the crowds of thousands, which grew as people continued to descend on Ferguson from all over the country and the world. The first night they shot tear gas at us, I didn't understand what was happening. I saw something move through the air, hit the ground and emit smoke. I figured the police had fired smoke bombs at us, but then I felt my throat tighten as if something were choking me. The skin on my face and exposed arms burned. I and the people near me ran, frantic to escape what we suddenly understood to be tear gas. This tactic may have thinned the crowds a bit, but most of us just moved a little further down the street and went right back to what we were doing.

As the protests progressed, police vehicles followed us as we ran, firing more tear gas as they pursued us. We were stunned, unaccustomed to this level of cruelty, but we kept on, and we stayed. Through it all, Jihad held my hand as the crowds surged, moving this way and that in response to the police attacks. He was by my side as the chaos of police dogs and provocateurs threatened to engulf us. It was Jihad who went to an army-navy surplus store in South County and found a gas mask for himself and a pink camouflaged scarf for me to cover my mouth and nose against the tear gas.

Together, along with the rest of the protesters, we learned that there were skills and tools we needed to participate effectively in what was clearly becoming a protracted battle in a war to win protection for Black lives and police accountability. We needed bandannas and other face coverings. No matter how hot the night was, we needed something to cover our arms against the sting of tear gas. We needed sturdy boots in case our feet got stomped or rolled over by a police car.

I never knew when I might have to run. I never knew if I might end up in jail. I just knew I had to be able to move with the moment. I started to see people with bags filled with bandages, burn spray, and first aid items to help people if they needed help, and I realized this was a way I could help, too. I didn't yet know what it was to be an activist, but I knew how to tend to people in crisis and I knew how to pray. I stayed out in the streets intending to do both.

In addition to the tear gas, the state and police had other means of trying to crush our spirits, our ability to mobilize. They tried to demonize us and intimidate us. They characterized our protests as violent when they weren't. They kept us from reaching or leaving demonstrations. They arrested people en masse simply for gathering. They charged people harshly for minor infractions, and they abused protesters while they were in custody.

On August 14, the Missouri Highway Patrol took over the effort to control the protests from the St. Louis County Police Department. Initially, they took a milder approach. But they were in a détente, and it didn't last long. The next day, police released a video they insisted showed Michael Brown Jr., and what he was doing, just before his encounter with the officer. At the same time, after days of public outcry, they released the name of the officer who had shot and killed Brown. The tensions between police and protesters immediately escalated again, and nearly two hundred people were arrested in one day. Our then governor Jay Nixon declared a state of emergency and set a curfew throughout Ferguson. The National Guard and Attorney General Eric Holder arrived soon after.

On the ground, we were taking in the changing landscape and getting organized. One local elected official started a group to discuss strategy and organization. It met in a small shopping center near where the protests were on West Florissant Avenue. Nearby, behind the vacant and boarded up Ponderosa Steakhouse, a group of young people in their late teens and early twenties had set up a protest encampment. They met during the protests and decided they weren't going to go home until there was justice for Michael Brown Jr., and so they occupied the space for twenty-four hours a day, every day. Some of them quit their jobs or were fired for their part in the protests after being seen on TV. They called themselves the Lost Voices.

I met Ciera, who was living in the encampment, at a table during a meeting with a local politician. I had seen her before, when I'd visited the tents while I was working with the mobile response unit. I'd taken food and supplies to Lost Voices, but they refused to

take them. They were skeptical of our motives, and I could understand why. People had quickly started to use the protests to advance
their own agendas. Drawn by the news cameras and promise of a
spotlight, people held photo ops, sought out media interviews, and
hosted indoor events not for protesters but for business leaders,
clergy, and politicians who wouldn't stay around long and wouldn't
be with us at night, when much of the police terror took place.

Now that I was off duty, I tried again to connect with Ciera. "If
you all need anything, let me know," I said. She told me she remembered me stopping by, and she encouraged me to come back again.
Later that same day, I walked over to the encampment. There were
maybe eight tents there, each a different style and color, and about
a dozen people milling around. I met a fifteen-year-old boy with a
road rash that coated his right arm. He had fallen while playing
around on a go-kart, he told me. I helped him tie up a bandage and
then tended to someone suffering from stomach pains.

It was here that I met Cathy Daniels, known to many as Mama
Cat. She arrived at the encampment that day holding large alumi-
num trays, weighted down with fried chicken wings and greens.
"Get some food!" she called to everyone. I fixed myself a plate, looking at Mama Cat in surprise. Soul food on the street at a protest? "I
do what I do," she told me. "Our people need nourishment." And I
agreed, delighted. Several more protesters came over to grab plates,
and we all shared stories of our experiences from the previous days.
I was meeting people who would become family to me.

I learned that day that Mama Cat had been cooking for Lost
Voices daily since she'd encountered their encampment. Struck
by their commitment to the cause, she had asked how she could
help, and they told her that a home-cooked meal would be nice.
They'd had no idea of the quality of the food they were about to get.
Mama Cat was a star student at the Culinary Institute of St. Louis
and would use the professional kitchen there to prepare meals for
the movement. At fifty-three, she was also a longtime Red Cross
employee who was used to working in areas of massive upheaval.

She had run shelters for the survivors of Hurricanes Katrina, Wilma, Irene, and more. A New York native, Mama Cat had moved to the St. Louis area just a couple of years before. When she'd seen the coverage of Michael Brown Jr.'s death on CNN, she felt compelled to come out and help fight with her community. She was a Black woman with sons and grandchildren, and the police killing of the eighteen-year-old hit too close to home. He could easily have been one of her own. She became our protest chef, serving us food at the front lines.

The police tore down the encampment a few days later. They came and wiped it out, confiscating tents and throwing away everything that Lost Voices couldn't grab and move in five minutes. Some people were arrested. All of us were outraged. Lost Voices wasn't causing any harm. What had they done to warrant this treatment?

Donations of food and water flooded in for those among us who had made holding physical space at the site of protest their full-time jobs. I came to see that I was more aligned with my protest family, people with whom I shared nothing but love, than with others who might be considered my peers—namely, some of the preachers who began showing up in the streets.

Some preachers didn't come to meet us protesters where we were. They didn't want to follow the lead of anyone on the ground or to learn from us. They came to be the "respectable" counterparts to the chaos they thought we represented. They wanted to show us that they were the leaders in our community, and their disdain for me was palpable. Often, people I knew from the church community wouldn't speak to me or acknowledge my presence on the ground. But later, I'd get calls asking for readouts of what was actually happening. They would turn around and pass these readouts off as their own in the media or at community gatherings. They held clergy meetings about the protests and never invited me. All the while we were out there experiencing the brunt of police backlash, one terrifying night after the next. I was putting myself out there, taking care of my community and afraid for them, and traumatized by the sounds of tear gas, rubber bullets, real bullets, and police dogs. Those preachers spent their evenings sitting safely in their homes or at meetings with one another.

They also didn't consider me a real pastor. I was still unmarried, and on top of that I didn't have a physical place to house my ministry. Since my ordination, I'd been Pastor Cori to my congregation and to many outside my immediate flock. The clergy in St. Louis addressed each other as "Bishop," "Pastor," "Minister," "Reverend," using the appropriate title. But when they called me, when they wanted to find out what I knew about the ongoing protests, they called me "sis." Some might chalk it up to misogyny, and certainly that was part of it. But there were women among the clergy who treated me that way too.

For a stretch of weeks in late 2014, I led prayer services in a classroom at Greater St. Mark Family Church's adjacent school building in St. Louis County, just minutes from the protests. The church served as a safe refuge for protesters. But I was not recognized as a woman of the cloth in many other preachers' eyes.

It seemed they felt I was unpolished. They deemed it beneath them to be out in the street protesting as I was. I believed that being a protester was an honor, but I heard a few of the preachers call us devils and terrorists. Rather than calling out the police violence that plagued our community, they told us that we were the ones in the wrong.

In fact, we were simply calling out problems that had festered for too long. Darren Wilson had killed Michael Brown Jr. after pursuing and trying to detain him, and far too many others in the community had unnecessary contact with police that put their lives at risk. We knew that Ferguson police targeted Black residents. They regularly issued citations and tickets for minor infractions. Black residents endured near-constant police surveillance and harassment. They made up two-thirds of Ferguson's population, but accounted for 85 percent of vehicle stops, 90 percent of citations, and 93 percent of arrests made by the Ferguson Police Department between

2012 and 2014. When officers documented their use of force during that same period, 90 percent of the time it was wielded against Black people.

But the pastors seemed to be more concerned about us protesters than they were about these systemic injustices. They didn't like where we marched, or how we marched. They wanted us to stop cursing, stop yelling our demands at the police. To us, there was no book, no instruction manual that laid out how to respond when the state kills somebody, one of our own sons, and tries to pass it off as a justified death, to cover it up. I realized I didn't need these preachers to validate the work we were doing. They didn't call me, equip me, nor did they put me on this assignment. My instructions came from the Lord. Thankfully, there were other preachers who did accept me, and our protest movement, just as we were.

In our movement, there was no one leader, and that was part of the beauty of our organizing. The police couldn't just brutalize or intimidate one person or another out of protesting and diminish our power. The group I organized with, we called ourselves Ferguson Frontline. We were the activists who consistently showed up, even during what others viewed as lulls in the action. Our space was open for people to show up however they felt they were needed and do whatever was natural to them. That was how we kept our momentum going on the ground. Each of us played a role, and we came to regard one another as family. There were those of us who would chant or serve people, drum or speak. Some served as medics, some as jail support. Others planned protests. We often heard that we were a leaderless movement, but the reality is that we were all leaders in our movement.

When we saw a need, we stepped up to meet it. At an event in Ferguson during one of those endless August days, I ran into someone I'd gone to high school with, Dr. David Ragland. David was an educator and an academic specializing in peace work, human rights, and racial justice. We talked about what was unfolding around us and reminisced about the past too. Mostly, we discussed how disturbed we were by what the media was saying about Michael Brown. He'd been "no angel," pundits said, before his death at the hands of police just days ago. This portrayal was a stark departure from what we heard when listening to his family and neighbors talk about the "Mike Mike" they'd known.

David and I lamented that members of law enforcement are the first to hop on television and they were rarely if ever fact-checked. It didn't matter if that same spokesperson came back a few days later and acknowledged that some detail or piece of information had been incorrect. By then, nobody was paying attention. The work of the smear, the damage, was done.

David told me of an idea he had to get the voices of the affected families into the national conversation. He wanted to humanize the victims as others tried to demonize them. I agreed, and we decided to work together. Too many members of the media filled their articles and broadcasts with police quotes and official statements. They didn't do enough to lift up the perspectives of the victims' family members. They left out important context about police violence, and the criminalized people who suffered it, implying that their deaths at the hands of police were somehow of their own doing. Someone needed to change these narratives. To do so, we cofounded the Truth Telling Project, along with a few of David's colleagues from academia.

As part of our mission, we reached out to affected family members and assembled a summit. We invited people who did peace work from all over the country to come help bring healing to our community. Our model was based on truth and reconciliation, but we knew we needed to end the killings first before there could be any progress, before we could truly alleviate people's pain, before there could be any reconciliation. We needed to center the very real trauma that surviving family members faced in the midst of police violence.

We invited the media there to help amplify people's stories, and we invited protesters to be on hand for support. The information we gathered was later turned into a tool kit for educators and college curricula across the country. We saw biases in how dominant narratives were formed, and we worked to create a corrective.

.　.　.

AS SUMMER TURNED TO autumn, our protests entered a new phase. Many of our actions moved to South Florissant Road near the Ferguson Police Department. We learned that the Subway sandwich shop across the street had a sympathetic manager who would let us use the restaurant's restroom. A nearby tire shop let us use its parking lot, and this became a place where protesters could gather to sit, eat meals together, and get to know one another. Mama Cat and Grumbles, another chef in our movement, set up stoves and served a weekly Sunday dinner for protesters. We enjoyed veggie lasagna one week and spanakopita and baklava the next.

But even as our movement proliferated nationally, the day-to-day challenges of our local organizing began to take a toll on me. We were still on the streets every day, twenty-four hours a day. Some days, I questioned whether I should keep showing up the way I did. So many of my protest family on the front lines were struggling; too many of us were getting evicted or couldn't make enough money for our food or to pay our bills. As a working professional who was slightly older than the younger people who made up the front line, I was often serving as a caretaker for some of my protest family while I struggled to provide for my own household and my own kids. I was spread too thin, and I considered quitting. I asked God to show me what to do. At one protest at Ferguson October, He did.

Ferguson October was a four-day series of events that brought people from all over the country into St. Louis for a weekend of resistance. We marched, rallied, and sharpened our political analysis with like-minded people. We knew the grand jury was deliberating on whether to indict Darren Wilson, and we wanted to send a message to them, to show them that the world was still watching. Protesters made themselves impossible to ignore at unexpected places, including during a performance of the Saint Louis Symphony, at a Cardinals' playoff game at Busch Stadium, and at a Saint Louis Rams game. We were everywhere.

One particular day that weekend, during a march to the Ferguson police station, a group of folks from out of state brought with them an enormous speaker system. They rolled it out through the streets on a dolly as we moved toward the building that represented the injustices we were up against. The booming system blasted modern-day movement anthems, songs from N.W.A and Public Enemy. Listening to those anthems in my community gave me hope. The 1989 classic "Fight the Power" came on. We had listened to that song probably a million times on the front lines, but as I stood alongside people from all around the country again, who were there to fight the power with us, it felt special. Ferguson Frontline needed support. We were all spent and traumatized. But, in this moment, my heart filled.

We rode the waves of Chuck D and Flavor Flav's voices, throwing our fists up in the air. I looked around me and thought to myself, "These are my people. Something is still happening here. This is real. This is our movement." It was then that I felt God's answer for me was clear: I needed to keep marching, keep protesting. Yes, I was tired, and yes, I was sick of all the ways we were dismissed and vilified. I was sure then of what I felt in my heart. We were all leaders out there, and we needed to continue on our paths. The criticisms were the natural responses of the powers that be, those who were threatened by what we were building together.

Ferguson Frontline, my movement family, became well known in the media and well known to police. We paid a price for our visibility and dedication to the cause. Our lives and livelihoods were endangered. Some of us lost homes and jobs. We were followed out of town and harassed on flights and in airports.

One evening, I was leaving a meeting of activists and lawyers who had gotten together to collaborate on a challenge to police violence. After pulling out of my parking spot, I looked in my rearview mirror to see a car with no headlights pull up close behind me. The car started driving faster than I was, riding my tail. I sped up and moved into the next lane, but the car moved with me. I realized that whoever it was, they were chasing me.

My heart raced. I sped down Kingshighway Boulevard, a major artery that runs through the west side of the city. I was driving too fast, weaving between lanes, and putting my own life and others' at risk, all in an effort to escape from my pursuer. To my right were businesses and homes. To my left, a median with large traffic barrier planters that could have flipped my car if I got too close. I was stiff with terror, aware that one false move and I'd be in the middle of a tragedy. I saw a red light just up ahead. I was forced to stop so as not to collide with the cars right in front of me. My tail stopped too. I looked to my right at a dark-tinted car. The driver rolled down his window partway, and I could see the top of his brow. When the light turned green, he sped off. The car chase had ended, but fear still gripped me.

Despite the threats to our safety, we persisted. We started livestreaming the protests to show people what was really happening. The media spun a narrative that looked different from what we knew on the ground. The way we were being treated by the police was never shown on national television. We decided we had to be our own media. We wanted people around the country and the world to see what was happening for themselves. But we didn't usually want to be named, nor did we want to be made the face of the movement.

The violence, harassment, and intimidation by the police took its toll on us. Our shared trauma bound us even more closely together, and for many of us that trauma left untreated would eventually settle into a chronic PTSD. The trauma manifested itself in different ways.

When I wasn't in Ferguson, I would still see armored vehicles, even when they were not there. At random moments in the day, I would smell tear gas, even when none had been sprayed. Hearing a helicopter above me would cause me to visibly shake, and the sound of bangs like those of tear-gas canisters being fired, or rubber bullets being shot, made it difficult for me to tolerate loud noises.

I felt crippling guilt about going to work at my day job while my protest family was still out there on the streets, and I carried that with me. I fretted while I was away. I rushed back out after work, just to see for myself that they were safe. And I would stay late into the night because I didn't want to leave knowing they would still be there, vulnerable to police attacks. Even when I wasn't protesting, the effects of being out there stayed with me in my daily life.

Ferguson Frontline was often criticized for never forming an official organization. But setting up a nonprofit would have meant losing some of the advantages and power of our leaderful, decentralized movement. It granted our protest family levels of anonymity and protection against police targeting.

Without the benefit of much funding, we tried to meet people's needs ourselves. We didn't know any other way. The activists who'd lost their homes and jobs because their landlords and bosses didn't agree with the fight? We did our best to take care of them. Some people slept at the protests. That's where they lived. Others asked for enough money to ride the metro bus system to Ferguson or to buy diapers for their kids.

Mama Cat bought many of the ingredients for the food she cooked for everyone herself. Those of us who had something to spare gave it willingly. I enjoyed my full-time nursing job and knew that if I had $40 to get my kids and me through the rest of this week, I could give up my spare $40 until I got paid again. If I needed to bandage someone up or give them aspirin, I went to the store to make sure I had what I needed. I would go to the dollar store, pick up a box of tampons, and hand them out while on the street. I knew many were going without the basics they needed. People came to my house to sleep when they needed a place to crash. We were struggling, and even though there was some money coming into other organizations, it hurt that they did not offer it to help those on the front line who needed it the most.

We were broke, but people came to our aid in other invaluable ways. It's no surprise that the most meaningful support came not from celebrities or philanthropists or local pastors. It came from those who had struggled as we were struggling. A Palestinian delegation once came to Ferguson to meet with us. We sat together in the grass at the Canfield Green apartment complex. They advised us on how to protect ourselves from police attacks, and specifically on what to do when we were tear-gassed. We didn't know water only made the gas hurt more. Instead, they told us, we should use milk of magnesia to clean our faces, and regular cow's milk if we didn't have that. Water does little to neutralize the poison. Beyond the practical matters of how to defend ourselves, the delegation talked to us about the struggle for rights and liberation in Palestine and Israel.

As the days and months of protests went on, I got to know members of our Palestinian community in St. Louis. Even though they weren't the ones disproportionately killed by police in our city, they came out regularly to stand with us. Our conversations about the oppression they and their family members experienced opened my eyes. I saw that so much of the militarized state violence we face as Black people in the United States is similar to what Palestinians face from Israel. I'd never thought about this before. I remembered hearing at church that it was our duty to stand with Israel, that the Jewish people are God's chosen people. There was never any exploration or discussion of how that belief was wielded in our world, geopolitically, or against Palestinians. I didn't know that to stand with Israel, no questions asked, meant that we were upholding and perpetuating the subjugation of another group of people.

Those months of protest deepened my perspective on the harm of oppression across our St. Louis communities. I got to develop deep personal and organizing relationships with members of our

LGBTQIA+ community, our Asian American and Pacific Islander communities, our Latinx community, our Jewish community. They were all made up of people who showed up for us, day in and day out, continuing a long American tradition of multiracial and multiethnic solidarity for justice in the face of white supremacy. For the first time in my life, I was in a deep, intimate protest community with people of various backgrounds and identities who could share how hate and state violence harmed them. We experienced this in different ways, but ultimately we were connected.

The truth is, the St. Louis I grew up in oftentimes felt very disconnected. Sometimes it was as if our communities existed in silos, segregated by race, religion, ethnicity, or class. The protests brought us out of our homes, our neighborhoods, our places of worship, and gave us an opportunity not only to come to know one another's pain but to imagine what a future of collective liberation could look like.

When we're all so privately caught up in our struggles to survive, we become deprived of those moments as a community, those moments of having the space to learn about one another and imagine a different world that can work for all of us. I didn't know much about how different and yet how shared our struggles were in St. Louis, and not just in St. Louis, but across our country and globally. I didn't know, because I'd been focused on how to keep my son alive and my daughter safe. I was just trying to survive. Now I was standing shoulder to shoulder with others who'd been doing the same, and our solidarity in struggle transformed what we thought was possible for our communities. At the same time, we never lost sight of Michael Brown Jr., who had so tragically not survived St. Louis as we had been so fortunate to do.

. . .

ON THE NIGHT OF November 24, 2014, we learned that Darren Wilson, the police officer who killed Michael Brown, was not going to face criminal charges. But before we learned of the grand jury's decision, we had spent weeks waiting, anticipating the news.

Earlier we had noticed tanks in places where we hadn't seen them before. The National Guard had established a presence across St. Louis. Sand-colored tanks rolled onto street corners and squatted there, as if readying for a battle. They reminded me of the footage I'd seen on TV from Desert Storm back in 1990 and 1991, when the U.S. government challenged Iraq over its invasion of Kuwait. But here, the heavy artillery was set against the familiarity of my home-town. That night, while protesting in Ferguson, I looked up to see a sign that read "Season's Greetings." Cheerfully, it stretched from one side of the street to the other. As was typical this time of year, the city was decked out, projecting a benign, Mayberry-like appearance. Yet the tanks just near the sign belied the truth. And here we were, as if at war, poised to protest the court's failure to hold an officer accountable for taking a young person's life.

The fall weather was cool, but not yet cold enough to merit my wearing a coat. I had on a black jacket, long-sleeved shirt and pants, both black, and boots. I'd packed my dark-colored nurse's back-pack with a hazmat suit, milk of magnesia, plastic gloves, bandages, Band-Aids, Ace wraps, burn cream, wound spray, surgical masks, bandannas, hot and cold packs, and protective film, in case I needed to create a barrier while giving mouth-to-mouth resuscitation. It was late afternoon and still light when I headed out into the streets. I knew that people would be flocking to St. Louis and that some would be unprepared for the magnitude of the police terror they'd be facing. They would need medical attention, and I was ready to provide it.

By nightfall, the protest had grown thick, and the police were tear-gassing us relentlessly. Typically, the gas didn't affect me much anymore. Because I have asthma, I knew to wear a bandanna or two in layers to protect myself. But this night, the tear gas lay so heavy in the air that even with my bandanna wrapped tight, I couldn't breathe. The illuminated "Season's Greetings" sign shone brightly through clouds of tear gas that resembled smoke, a line of police in riot gear wearing gas masks beneath it. They beat their batons in unison against their shields, chanting "Move! Move! Move!" in time with the crack of the surfaces making contact. I moved away from the front lines to get some fresher air, and I walked in the direction of my car in an effort to catch a break and collect myself.

That's when I heard someone yell, "Help, help! My mom is having a heart attack." I figured it was an ambush. I was jaded by previous encounters with police tactics of sabotage, and so at first I didn't even slow my stride. I was used to fire trucks or police vehicles with sirens blaring, suddenly rushing through our energized protests, no emergency in sight, merely to worry and distract us. I was used to exchanges with people who weren't who they said they were. They were usually exposed later as undercover cops. At first, the shrieks I heard as I tried to find some respite from the tear gas seemed like just another dirty trick that I should ignore.

But then I heard my name, "Cori, Cori! Come help! We need a nurse!" I turned and saw people I recognized standing around a woman whom I guessed to be in her mid- to late fifties, slumped against a car. I ran toward her and caught hold of her just as she was collapsing onto the ground. She called out the names of two medications, one of which I knew to be a blood thinner, the other a medication to lower blood pressure. "Yes, she might be having a heart attack," I thought as I eased her to the ground. Her eyes closed, and she went limp. Still, I could feel that she was breathing, and she had a pulse. Another woman nearby identified herself as her daughter and told me the woman's name: Lisa. I called her name and tapped her face with my hand, but to no avail. I placed the knuckles of my closed fist on the center part of Lisa's chest to see if the pain would stimulate her to wake up and talk to me, a technique used to assess level of consciousness.

Given the dense crowds, we knew that an ambulance wouldn't reach Lisa in time. Several protesters agreed to carry her to where the paramedics were, just behind the line of police guarding the Ferguson Police Department. In doing so, we risked them framing us as aggressors and shooting at us. But we had one potential ally on our side. The national media were back in town to report on the grand jury's decision. We decided to carry Lisa through the tent where outlets were broadcasting live. If the police shot us, at least it would be captured on screens worldwide. I continued saying Lisa's name loudly while alternating between rubbing her sternum and smacking her lightly on the face, in an effort to rouse her. She stayed still.

Meanwhile, eight or so people carried her toward the broadcast tent and toward the paramedics who might save her life. They shouted, "Help her! This woman might be having a heart attack!" "I'm a nurse, this woman needs help!" I yelled out. But the law enforcement officers who stopped us ignored our efforts to get Lisa to safety. Instead, they pointed their long guns at us. "Drop her!" they shouted, again and again until Lisa's rescue squad did just that. But I wasn't ready to stop the interventions my training had taught me. I continued trying to rouse her. I said, "I'm the nurse helping her. I'm not letting her go. You are not skilled to help her in this moment. She needs a medic!"

Then I remember seeing stars. Not cartoonish stars or some other abstraction. I saw the actual celestial expanse. I felt the sky getting closer and closer, and it wasn't until I flipped and the ground started rushing toward me that I realized what was happening. "Oh my goodness. How much is this about to hurt?" Then impact.

I hit the ground. Half a dozen officers surrounded me in a circle, stomping and kicking me as if I were nothing. Boots rained down on my body, kicking me from all angles and grinding my face and abdomen into the asphalt. My body jerked from side to side as it absorbed the impact of the officers' boots. I wanted to yell, cry out to my protest family. But not only could I not see them, what could they do? "Who do I call out to for help when it's the police who are assaulting me?" I wondered. I remember telling myself, "If you don't get up, they're going to kill you."

I jumped up, still numb to the pain in my body. I don't know how I had the strength to get up off the ground, other than with the help of the Lord. The police had tear-gassed Lisa and me, but my body hadn't recognized the signs yet. Now up on my feet, I stretched out my arms and yelled, "Stop! I'm the nurse helping." I couldn't say one more word. I felt my throat begin to tighten and I felt burning. My throat was on fire. That's when I realized my bandanna had fallen from my face and I was feeling the tear gas flooding my airways. I yelled, "I," and took a shallow breath. "Can't," I managed. Took another shallow breath. "Breathe!" I got out to the officers. "I-HAVE-ASTHMA!" I said between more shallow breaths. One responded, "She's lying. Arrest her!" They grabbed me and I went limp too.

When I woke up, an oxygen mask covered my face and I saw a paramedic standing over me, tending to me. I could breathe better, but I felt an uncomfortable pressure on the right side of my head. I realized that that pressure was the barrel of a gun. "I told you she was lying," said the police officer responsible for threatening my life as I came back into consciousness. The paramedic said that I wasn't and knocked the gun away from my face. Eventually, the officer left. I never found out what happened to Lisa. I know that we were tear-gassed together, but she wasn't there when I finally came to.

The next twenty-four hours are a blur of activity. Adrenaline pumped through me and I walked, stood, and moved until a friend finally made me sit down by sitting on me. Bruises covered my arms and knees, but I escaped the abuse without too many more severe physical injuries.

The psychic injuries remained, however. A few days after the incident, my children and I stopped at a gas station. A patrol car pulled up next to the pump where we'd parked to refuel, and I panicked. I swiftly put the car in gear and peeled out of the lot in search of a different place to fill our tank. My kids asked me frantically what was wrong, but all I knew was that I couldn't be around police.

It took me a few days, but I did eventually join the protests again. I always did. There were other times when I told myself that I was too tired and needed to stop and rest. Whenever I wanted to stay away, I was haunted by the fear that the police were hurting my people.

I talked with Angel and Zion about why I was out there protesting every day. Worrying about police violence was just part of our daily lives. We talked about what they were to do during a traffic stop, even when they weren't driving. I let them know they had to be careful about whom they were in the car with. During a stop, any blame for perceived wrongdoing could fall on them. I had a lot of anxiety about them getting their driver's licenses, especially my son. I wasn't going to hold them back from learning to drive; I just didn't push it as their sixteenth birthdays neared. I was walking a thin line. I wanted them to be prepared to handle themselves with dignity and know their rights if a police officer came at them. But I was also careful about what I said, because I never wanted them to seem unnecessarily antagonistic or rude to the police and end up hurt as a result.

For the most part, while I was out protesting in the streets, my kids were home. Sometimes, racked with the creeping guilt that all working parents know, I would ask my kids, "Has Mommy been gone too much? Do you want me to stay home?" They'd always tell me no and that they understood. And I made sure we kept our traditions.

Just as my parents and siblings had enjoyed our weekly pizza night when I was a kid, my children and I had ours. Wednesdays we ordered pizza and watched a movie. We had a standing order with Domino's. At the entrance to our apartment complex, there was a video store, where we'd rent our movies. On those Wednesday nights, I headed out to protest again, fortified by the time I'd spent relaxing in the company of my children.

Occasionally, Zion and Angel joined me. I didn't know if there would ever again be a time when thousands of people would be in the streets fighting for justice, and I wanted them to be a part of the moment, to experience it. They became involved in their own ways, joining other youth in the movement, including Michael Brown Jr.'s sister, in filming a short documentary about the Ferguson uprising.

. . .

By December 2014, a lot of the protesters returned to the routines of regular life. Most of the national media had gone home, too, or moved on. But Ferguson Frontline, we stayed out, continuing to speak truth to power out in the streets, in the rain, sleet, hail, or snow. We were no longer there all day and every night but we stayed active. We organized daily actions. Allied demonstrations had taken root around the country by this point too, from Philadelphia to Seattle, New York, Cleveland, Los Angeles, Oakland, Minneapolis, Atlanta, Chicago, Boston, and beyond. People had started protesting against police violence in their own communities.

. . .

Twenty fifteen marked a shift for me. That year, I picked up the bullhorn. I started leading in my community in a different way from what I had done before.

In March, I organized a silent march with the Truth Telling Project in downtown St. Louis. I went to the dollar store and bought markers, glue sticks, black tape, and black and white poster board. I put together all the signs by hand so they'd be ready for the people who showed up. I drew them all in black and white.

That day, protesters gathered on the front steps of the Old Courthouse, where slave auctions were routinely held in the antebellum period. It was also where Dred and Harriet Scott sued for their freedom in 1846, arguing that because they had lived on free land, they were free. The enslaved couple's struggle for freedom ended in 1857 when the U.S. Supreme Court ruled that citizenship was out of reach for African Americans. That ruling hastened the Civil War. At our action, marchers wrote messages on pieces of black tape, then used that tape to cover their mouths, rendering themselves speechless. That's how some of us felt after witnessing months of inaction in the wake of Michael Brown Jr.'s death.

I picked up that bullhorn, my first time, and pulled everybody together. I welcomed everyone and laid out the plan. I invited a few speakers to energize and inspire the crowd. We held our signs high as we walked through our city's streets. That day marked a turning point for me.

That same month, I co-organized a trip for a group of Ferguson Frontline activists to Selma, Alabama, for the fiftieth anniversary of Bloody Sunday. We joined others from around the country and around the world to commemorate that day in March 1965 when more than six hundred protesters, demanding voting rights for Black Americans, began their march from Selma to the state's capital in Montgomery. Famously, as they came across the Edmund Pettus Bridge, they were met by white supremacist police officers and vigilantes, and they were brutalized.

We arranged for a van to take about ten of us south for the commemoration. On our first or second night in Selma, we all packed into a motel room to talk about what we wanted to accomplish while we were there. We were Frontline, family, and were used to being in close quarters. This was no different. Some of us sat on the floor, and others on the beds, chairs, and dressers.

We made this trip because we wanted to, not because other organizers had invited us. We needed to make clear to those who were gathering, those who had been a part of the movements that came before ours, that what had happened on the Edmund Pettus Bridge in Selma, Alabama, five decades ago was happening now in the streets of Ferguson, Missouri. We honored the achievements made and the bloodshed suffered by activists of the civil rights movement.

But we had shocked the world when we came out to protest the way we had, and by then we had sustained our uprising for several months.

Too few people in some of the legacy civil rights organizations saw the connection between what we were doing and those earlier struggles in the centuries-long war against white supremacy and state violence. We were still inside those first four hundred days, and we'd been fighting. We'd been beaten with batons. We'd lost fellow soldiers to death and jail. But we hadn't been invited to Selma as contemporary freedom fighters.

Our T-shirts, jeans, and bandannas made us hoodlums in the eyes of some in older generations. We didn't wear suits and dresses as they had in the 1950s and 1960s, and so we weren't seen as dignified. We didn't typically walk in formation, holding hands and singing as they had, and so we weren't seen as respectable. We didn't always disavow the violence that happened at protests, so to them we were loose cannons playing at revolution. We didn't have one person who led our movement, so to them we lacked focus, goals, and organization.

It was hard to feel their disdain, their reluctance to claim us. But we wondered why we couldn't be who we were, why we had to show up and look like someone else's idea of serious. Our movement looked different from theirs, and we were fine with that.

Mike Brown Sr. and his wife, Cal, were with us that night in the motel room at Selma, and knowing that we had his blessing was a great feeling. He spoke to us from his heart. He expressed his appreciation that we were there trying to keep his son's name and legacy alive. Our meeting complete, we filed out onto the building's second-floor balcony, chanting as we stepped into the night air: "Turn up, don't turn down! / We do this for Mike Brown!" Someone held the American flag upside down and our voices rang out, affirming the sense of community and security we had with one another. "Who shut shit down? We shut shit down!" We moved from chant to chant, being who we were on the streets of Ferguson right there in Alabama. "Whose streets? Our streets!"

We brought this same energy to the formal commemorative events we attended. When we heard that the president was going to be speaking, we knew we needed to make our presence known. If ever there was a moment in our lifetimes when it should truly matter that we had a Black president, now was that time, we felt. But President Barack Obama had not shown up for us. Why hadn't he come to Ferguson to be on the ground with us? He hadn't acknowledged Frontline's leadership. He'd had a meeting at the White House in December 2014 with activists from our movement, but not one person from Frontline had been invited. Why hadn't he opened the door to all of us?

Here in Selma, we had the opportunity to make it known that President Obama had not met the moment. I expected him to show up for us, to come to what we called "ground zero" so that we could tell him what was really happening. I believed if he set foot onto West Florissant Avenue in the early days of our protests, or onto South Florissant Road, where the protests had moved to, the aggressive and violent treatment of protesters would cease. Maybe he could ease some of the burden that Michael Brown Jr.'s family carried as they were villainized while working to seek accountability for his death. He was a Black president, and regular, everyday Black people needed him just to show up. Presence can speak volumes.

This was a job that called for Drummer Boy. Drummer Boy was young, in his early teens. He was a talented percussionist. He had been a fixture at protests back home, banging his drumsticks on anything that made noise, and eventually, once he got a drum, he used it to punctuate our chants, elevate our spirits, and ground us with his steady rhythms. He was with us as we joined thousands of others at the outdoor event where President Obama was due to address those gathered. Dignitaries, community leaders, elders who had themselves played a role in the civil rights movement, crowded into the Selma streets eager to hear what the president would say. We couldn't even see him from where we stood, far away from the stage. But the sound system brought his impassioned, lilting voice to us.

The moment President Obama started to speak, Drummer Boy started to drum, and we started chanting. A group of older Black men descended on us, swiftly, rushing toward Drummer Boy, trying to pull his drum away from him and stop him from interfering. A big commotion ensued. But we were undeterred. "You need to listen to why we're doing this," we explained to anyone who'd listen.

One of the men who came to quiet us turned out to be Bernard Lafayette from the Southern Christian Leadership Conference, or SCLC. After we first made it clear that they were not to touch any of us, Dr. Lafayette agreed that this wasn't an appropriate response. We all stopped and listened to one another. We made clear our frustration with feeling overlooked and disrespected by those who we thought would embrace us. Dr. Lafayette promised to keep the doors of communication open. Obama kept speaking, but we'd disrupted the narrative.

.   .   .

THAT SPRING OF 2015, Ferguson activists were tired and worn. We didn't seem to be any closer to finding justice for Black people in this country. Police killings still took place, locally and around the country. Protesters suffered. Some were fighting criminal charges from arrests. Many Ferguson Frontline folks were still struggling financially. Then we learned that some activists were being paid. It broke my spirit when I found out. I felt betrayed, and so did many others.

The movement needed help; the work was not done. The organization I'd helped co-found, the Truth Telling Project, spent countless hours trying to find ways to support families of victims as well as the protesters. We decided to see if Dr. Angela Davis would come to Ferguson to encourage us and help us mend what had been broken. I knew we needed two separate events. One was to be an intimate gathering with Frontline activists. There would be no cameras, no press, no outside folks, just the activists and organizers who had been on the ground in a setting where we could share and learn freely. Then we'd have a public event free and open to anyone who wanted to attend. She accepted the invitation, and in June we welcomed to St. Louis a freedom fighter from an earlier generation who saw us for who we were, just as we were.

She met with us Frontline activists at Merhaba, an Ethiopian and Eritrean restaurant that had always opened the door to us. Then we moved to my alma mater, Cardinal Ritter College Prep High School, for the event with our community. Local Black vendors displayed their wares on tables that filled the school's hallways. People from across the region, from Arkansas and other neighboring states, had traveled to hear Dr. Davis. The large auditorium was filled to capacity.

When it came time for her talk to begin, we announced that activists should move to the front, and she spoke directly to us. She talked about recent trips she'd made all over the world and how, regardless of what she'd initially been invited to speak on, everyone wanted her thoughts on Ferguson. "This movement is worldwide," she said. She continued, "For me, as well as for people throughout the world, the very mention of Ferguson evokes struggle, perseverance, courage, and a collective vision of the future.

"I want to thank you, Ferguson activistsß who refused, who refused to put down the torch of struggle. Who made Ferguson a worldwide symbol of resistance and who did this at a time when we were urged to search for easy solutions, for fast answers, for formulated resolutions. Ferguson protesters said, 'No, we will continue to make the issue of violence against Black communities visible. We will not accept a simplistic answer. We will not allow this issue to be buried in the graveyard that has not only claimed Black lives but also the struggles to defend those lives.' So, thank you, for not giving up, for not going home, for staking our claim to freedom on the streets of Ferguson, Missouri, with such great power, with such great power that Ferguson has become synonymous with progressive protest from Palestine to South Africa and, indeed, all over the world.

"But when Mike Brown was killed in Ferguson, the movement refused to disband. Even when the police attacked, the movement refused to disband. Even when some people's rage led them to respond in ways that may have been counterproductive and that almost always happens, the movement still refused to disband. When people tried to discredit the protesters, the movement refused to disband. Even when people asked, 'Where are the leaders? Where are the leaders?' The movement said, 'We are the leaders!'

"I love Martin. I deeply love Malcolm. But this is the twenty-first century, and we have learned that leadership is not a male prerogative. I know many of the brothers in this hall today know that women have always done the work . . . so women should also be in the leadership!

"When Black women stand up as they did during the Montgomery bus boycott, as they did during the Black liberation era, earth-shaking changes can occur," she ended.

If at no other time before, when Auntie Angela finished speaking, we felt validated and heard. Now we could find the strength to go on, to persevere, and to continue what we had started.

Chapter 7

LEGACY SOCIAL JUSTICE AND civil rights organizations continued to have an ambivalent relationship with the movement that we'd birthed in Ferguson. In July of 2015, one month after Dr. Angela Davis came to town and buoyed our spirits, I was invited to Baton Rouge to attend a convention put on by a legendary civil rights organization. I was giddy with excitement. This was my chance to talk to some heroic organizers—the people who came before us, and whom I looked up to.

I'd been invited to speak at a plenary, about our activism at Ferguson. I knew I was also being tasked with closing the generational gap that kept people from seeing and believing in us. Here I would have a platform. I anticipated that I would walk into a space that would be friendly, where people would be open to solidarity and allyship. Instead, I was met with open hostility.

I wore a T-shirt and jeans—my protest uniform. As I entered the lobby of the hotel that was hosting the plenary, I noticed that everyone else wore business attire. I hadn't been told that the event would be formal. People turned their heads to look at me with disdain, regarding my appearance as though I were too hood, or dirty, or trash. I had gained some visibility in the media by then, and people knew who I was. But they wouldn't speak to me, and turned up their noses at me when I passed.

After the many months of protest in Ferguson and other parts of
St. Louis, I did not expect to continue to encounter activists who
seemed to have no interest in connecting with those of us who were
on the ground to find out more about how our movement operated
and why, or to build relationships and share ideas with us. Instead of
standing with us in solidarity, they were critical. Many of the people I encountered at the convention had never set foot in Ferguson
and parroted what they'd heard from television commentators who
themselves had never been there. They felt justified in sneering at us,
and belittling us. And it wasn't just the elders. People in their twenties and thirties were expressing empty, elitist opinions. "It's fine," I
thought, taking it all in. "When I give my speech, they will hear the
truth about Ferguson and the protesters there."

On the last day of the convention, I attended a luncheon in one
of the hotel's huge banquet rooms. I was due to speak on the truth
about our protests back home. I was planning to dispel the lies that
had circulated about our movement being leaderless and made up
of violent protesters. But just before it was my turn to speak, I was
notified that my speech had been cut due to time constraints, sup-
posedly. The convention's organizers asked me to instead speak on a
panel highlighting youth activism.

I was frustrated. I had traveled all the way to Louisiana. I had
left my kids in the care of my parents. And, here I was being treated
this way? Instead of getting my message across, I would have to be
in conversation with the same young people who had been making
nasty, snobbish remarks at me. But I agreed. I'd stay to participate,
and then I'd leave, I told myself.

Later that day, there was a formal dinner. I sat at a large round
table, listening to the overlapping conversations of the hundreds of
people packed into the banquet room around me. People's voices
mixed with the clinking and clanging of glasses and silverware. I was
near the front of the room with my back toward the lectern, which
meant that I had to pivot in my chair to see who was speaking at any
given moment. I wasn't too interested in being attentive, though. I

was disappointed, and it had become clear that not one person at the table I was seated at would engage in any type of conversation with me. Some of my hello's fell flat without a response. I looked down, and played with my butter knife, and my fork. I needed something to do with my hands, a way to rid myself of the disgust and annoyance mounting in my body.

The emcee announced that next we'd hear from a presidential candidate, a U.S. senator from Vermont. The politician's name wasn't familiar to me, but I turned around to see if I might recognize him. I didn't. I saw an older white man with white hair. His wife smiled and waved in my direction. I turned back around and returned to fidgeting with the flatware. As he spoke, I listened, but I would be lying if I said I was engaged. But then I noticed that he was speaking frankly about the connection between racial justice and income inequality, and I heard him name mass movement as a solution. "We need to bring people together to take on the powers that be," he said. "When thousands and millions of people stand together, there is no stopping us. We can succeed." He had other clear ideas for solutions: "We need to demilitarize the police," he told the crowd, and finally, I heard him say, "Black lives do matter." I spun around. I couldn't believe what I'd heard.

Every single other candidate refused to acknowledge the particular precarity we face in this country as Black people. The candidate Hillary Clinton had come to St. Louis and told us that "All lives matter," while we chanted and marched in the streets every day demanding justice for Mike Brown Jr. In that banquet hall, I wanted to jump up. I wanted to stomp, and cheer. I felt vindicated and validated. Here was this older white presidential candidate telling a Black room that Black lives matter, when I'd been bringing that same energy throughout the convention and been shunned for it. Satisfied, I readied myself to go.

As I was leaving, a representative of the organization stopped and introduced himself to me. Reverend Jones was a high-level staffer. Part of his job was to aid in setting up local chapters of the organization around the country. "If you ever think of starting a chapter, let me know," he said, and handed me a folder of materials. Despite my disappointment that weekend, the idea of possibly opening the eyes of those who misunderstood us, and uniting in the fight for justice intrigued me. I saw the potential benefits of a partnership. In St. Louis, we could expand the spaces where racial justice work and Black liberation theology could grow, a place where someone like me, an activist, could play a part. And we wouldn't have to start from scratch.

I returned back home after the weekend, and went right back to the streets, to my kids, and to my job at the New Day Behavioral Health Center. A few months later, I coordinated a meeting between Reverend Jones and a group of local pastors. We started laying the groundwork for forming a chapter. But then, something happened that put everything else in progress on pause.

. . .

I WAS ASKED TO run for office. This wasn't a recruitment to try for alderperson or mayor of a local municipality or for a city or county office. It wasn't a nudge to run for a position in one of Missouri's state governing bodies. It was a call to run for the U.S. Senate.

The Chicago multimillionaire and McDonald's franchisee Willie Wilson had launched a campaign for president on the Democratic ticket. One early Wilson supporter was the Charleston Black Lives Matter activist Muhiyidin d'Baha. Muhiyidin's image would go viral in 2017 after he hurtled through police tape to grab a Confederate flag from the hands of a South Carolina Secessionist Party member. When Wilson made a stop in St. Louis while campaigning, Muhiyidin came with him. He reached out to me during that trip.

Muhiyidin had heard about me and my work with Ferguson Frontline, he told me. He talked to me about the lack of representation in Congress, specifically in the U.S. Senate. Cory Booker was the only Democratic Black senator, and the Republican Tim Scott was there, too. The only Black woman to serve as a senator at that point had been Carol Moseley Braun in the 1990s. "We need more Black women in the Senate," he said. "You would be the perfect person to run because of your voice and your activism and your boldness."

The idea was so far-fetched that I burst out laughing and told him no. But the next day, he called and brought it up again. My answer hadn't changed, but his phone calls kept coming. He was an activist from another state who had never met me face-to-face, but still—he was someone who believed I should run.

Later that morning, I was getting my breakfast together in our break room at New Day when my phone rang. A few local community leaders, including veteran activist Zaki Baruti, were on the line. They had gotten together to reach out to me. They'd also talked with Muhiyidin, and he'd gotten them excited about the prospect of my running. They told me that if I ran, they would help me to assemble a team, and build me a fundraising structure. I stood there at the table, stirring my oatmeal, stunned that this question was once again asked of me. I knew I needed to finish the call before getting back to my desk and my day, and I got ready to repeat the answer I'd prepared: No. But I felt something rising up in my spirit. "Give me twenty-four hours to get back to you," I said.

As the day went on, questions swirled in my mind. How could I run? How could I not? What if my son became the next hashtag? What if he was gone and there was more I could have done to keep him here? What if I had the opportunity to make change but didn't give it my all, because I felt unprepared for the position? I thought not only of Zion but also of my daughter, Angel, and about all the young people I knew who could become the next hashtag. I decided I needed to do everything I could to save my children's lives. Being in the halls of power, I thought, would help me ensure that all the work we'd done at the Ferguson uprising could be at the forefront of policy making. By being at the table, I could make sure our demands remained central to conversations taking place all over the country and the world. I was flooded with feelings of apprehension, inadequacy, inferiority, and impostor syndrome at the very thought of running. But I knew I had to push past them.

Twenty-four hours later I was back in that same break room on the phone. Adrenaline coursed through my body. I'm not a coffee drinker, but I made myself a cup. I called back Brother Zaki, and gave my answer. I was going to do it. I was going to run for the U.S. Senate in Missouri.

My next call was to Reverend Jones. I let him know that I wouldn't be able to start a new chapter of his organization in St. Louis now. I told him about the decision I'd just made. "I know that this is what the Lord is telling me to do," I told him. Reverend Jones had been in politics himself, and at twenty-six, he had been elected to the Kansas State Senate. At that time, he was the only Black state senator there. "I thought I was coming to St. Louis to get a chapter started, but maybe I need to come to St. Louis to help *you* get started," he told me.

Reverend Jones was of my father's generation. Like my dad, he'd campaigned for the Reverend Jesse Jackson when Jackson ran for president in the 1980s. Hearing that Reverend Jones wanted to help me get started was music to my ears. This was going to be a huge undertaking. And with his help, I could get some things set up and ironed out before presenting the idea to my dad. I didn't want my dad to feel pressured, or obligated, to help me when this work was so different from what I had done before.

My father wasn't always happy about my decisions. Sure, I was no longer stuck dating one man after another who brought heartache and trouble into my life. I had steady, meaningful work that I excelled in. I supported my kids, and we shared a happy home together. But I had started the church and poured so much effort into it, only to have it disband. When I started participating in protests, my dad had worried about my safety, and he didn't like the strain my activism put on my emotional and mental health.

I knew my dad would show frustration and disbelief at the news that I was running for the Senate. He was all too familiar with the challenges that running for office could bring—the long hours, the fundraising needs, and the scrutiny. "What are you doing, Cori?" I expected he'd say. "What are you going to stick with and give your all to?" It would take some time for me to see that the church and the protests were all part of the journey that would bring me to where I needed to be. At the time, all I knew was to follow my heart. I didn't fully understand where I was headed. I didn't expect it to make sense to my dad either. When I told him my plans, his response was the one I expected from him, but not the one I'd hoped for.

I wanted him on board. I organized a meeting with my dad at Merhaba, the same supportive East African restaurant where Frontline had met with Angela Davis. Reverend Jones was now serving as my interim campaign manager and chief adviser. His deputy campaign manager was LaTonya Jackson, who worked with my dad at Better Family Life, the community development agency. She was building expertise in community banking as part of her day job, and she was someone I could trust to have on my campaign. Our goals were clear: explain to my dad why I was running and show him that I wasn't going into the race alone.

My new team and I sat at a table, nervous, waiting for my dad to arrive. He walked in wearing a gray jogging suit. The hood of his sweatshirt was pulled up on his head, obscuring his face as if he were a boxer entering the arena. I watched him approach and thought, "Here comes Rocky, ready to fight us all." He slid into his seat, his discomfort obvious. After he took off the hood and trained his eyes on us, we began.

We presented what we had worked on, why now was the time, the structure we planned to put in place. As we spoke, he was silent. Eventually, we finished making our case and asked if he had any questions or advice for us. His face was still blank, illegible. Then finally he spoke. "I just don't want my daughter to be the sacrificial lamb," he said. "I don't want my daughter running for this seat, opening herself to harm and criticism, when there's no real way to win."

Through all his years in local politics, he had weathered many attacks. Given the scale of the race I was about to take on, I realized he worried that he wouldn't be able to protect me, that no one in my circle would be able to. He had been at the center of or worked on campaigns where he had personally seen people make promises they couldn't or didn't make good on, leaving the candidate to shoulder the burden. He continued, probing us on the specifics: How would we raise enough money for a U.S. Senate race, which required that I travel throughout the state to win votes?

Reverend Jones, LaTonya, and I leaned back in our seats. I knew his concerns were valid. And we knew that with his experience came wisdom. But I could barely register the practical pushback he was offering. I felt I had disappointed him. Again. I wanted my dad to be proud of me. I wanted to make him proud of me. I quieted the part of myself that wanted to make it okay with him, the perennial good daughter who wanted to stay in her dad's good graces, whatever the costs.

I let my team reassure him that they would see to it that I was safe, that they were serious and hardworking and would stay by my side through the end. "We've just got to get started," they said. "We can show you better than we can tell you." He listened as they made their case, but he left the restaurant that day unconvinced. "I just don't want my daughter hurt," he said again, as he stood up to leave. We sat there in a daze. We hadn't even put a dent in his skepticism. I excused myself to go to the bathroom. Over my shoulder I heard every member of my team move to the bar and say in unison, "Top shelf!" We'd all been through the wringer, and I was grateful that the task of convincing him hadn't fallen to me alone.

That meeting with my dad turned out to be a preview of what was to come. Again and again, I'd tell friends, family, and other people who had always supported me that I planned to run and was met with incredulity: "Black people can't win a statewide race in Missouri. You shouldn't run," they'd say. Or: "A Black woman running for the U.S. Senate? You'll never win in Missouri." The kindest variation on the theme went something like, "Well, you won't win, but this is a good way to get your name out there." As I geared up for my launch, very few people took me seriously.

In December 2015, I announced my run for office with a press conference in front of the Ferguson Police Department. I was surrounded by a small crowd of my fellow activists. Many didn't come, because they didn't understand why I was trying to be part of the system we had been fighting against. I understood their reluctance and distrust because of how often we had been let down by elected officials during the protests and prior to them. But for me, an inside/ outside strategy was necessary. If people on the inside are the ones who write the laws, appropriate the money, and vote in favor of a particular agenda that those on the outside have to live out each day, people with the heart of those on the outside must be in both places.

The presumed front-runner in the Democratic primary was Jason Kander, a young white politician who at thirty-one had been elected Missouri's secretary of state and who had previously served in the Missouri House of Representatives. I knew I couldn't beat him at his own game of coming up through the established party ranks. I had a model, one person who served in the U.S. Senate who I knew believed that the kind of change I wanted to see in my community was not only possible but also necessary, a moral mandate.

I hadn't known anything about Bernie Sanders before I saw him onstage at the conference, but his boldness that day had opened my eyes. With his wild gesticulations, and unapologetic manner, he'd shown me that I didn't have to temper what I believed, even in a staid environment. From Bernie, I learned that I could run as myself. Now that I was vying for a Senate seat, I looked him up and scoured his website to learn more about him.

Later that year, Bernie's campaign took off, and with it grew a nationwide movement of supporters committed to his brand of truth telling and democratic socialism. Less than two months after my December 2015 campaign launch, the St. Louis for Bernie group asked if I wanted to endorse him for president. I immediately agreed, which made me one of the first candidates in the state to support him. In March of 2016, I was among the speakers who took the stage at a Bernie for President campaign event held at Southern Illinois University Edwardsville, just beyond the outskirts of St. Louis. Bernie wanted to make his support for the Ferguson uprising clear, and I was one of four activists from that fight to take the stage and ready the crowd for him. When my team and I got there, we were ushered past a long line of people waiting to get into the auditorium, through a back door that led to the speakers' greenroom. This was my first experience as a speaker at this type of a big, political event, and I was honored. I had met Bernie once before, briefly, and I hoped today might be an opportunity to have more time to connect.

I'd been given two minutes to speak, and Reverend Jones and I crafted a short speech that I read over on my phone as I waited to be called to the lectern. I stood just offstage watching the crowd. I was nervous. But when the emcee called my name, my anxiety melted away. I walked out onto the stage, looked out and saw the sea of Bernie signs, heard the cheers, and felt the crowd's high energy, like a crackling electric current. I'd never seen a big crowd so hyped before. People weren't just cheering, they were really hyped, and for a candidate for office. At the lectern I took a deep breath. "We love you, Cori!" someone yelled from the floor. I swelled with feeling for the people of St. Louis, for the people within and beyond my community who believed that another world was possible and within reach. These were my people, and I appreciated them. "I love you, too!" I called back. From there, my words flowed, effortlessly.

And with that, I was ready. "My name is Cori Bush. I am running for the United States Senate, and I am feeling the 'bern'! I'm a single mother, I'm a registered nurse, a Ferguson activist, and I'm an ordained pastor, but I do understand what it's like to work forty hours a week and still live in poverty. I know what that feels like. For some reason, my round hips and my dark skin says that I must make less money than my counterparts, and I don't understand that. When I stood with others in Ferguson against the tanks and the tear gas after the death of Michael Brown, I was standing against years of injustice—standing against years of racial inequality. I was standing against racial divisions and out-of-control violence in cities like St. Louis, Missouri. My state of Missouri, which has a D rating in education, is number one in African-American school suspensions, number one in violent crime, number one in murders, a national leader in the school-to-prison pipeline, and last in preschool enrollment. But today, I stand here not against something but for something. I stand here, I stand here for someone, someone that I believe in. I stand here for a leader who I know will challenge the status quo. I stand here for Bernie Sanders." The crowd roared.

My appearance at that rally generated a lot of media, more than any I'd had before. I welcomed the publicity because of the boost it gave my campaign. But I also welcomed the opportunity to disrupt the facile narrative that Senator Sanders's support was made up almost entirely of so-called Bernie Bros, deemed aggressive white men who lacked a serious awareness of racial or gender politics, let alone any firsthand experience with race- or gender-based oppression. Not only was I a Black woman. I was a Black woman activist who had come straight out of the Ferguson movement. I was happy to talk about how Bernie supported us when other politicians with aspirations to higher office refused to.

On the campaign trail, I was traveling and giving speeches in front of crowds to talk about my story, why I was running and my policy priorities, not about Bernie Sanders. We opened a campaign office in Ferguson as a reminder of our mission to end police violence and fight discrimination, injustice, inequity, and inequality. We spent much of our time there when we weren't in the streets knocking on doors or on the road. My campaign manager would meet me at New Day just as my day there was ending. I would change out of my work clothes in my office and run down the parking lot to the car, sometimes while still putting on my blazer. Reverend Jones, my assistant Rnesha, and I traveled all over the state together, often taking hours-long drives so I could speak for fifteen minutes before turning around to return home to St. Louis.

One drive in particular led us to a local buffet restaurant in a rural town in Central Missouri. Inside, a Democratic club meeting for candidates for statewide seats was being held in a private party room. Reverend Jones's wife came along on this trip, and the four of us campaigning there made up 100 percent of the Black people in the room of at least sixty people. Everyone else was white. It was an uncomfortable space, and tensions were high. Or so I gleaned from the folded arms and angry looks I received from a few of the attendees. I was unbothered, knowing I belonged just as much as the other candidates.

Once my name was called, I stood in front of the audience, the team within a few feet of me, and I gave my stump speech. Throughout, I noticed heads nodding in agreement, I saw arms unfolded, and I even heard some laughter. At the end, I received a standing ovation. People came up to me afterward, to shake my hand and to speak with me. An older white woman approached me, interrupting a conversation I was having, and grabbed my left hand with one hand, and with her other hand, she started to rub the back of my hand with her fingers in a circular motion. I looked at her in astonishment, feeling a bit violated, and withdrew my hand. I asked her what she was doing, and she responded, "I wanted to see if it rubs off." I froze, in shock, my mouth partly hanging open. A few others who stood near us and witnessed our exchange looked mortified. I took a second to think before I responded, and I realized I was dealing with ignorance. I said to the woman, "No, it doesn't rub off. It's the color of my skin." "You have to understand," she replied, "We've never seen Black people before. Everything we know about Blacks is from television, that all of you are thugs, gang members, and murderers or on welfare. But that's not true at all! Look at you!"

I encountered a number of strange and surreal moments on my trips campaigning, and some incredibly gratifying moments too. But regardless, I'd get back with just enough time to check on my kids, look over homework, make sure the meals I'd prepared for the week were stretching as they needed to, and fall asleep, only to do it all over again.

Looking back, I wasn't doing everything I needed to run for the U.S. Senate. I didn't really know what was needed, and none of the power brokers were inclined to clue me in. My team was left out of endorsement meetings with organizations and publications. We'd find out other candidates were speaking before editorial boards and party groups, and we'd ask if we could have our turn. "There's no point in you coming," they'd respond. "We've already made our decision." We started late and learned as we went, never quite catching up. But, still, I believed I was meant to wage this campaign, and I wasn't going to quit.

We leaned on social media and grassroots fundraising. I didn't hire fundraising consultants, and I didn't meet with the wealthy donors who power successful campaigns. We didn't raise much money, and we didn't realize early enough how much we needed. We also didn't factor in the personal cost I would have to carry. In fact, I put a lot of my own money into the campaign. It's expensive for a woman candidate to be picture ready for the various campaign functions on a daily schedule: for prayer breakfasts, for knocking on doors in all types of weather, and for media interviews, outdoor events, fundraisers, and endorsement meetings. Working in the humidity, rain, or heat meant I had to get my hair done sometimes more than once a day. I needed to apply and re-apply makeup and change my clothes a few times a day. A man can put on a white shirt, a suit, and a tie and be seen in the same outfit multiple times in a week. When a woman is photographed wearing the same blouse a handful of times over the same period, she's criticized. I might spend $30 at the thrift shop on a new suit and $50 on shoes that were professional and comfortable enough to stand and walk in for hours at a time. That was $80 I simply didn't have.

All of a sudden, I needed a budget for hair, makeup, jewelry, and nails. I had to spend money on eating out because of the long and unpredictable hours, while also buying groceries for my children at home. After spending years in boots, T-shirts, jeans, and scrubs, I had to consistently look as though I belonged in public life. The hidden costs of entering electoral politics were many.

I didn't have much extra money to spend prior to running for office, so the costs of extra gas, eating out, and new (or, new-to-me) clothing made it increasingly difficult for me to make ends meet. A few times, I came home to find that my electricity had been shut off. Or I'd find that the stove wouldn't come on—because the gas was disconnected. Or there would be no hot water running from the faucets. Sometimes, I simply didn't have money to pay a bill on time. But on at least one occasion, I was just too busy to keep my mail straight. One month, I paid the electric bill twice and the gas bill not at all. That kind of thing is an honest mix-up, but any mistake knocked me off my square.

Despite what we'd told my dad that day at Merhaba, my team didn't have a proper fundraising structure. I wasn't prepared for what he'd warned me about. I was running in a Democratic primary, so I didn't have to steel myself against attacks from the right. Instead, just as I'd been stung by civil rights organizations that criticized the Ferguson uprising, I was hurt most by people within the Black community who I thought would be allies. Many turned their backs to me, or actively worked against me.

The activism work I'd been a part of was precisely the problem for many of my critics. That I had raised so little money was enough to make me seem like an illegitimate candidate to members of the Democratic establishment. I was also too progressive in their eyes, a protester who knew plenty about marching in the street, but not enough about policy. And I was strongly affiliated with Bernie Sanders, and Bernie was not favored locally by many in the Black community.

In 2016, like Bernie, I was considered fringe, a disruption and a distraction. But despite these criticisms, I knew that I wasn't alone, and I leaned into the people who remained by my side: my team, other local candidates like Bruce Franks Jr., an activist from the Ferguson uprising who also decided to run for office at the same time and who also backed Bernie, as well as the progressive movement in St. Louis. I chalked up any attacks or lack of support to fear and ignorance, and campaigned with a fury—working to change people's minds.

It wasn't enough. I lost to Kander in the primary, which was held the second day in August 2016. The night of the loss, Bruce and I combined our watch parties mainly because we shared so many of the same friends and supporters. I stayed out dancing in the street at Yaquis with family, friends, and supporters on Cherokee Street, licking my wounds with my team late into the night. David Ragland, my friend from high school with whom I'd cofounded the Truth Telling Project, drove me home from the party where we'd watched the returns come in. I stepped out and thanked him for the ride, turned around, then noticed that my car was gone. On top of a stinging loss, someone stole my car, I thought to myself and stewed in frustration. But the next day, I learned my car had been repossessed, not stolen. The campaign that had wrung me dry was over.

·   ·   ·

THAT YEAR BROUGHT US Ferguson veterans a mix of victory and tragedy. Bruce won his seat in Missouri's legislature. He was representing the 78th District in St. Louis. But five weeks after my primary loss, on September 6, I woke up early with a sense of foreboding. I pushed the thought aside and gave myself a pep talk. In a matter of hours, I got a call. Twenty-nine-year-old Darren "King D"

Seals had been killed. His body had been found inside a burning car that morning. He'd been shot, then set on fire.

I knew Darren because he had been a consistent presence at Ferguson protests. He'd comforted Lesley McSpadden, Michael Brown Jr.'s mother, the night we'd learned the grand jury would not indict Darren Wilson. Darren held her as she wept. Since the protests peaked, he had been outspoken about being targeted and stalked by police. On social media he posted about these encounters. Now he was gone, and protesters were at the scene where his body was found, livestreaming and posting photographs of the bullet shells that littered the ground.

At work that day I followed the livestreams and mourning with a heavy heart. I was broken by Darren's death and by its eerie similarity to a previous death of another young Black man in Ferguson. The same day the grand jury had made its crushing announcement of no indictment for Darren Wilson, twenty-year-old Deandre Joshua's body had been found in a burning car, blocks from the protests, a bullet wound in his head. I hadn't known Deandre. Still, it was too much for me.

Throughout the day, I would go into my office and shut the door behind me to cry. I texted and talked with a friend who encouraged me to turn my attention elsewhere for a while. Still not able to look away from the digital memorial to Darren, I kept scrolling through my social media feeds. That's when I saw a post from a preacher I knew. He had started a clergy group I worked with from time to time. His post said he had a couple homes for rent and was available to show them if anyone was interested. I let him know that I was, and went to view one as soon as I left work. That was the fateful evening when I was raped.

The last four months of 2016 were some of the toughest of my life. In the new year, a key volunteer on my Senate campaign asked me to run for Congress again, this time for the House. I knew J.T.'s father through the Truth Telling Project. I listened to him and respected his read on the political landscape, but I said no. I wasn't ready to re-enter public life after my assault, I hadn't even gone back to work yet. It was difficult for me to be around people without being triggered. Panic and anxiety would overtake me in an instant. I was hypervigilant, extremely sensitive to my surroundings and people's tones of voice, and on guard for potential threats. I would dissociate and have flashbacks where all of sudden I was thrust back to the assault, to the moment when the pastor was holding my wrists so tightly that I felt trapped knowing the worst was about to happen. I was emotionally numb, unaware of who I was, when a committeewoman in the Democratic Party hierarchy reached out and asked me to run for the seat. Again, I said no. Bruce Franks Jr. tried next. "Cori, we need you to run for this seat," he told me. "I know you're still dealing with what you went through. But you're the person."

I gave Bruce the same answer I'd given J.T. and the party functionary. I was still fragile. By the time he asked, I had just returned to work at New Day after a four-month break. I was just beginning to find my confidence, and to feel that I could get through a workday again. Because I still worked in community mental health, I was often triggered by the struggles of my patients. I'd slip back into the quicksand of despair. But I moved slowly and took things day by day.

I'd entered the Senate race because I wanted to be able to ensure the safety of my son, my daughter, and all of my loved ones. With this new call to serve, a specter of police violence hung over my decision, but so did everything I had gone through with the rape. My rape kit—the collection of which had been a painful and humiliating process—was left to sit on a shelf for four months before it was tested. In addition to surviving and healing from their trauma, victims are tasked with navigating society's stigma and disbelief. I had gone to court multiple times in an effort to get an order of protection against my rapist. He avoided being served the documents, enlisting his neighbors to help him dodge the process server I paid and who repeatedly tried to deliver the order. I found no justice.

I had had so much help, so many advocates throughout the community: even the circuit attorney tried to help me. What about people who don't have that kind of support? I wondered. Who in elected office is speaking about how police departments allow rape kits to sit unopened for months? Who is demanding that the criminal courts system change and effectively deal with sexual assault cases? Because the system gives victims and perpetrators the same rights, the judge explained to me, my rapist walked free after claiming we'd had rough consensual sex. A technicality kept me from being able to get even a modicum of protection against future harassment or abuse. It wasn't right.

I kept talking with Bruce, and we discussed what it would mean for me to challenge William Lacy Clay Jr. Clay had held the seat for many years. Before him, his father had won the seat in 1969, when the district sent its first Black representative to the nation's capital. That win, nearly five decades earlier, still mattered deeply to Black St. Louis. Taking on the Clay family's political dynasty would mean taking on the access and power that our parents' generation had fought for. My dad had worked on Clay Sr.'s campaign, and I grew up knocking on doors for both men. Our families were connected and had built familiarity and respect over many years. Bruce was a St. Louis native himself and knew what the Clay family meant to Black people in the district, especially in the northern part of the county, where my dad still held political office.

But we both also knew that Clay was not fighting for the things we cared about. Two months before Michael Brown Jr. was killed, Clay could have voted to demilitarize the police, but he hadn't. I thought about all the things he could've done differently to effect change for the most marginalized in our community. How his presence here with regular, everyday people would've spoken volumes to so many. Instead, he was known for being the absent congressman. All those times I'd been pummeled by high-interest payday loans, or struggled to balance my student loan debt and childcare costs with other household expenses, I'd wondered, "Who is speaking for people like us? Do our federal elected officials recognize how hard life is for so many of us?" I was tired of asking questions I already knew the answers to. It was time, I knew, for me to try to fix these injustices by stepping up myself.

I was going to enter the House race, but this time around, I knew how to do it better. I wouldn't be able to leave my full-time job and devote myself to campaigning full-time. I'd need the right people managing fundraising, communications, policy, coordinating volunteers, and field operations. If I needed graphics designed or a mass email sent out, I wasn't going to micromanage the process. I would have a team with me that I trusted.

A couple of months before I lost my Senate race, a group called Brand New Congress reached out to me about an initiative they were starting to get working progressive candidates elected across the country. They were just developing their program when they made a trip to St. Louis to my campaign office to learn more about my candidacy. Now this group was up and running and working closely with another political action committee called Justice Democrats. While encouraging me to run for the House, J.T., along with several of the PAC's supporters, had nominated me as someone whom the Brand New Congress should support. The organizations contacted me to say they wanted to endorse me and offer all the infrastructure I'd been missing that first time around. I was skeptical at first. "I've been there, done that," I said. "So if you can't really help me, I can't do this." They assured me they would have my back, that I could continue to work my full-time job, and we got started.

In March, I held my soft launch at UrbArts, a nonprofit creative space/art studio focused on marginalized youth and community development. The next month, I held my official campaign launch in a storefront back in the North Oaks Plaza, just minutes from where I grew up and where my dad still lived. The Northwoods location was in the heart of northern St. Louis County, and it represented my roots back to the penny candy and ice cream days. As a preteen, I'd gotten a second hole pierced in my ears at the beauty supply store there. I'd have my work cut out for me, persuading the incumbent's supporters to back me. But, at North Oaks, I was surrounded by people who believed in me.

Through my Senate campaign, I'd expanded my base of support. To my activist family, I'd added a bigger slice of the progressive community, including many who had worked for years with the unhoused. I had the backing of those who had been energized by Bernie's campaign for president, which included Black millennials and Gen Xers disillusioned with Democratic Party politics as usual despite their parents' leanings. I had support from the LGBTQIA+ community and from folks in the disability rights community and more. About a hundred people packed into the storefront ready to pick up right where we'd left off. I was coming back harder this time.

Brand New Congress and Justice Democrats gave my new operation "next level" sheen. We released our first campaign video, and printed an eight-by-twelve-foot banner featuring my smiling face. It hung from the wall announcing Cori Bush for Congress 2018. Tables were set up around the room. At one, we had merchandise for sale. It was piled with T-shirts, buttons, stickers, and bumper stickers. At another, a volunteer took donations and people signed up to host house parties or canvasses, eager to spread the word. Often political functions have the feel of subdued networking events. Not in my space. The atmosphere was electric. Folks were exuberant.

My friends and family gathered with me, and included among them was the person who'd always been fiercely protective of me: my dad. Finally, my dad could see that I was serious about politics and that people in politics were taking me seriously, too. A few weeks earlier, he was at home when he'd gotten a call from someone affiliated with Clay Jr. The person asked if my dad knew that I planned to challenge Clay for his seat. Upon hearing that my dad was aware of my plans and wasn't discouraging me, Clay's proxy reminded him of our families' long-standing relationship and asked him to keep me from rupturing it. In turn, my father reminded the person at the other end of the line that I was an adult, and I made my own decisions. The call ended soon after. Prior to that, my dad hadn't said much to me about what my decision to run for the seat might mean for the Clay legacy, or to him for that matter, considering he had helped to build that legacy. But my dad didn't like feeling strong-armed. He didn't like the caller's insinuation that there would be a quid pro quo. And he didn't like that Clay's people didn't reach out to me directly. He didn't like feeling like I had been disrespected. After that phone call, my dad was all in. He supported me with gusto.

That night at my campaign launch, my father took to the stage to introduce me. He was a City of Northwoods alderman, and it was the first time in his political career that he had publicly come out against the Clay family. If he felt any risk to his own political future that night, he didn't show it. Instead, he got up to the lectern and looked out over the crowd. He commented on how diverse the room was, how the room showed the support I had across racial and ethnic lines, across the generational and geographic lines that too often cordoned us off into separate camps. He choked up as he thanked everyone for supporting me.

As I looked at him, I could see that he was having a reckoning himself. He had seen this level of organization and coordination happen for other people through his many years in politics. Now he was seeing it happen for me, and not because I'd come up through the traditional channels. This was something new. "I've noticed what you all have done, the momentum that you have," he said, addressing the progressive organizations and activists in the room. "I'm not a progressive. I'm what you all call the establishment," he said. But he wasn't actually establishment. He was progressive in his values, but his affiliations and age made people assume he was a more moderate, corporate-backed Democrat.

Hearing my dad's words was a shock to me because I felt he was more closely aligned with progressives, those of us who wanted to expand what was possible in the Democratic Party and in the country. I began to realize that many people supported "the establishment," because that's all that had been offered as the way to be taken seriously and to win when they were making their way in the world of U.S. politics. A big-tent, well-funded progressive movement like the one we were trying to build, a movement that rejected corporate and super PAC money, hadn't existed here, not in this way before. That didn't mean that we should be on opposing sides. Not at all.

We shared values and wanted the same things for ourselves and our families, like ending poverty and discrimination, providing quality health care and education, protecting voting rights and reproductive rights, fighting for climate justice and equality. My dad and I believed in the same things. Like many people who are just trying to support themselves and want the best for their families and their neighbors, my dad was progressive in his thinking even if he didn't identify as such initially. And it didn't help the progressive movement to make people like him feel like outsiders.

My dad introduced me and then stayed onstage, next to me, as I gave my remarks. He patted me on the back and kept his hand on my shoulder throughout the speech, putting his pride and ever-present desire to protect me on display for everyone to see. When I was a kid, I would hop out of bed as I heard him coming in the door from working second shift at the grocery store. I'd run to his favorite chair in the living room to greet him, taking up his space for him. He was never angry. He played up his exasperation until we both laughed. Now here I was as a grown woman, still following his lead in many ways and taking up his space. I was proud of him, too.

I took the lesson I'd learned that night as I went door-to-door in the weeks and months that followed as I campaigned. I gained a lot of support in south St. Louis, a community known for its diversity, where many residents are immigrants and refugees from Latin America, the Middle East, Africa, Asia, and Europe. The area is also home to many progressive neighborhoods where I could expect peo-

ple to be empathetic to or themselves a part of social justice organizing efforts. People recognized me from Ferguson. There, people
wanted to talk about my activism and the uprising.

But in the district's predominantly Black neighborhoods, some
residents didn't like the negative media attention our activism had
brought to their communities, and they were up front with me about
it. Our four hundred days of protest seemed excessive to some. Several expressed the idea that we were unserious, that we were rabble-
rousers without any real plans. I made it clear that wasn't true of
the protesters, but I knew these criticisms just meant I had a lot
of work to do to make sure that people knew the truth about us. I
didn't want to be branded as ignorant or foolish before I could even
properly introduce myself. I also didn't want to be accused of being
unrealistic or pushing a white liberal agenda, which is how some
characterized Bernie Sanders's platform.

To me, Black people need quality health care and education, free
college tuition, and student loan debt forgiveness. We need a living wage, safe and affordable housing, reliable public transportation,
environmental justice, broadband access, economic equity capital,
and an end to mass incarceration and police violence. This was not a
white liberal agenda to me. It is an agenda that saves lives.

I learned at those doors and in those meetings that people liked to
hear about my experiences as a nurse. I talked about how I watched
my patients die because they didn't have access to the medication
that they needed. I talked about the young people I saw who were
dropped from their parents' health insurance plans just before their
first bout with an undiagnosed mental health condition. I talked
about how they struggled to manage health crises while uninsured
with testing, treatments, and medications being out of reach. I
talked about how I had worked in childcare for a decade but was
unable to afford health insurance for myself all that time. What I'd
been through and witnessed led me to support Medicare for All, I
explained. Then I would add that the same way that I fought for jus-

tice on the streets of Ferguson, I'd fight for them just as fiercely once elected to Congress.

I was making inroads, but the incumbent's father's legacy sometimes overshadowed me. One day I was knocking on doors in a neighborhood not far from where my dad lived, a neighborhood in which he had tilled soil for his own campaigns for three decades. These were the doors of his friends, his peers, people he'd sat with on PTAs and in church pews. I knocked on the door of an elder who asked what I was thinking challenging Clay Jr. He couldn't point to anything Clay had done that he supported. There was nothing positive, but nothing terrible either. There was no recent scandal that made this man feel it was time for Clay to go. "Don't you know that's a machine?" he asked. "I do," I said. "But I believe we're our own machine. The people are the machine, and we can accomplish whatever we want to if we show up to vote." We spoke for a bit, but it was clear the man's mind was made up: "My family's been voting for the Clays forever. Why should we switch our vote to you? You don't have anything, and who's backing you? The devil we know is better than the devil we don't."

That dynasty wasn't my only problem. That I, a woman, had the audacity to enter the race also rubbed people the wrong way. "Why are you running against a Black man as a Black woman?" these critics asked. "Black women are supposed to be there to support Black men, build them up." I wanted to go to Congress to tear down the structures that continue to harm my people, but all some critics saw was an effort to tear down a Black man. The misogyny ran deep. Here again was the problem of my marital status. People asked me, "If you win, what are you gonna do with your kids?"

The comments that really got to me were about optics, the deep-seated belief that a single woman shouldn't be in a position of great leadership. I'd heard it when I'd started my church and again when I ran for the U.S. Senate. Those roles were too prestigious for someone who didn't have "a head," as some put it, or a head of household. And then there is the misogynoir that took center stage on a regular basis. Folks have low expectations of Black women because they want us to be low—out of the way, silent, available only when called upon and just enough so that they can claim to support Black women. They give us a ceiling, and they are surprised, even angered, when we stand taller. They think we can aspire to and achieve only small feats because that's all they believe we deserve. Folks want to be in control of us and put a cap on our brilliance because of their own insecurities and shortcomings. Some people read my ambition and confidence as egotism. It made them uncomfortable. They wanted to know where my husband was. I took to responding, "God hasn't given me one yet. Do you have one for me?" That usually put an end to the questioning.

Other questions about my respectability circulated. Some in the Black community, especially some in positions of power, told people close to my campaign that I didn't look as if I were Congress material. My braids were unprofessional, they said. I first got braids in 2015 when my longtime hairstylist, Candace Smith, moved to Atlanta. I was a regular in her chair, every Friday morning at 9:00 a.m. To give myself time to find a good new stylist, I gave braids a try and loved them. This worked for my lifestyle. My scrubs were unprofessional, they said. Their concerns were superficial. How I dressed had nothing to do with whether I was right for the seat. But to some, my clothes and choice of hairstyle were evidence that I was too young for the position, naive. I wasn't playing the role of candidate correctly because I didn't know how, they believed. And they treated me like a kid stumbling about in my mom's heels. I was over the age of forty and running on the strength of my ideas. But some preferred to scrutinize my appearance rather than hear me out.

Just as we started to understand all that we were up against, the well-oiled machine that had so impressed my father at my campaign launch started to sputter and lurch. The collaboration between Justice Democrats and Brand New Congress, who had been acting as my joint national campaign team, worked well at the start. They built a campaign structure that made me feel we were on the right road. Fundraising started off well, social media was picking up. They connected me with other progressive political candidates nationwide. They'd sent me to a summit in Kentucky a few weeks after the launch. There I met other candidates they were endorsing, and together we talked about policy, did rounds of mock media interviews, and strategized about our campaigns. It was there that I met Alexandria Ocasio-Cortez. She knew about all that we'd accomplished in Ferguson, and I was immediately struck by her fierceness and clarity of vision. On that first day at the summit, she expressed that she wasn't yet sure whether she'd run. We sat together at dinner that night, and she spoke about the dynamics in her district. I pressed her to run and told her she was the person for that political moment and the person for that seat. We learned more about each other and bonded that night and in the days that followed.

But now these progressive groups were taking on more candidates, which thinned out their resources. They stopped managing my campaign, and suddenly things began to feel the way they had during my Senate run, with the weight of fundraising and day-to-day operations putting more on my shoulders than I could handle while working a full-time job. By the end of the year, I needed to find a new team, and the pressure was mounting. I didn't have time to waste.

I was determined not to give up. I spent the first three months of 2018 starting over almost from scratch. The primary was scheduled for late summer, so I had a small window to get things in order. In April, however, conditions went from bad to worse. I was driving near New Day one day when a car ran a red light and crashed into the side of mine, T-boning my cute black Jeep Cherokee that I had purchased only a few months prior, the first car I ever bought brand new.

The pain was incredible. I had micro concussions. I had more than a dozen areas of injury along my spine from my neck to my pelvis. The position of my pelvis was shifted from the impact. I couldn't walk but a few steps. I spent the first couple weeks in bed, lying flat on my back on ice packs. Because of the swelling, I could not walk using my left leg. That hip was in tremendous, unremitting pain because the ball would not stay in the joint. I was prescribed bed rest and visits to the chiropractor. I had to take leave from my job once again; there was no way around it. After some days at home, I set up an air mattress in my campaign office so I could at least keep up with the work there. It wasn't enough. I'd been knocked down right when it was time to ramp up my campaign. I couldn't go to endorsement meetings and sent people to represent the campaign for me. I couldn't go to the few donor meetings and fundraising events we'd set up.

My kids helped me go to the bathroom. My team organized meals for us daily. I wasn't eating much though because I couldn't really sit up in bed. After weeks of visits to the chiropractor, I was not getting much better. I wanted to quit. I didn't want to do a disservice to my supporters and the people I wanted to represent. But I realized the disservice would be quitting. So that July, I started having my team pick me up from home and carry me into the campaign office. They set up an extra-high air mattress, one where I would not have to move a lot to lay down on it, so I could at least be in the space with everyone. A few weeks later, on my birthday, July 21, Alexandria Ocasio-Cortez came to town to stump for me at a breakfast, a canvass, and an afternoon rally. It was the first time I had knocked on a door since my accident, and it was still too soon. I could barely walk. The ball was still out of the joint socket of my left hip. I was dragging my leg. As we went from door to door, Alex saw me struggling with tears in my eyes, trying to keep up. She decided she had to hold me up so I could knock on a few more doors.

By the afternoon rally, as happy as I was, the pain was becoming unbearable. I was sitting listening to the speakers, on camera, rocking back and forth in pain. I popped a piece of chewing gum in my mouth to take my mind off thinking about what I was feeling. After all the encouraging, heartfelt remarks from the wonderful and diverse speakers representing the beauty of St. Louis, Alex and Bruce Franks Jr. blessed me with their introductions. My dad and Bruce helped me to the stage, and I barely made it up the few stairs. I still delivered that speech in four-inch stilettos.

I tried to go back to work, too. But my job required a lot of fast-paced movement up and down hallways. As I walked down the hall toward my office, I needed to lean against the wall and finally dropped to the floor in anguish. I had to crawl. I knew my job was on the line, but I returned to bed rest. Eventually, the last week of July, I went to get an MRI. The imaging revealed that I'd been given the wrong course of treatment over thirty-nine chiropractic visits. My chiropractor put me in traction, and immediately my condition changed for the better.

On August 7, I lost the Democratic primary to Lacy Clay Jr. Until the very end, I believed the seat would be mine. I had put my name and reputation on the line, and I lost—again. I also lost my job. I was licking my wounds the day after the primary, at home, when New Day left me a voice mail, letting me know I'd been fired. They said I had been gone too long, and they needed to fill the position. I had been there five years. I'd be living on supplemental medical insurance. My finances were a shambles. And my political ambitions were dashed. And, most of all, I needed to heal.

Chapter 8

MY BODY AND SOUL were crushed that fall of 2018. I let myself fall into grief in the weeks following the primary. I wondered why God would tell me to run, only to lead me down another dead end. I felt guilty for pulling my family even more into the spotlight of public life. I felt I'd let down everyone who believed I could win and bring about the change we all wanted.

Running for office yet again was the furthest thing from my mind. First, I needed a job. I needed to catch up on bills. My teenage children were coming up on milestones, and my expenses were due to climb. Zion had just finished high school and was set to begin at a local community college. He'd chosen a path that wouldn't leave either of us saddled with debt, but I still had to cover all the up-front costs so that he could pursue his associate degree. Angel was headed into her senior year of high school, and that meant there were going to be college application fees, homecoming, prom, a class ring, and graduation.

Months after the crash, I could feel my body coming back to itself. Soon I'd be able to walk well enough to return to nursing. As soon as I was well enough to make it through an interview without wincing, I got out there. I was a high-tech nurse with management skills. I'd worked at a hospital, at clinics, and in in-home care. It didn't take long for me to get offers, and I accepted a job in the cardiac intensive care unit at a children's hospital. The onboarding process took a couple months. I was counting the days until I'd get my first check. By the time I started working, I was well enough to be on my feet for twelve-hour shifts.

It didn't take long before I was reminded that I was no longer just Nurse Cori. I was the former congressional candidate and Ferguson activist, Cori Bush. My patients' families would stop me as I made my rounds and ask to take pictures with me. People might FaceTime a friend or family member to tell them that I was their nurse while I was there in the room with them. Mostly the attention was fine, but sometimes it was a distraction. A family would get frustrated that I couldn't be their nurse during a particular shift, or they would demand a level of attention that went beyond what I was able to give while balancing their needs with other patients' too.

The campaigns I ran had engendered a feeling of familiarity and accessibility that made my return to civilian life challenging. Sometimes the policies I'd championed created problems. Once, a family member of one of my patients, who was from out of state, kept wanting to talk to me about my stance on police accountability, a position I had no interest in explaining to them while I was taking care of their child. I was outspoken about defunding the police, redirecting funds used for tear gas, MRAPs, bear spray, rubber bullets, and militarized weapons to social programs in education, healthy food access, mental health services, substance use treatment, recidivism reduction, community violence prevention, and housing. That person left and came back later that day wearing a hat and T-shirt emblazoned with the thin blue line, the pro-police symbol and a white supremacist dog whistle that appeared on the scene in response to the words "Black Lives Matter." The desire to intimidate me was obvious. I was able to work around such intrusions, but I knew that a single family member with an ax to grind could put my license at risk. I stayed vigilant.

Other times I had difficult interactions with family members that had nothing to do with my public profile but one that was all too familiar. Once, I walked into a patient's room, greeted the mother, and introduced myself to her as her child's nurse. "I want the real nurse," she said. I responded that I was the real nurse, but the mother was adamant: "No, the other one. The one who was just in here who emptied the urine." I explained that the young white woman she was referring to was the patient care tech and would also be helping the child. "Get out," the white mother told me.

I respectfully left and went to my supervisor to explain the situation. She was sympathetic but frustrated. During my interview process, the leadership team on my unit had been excited about my background and experience pointing out racial disparities and pushing for solutions. They'd wanted me to help the hospital recruit more Black nurses, since I was one of very few in a staff of more than a hundred. They'd been eager for me to introduce my ideas around clinical care and cultural competence to the rest of the hospital staff. Still, I learned then that management was not equipped to support me when I came to report a racist incident that kept me from doing my job.

Would the experience I'd gained in street protests and on the campaign trail make me a liability as an employee? I knew they wondered about me. And at the same time, I became less confident that the people I worked with had my back. I would step to the nurses' station and ask for help with a patient, and no one would volunteer, but they were eager to help a white nurse. I would ask for someone to relieve me for lunch, and a whole table of nurses would look at me but not utter a word and would then go back to their conversations. A white nurse could ask the same question minutes later, and more than one person would respond to help. I spoke with other Black staff and found they had similar stories. It was blatant racism.

I told my supervisor I didn't want to work in an environment where I had to fight just to perform the basics of my job. I couldn't provide quality care this way. Those babies' lives were on the line. "When I go home, I have to fight," I said. "I don't want to do that while I'm at work too." It was also difficult for me to return to a staff nursing position after I had spent years in management. Many of my peers were right out of nursing school and more than a decade younger than me. They'd try to correct me when I used a technique they hadn't learned yet, and I was too often on the receiving end of doubts, criticisms, and pushback that weighed on me.

I kept hoping that conditions at the pediatric hospital would improve, but they didn't much. I worked there nearly three months before I knew it wasn't going to work out. By then I'd decided that I was going to run for office yet again. Balancing a job with a campaign was going to be an issue working on this floor. At New Day, I had an hour lunch break when I could get things done, and I could go to the break room and take a call if I needed to. But at this hospital, I was unreachable for as long as twelve or sixteen hours during my shift.

That wouldn't do. If I was to challenge Clay again, I needed for my race to be my focus. At first, I'd been reluctant to campaign again. I was stung by my loss, and I wasn't sure I had it in me to go back out there after everything that had happened. It was harder dealing with the criticism and attacks since the assault. There was still a lot of trauma I needed to work through. My father understood that I needed my rest, but he was insistent. "Get yourself together, because you are going to run again," he said to me soon after the primary. He let the conversation quiet for a while, but by the end of 2018 he was back at it. I knew members of my team had continued to meet and organize, hopeful there would be another race. "When are you going to start working with the team?" my dad would ask. "We've been working, so when are you going to get started? You don't need to take off for two years and then run again."

Not only did my father believe in me, but my team did, too. Many of them had never stopped working, confident that I should be the one to carry into Congress the vision we'd crafted together. I started believing in myself again. One question kept coming back to me: Did you accomplish what you set out to do? I hadn't. I hadn't accomplished my goal of making sure that the people in my community felt represented at the federal level. I hadn't done what I needed to to keep my son or daughter from becoming the next hashtag, or to make sure another assault victim's rape kit didn't sit on the shelf untouched for months. I prayed about my decision, and I asked God to fix my heart to be able to run again, prayed that God would allow me to be as connected to and invested in the fight as I'd been before. "Lord, as I step out, give me what I need to be able to do this." And then I stepped out.

.   .   .

ON A GLOOMY, BITTERLY cold day in January 2019, my team and I visited a building in downtown St. Louis that, until April 2017, had been the only twenty-four-hour walk-in shelter for unhoused people in the city. The building needed a lot of upgrades and repairs, and the shelter's operators had tried and failed to raise enough money to cover the work. In 2017, the city threatened closure, citing a litany of code violations, but put no contingency plan in place for the shelter's residents. We felt their efforts were insufficient and unsatisfactory. We staged a protest, marching in the street and camping out on the sidewalk in front of the building. It was no use. The city closed the shelter, pushing even more unhoused residents into the streets. Nearly two years later the building was a hulking, empty shell on the corner of Locust and 14th Streets, a reminder of the human costs of failed leadership that believes in property over people. I sat on a bench out front, next to a sculpture of a sleeping person, and there I announced my candidacy and my run for the U.S. House of Representatives one more time. A member of my team recorded a video we then posted to social media.

The next day I flew to the Sundance Film Festival for the premiere of *Knock Down the House,* a Netflix documentary that tracked my 2018 primary campaign along with those of three other progressive women who had challenged centrist Democratic incumbents for their House seats that cycle: Amy Vilela in Nevada, Paula Jean

Swearengin in West Virginia, and Alexandria Ocasio-Cortez in New York. All of us had been endorsed by Brand New Congress and Justice Democrats. The film covered our campaigns and put on full display our common desire to make Congress a place where regular, everyday people are represented by regular, everyday people who know and better understand their struggles. When the director, Rachel Lears, approached me about being in the film, I had no idea of the impact it would have. A lot of people shared with us, from all over the world, how the movie changed their lives and, in many ways, moved them into action. Several ran for office.

In the moments after the movie premiere, I stepped to the front of the theatre with Amy, Paula, Rachel, producer Sarah Olsen, and producer/editor Robin Blotnick, and I announced my candidacy again, this time in front of the press, amplifying the message we'd put out on our social media channels just the day before. *Knock Down the House* won the Festival Favorite and U.S. Documentary Audience Awards at Sundance, and I left the festival energized, ready to go get the seat I knew would be mine.

Off the bat, I made sure that people understood that I wasn't going anywhere. I had canvassed in two previous cycles, and I had already worked the land and tilled the soil. I let it be known that I wasn't running again as some sort of vanity project. The people wanted me to run, and I was ready. I was open about having had a car accident that took me off the campaign trail two and a half months before the last primary. I talked about how I now had an experienced team that had weathered the storm once and would stand by me.

At doors, I noticed a new response to my candidacy from some of the same people who had before expressed undying devotion to the Clay dynasty. The insiders knew that by the time I announced my intention to run, we had exceeded our fundraising for our last race. There was no need to ask why I'd challenge Clay. The difference between our policy positions was clear, and two years into the Trump administration it was obvious to people why we needed unapologetic progressives in the House. The vile, white supremacist, sexist, bigoted Trump administration spewed lies, targeted Black and brown women elected officials, made a mockery of our democracy, and emboldened fascists.

Of course, some of the more notable in my district felt that even if they planned to vote for me in the privacy of the polling station, they couldn't have a donation to my campaign show up on a Federal Election Commission report. They couldn't publicly pledge their support. The stakes were too high for them should I lose once again. But for me, every bit of help mattered.

I also accepted that some folks just didn't want to associate with me no matter what and I shouldn't waste time trying to go after them for an endorsement. When I ran for the Senate in 2016 and the House in 2018, I'd spent hours talking with people I was told I needed to win over if I had any hopes of winning. More often than not, my efforts didn't work. I decided that I'd take whoever was with me and wouldn't worry or be upset about those who weren't. I focused on the doors that were already open and the prospective voters who had felt as though they were overlooked for so long.

I carried with me a new confidence born from the experience of my losses. People's swipes didn't touch me the same anymore. I learned that no matter what I did, people were going to have their opinion. I stayed genuine, and I wasn't going to be afraid to mix it up. I wore jeans to one event and a suit to another. What mattered most to me was that I was comfortable in my skin and that others would see that.

More and more, people wanted to be a part of what we were building and look the part. I encouraged the members of my campaign team and our volunteers to wear their purple "Cori Bush for Congress" T-shirts everywhere: Dress it up for formal campaign events with a blazer. Wear it to the grocery store. I wanted to brand us, and it worked.

The shirts became trendy. People came to our campaign office because they wanted to be part of the T-shirt gang. We weren't so formal; we weren't always buttoned up in suits and pearls, as had been the norm for candidates. We were down-to-earth and relatable.

I knew that to run a truly inclusive campaign, we needed to do more than look the part. People in the community, particularly Black residents, often told me that they wanted to be part of our efforts but just couldn't afford to. They wanted to knock on doors, but they were working two jobs or had kids to care for. We knew it was a type of privilege to be able to volunteer on a campaign, so we decided that we needed to create another way for people to get involved. As 2019 drew to a close, we announced that we would hire canvassers to knock on doors and pay them $17.50 an hour. We offered four-hour shifts every day for three weeks and weekly pay.

The winter holidays were right around the corner. And the response to our efforts was tremendous. People signed up and came out in droves. It was heartening, but it also broke my heart to see so many show up for a job that would last for only a few weeks. People were hungry for good work that didn't pay poverty wages.

The backlash was immediate. On social media, commenters announced that I was stupid and naive for thinking I could hire people to canvass. They mocked my campaign for thinking that door knocking should be paid, and for our paying anything more than minimum wage, if we were offering anything. But I was firm: If we want to open the door to more people who want to work on our campaigns, we must make campaigning accessible. And what would I look like if I was championing at least a $15 minimum wage, an ally to the Fight for $15 movement, but I was unable to pay campaigners on my congressional campaign at least that much?

By paying our volunteers as employees, we were able to open political work to a wider range of people in the district. One man, in his forties, who signed up with us said he'd never made that much money on a job in his life. A mother of a newborn knocked on doors with her child in her carrier and said she was happy for the opportunity to make money that she didn't have to turn around and spend on childcare. We connected a canvasser who was facing evic-

tion with full-time work that he could pick up after his time can-
vassing with us ended. He was able to stay in his home.

We brought other innovative approaches to the campaign and,
in doing so, threw open the doors of electoral politics to those who
might otherwise not have chosen to take part in a congressional
race, those who see politics as being distant or removed from their
own lives. In December 2019 we held an interfaith, multicultural
community event. A couple hundred people joined us at our office
for a holiday meal. We arranged to have a Black Santa on hand to
hear about wish lists, pose with kids for photos, and read "'Twas
the Night Before Christmas." We set up a craft table where children
could make angels and gingerbread figures as ornaments. We had a
DJ playing music and a buffet-style spread. We gave families enough
food for a full Christmas meal, including a turkey. I borrowed my
dad's collection of Kwanzaa table items that he had been assembling
since I was a child, and a local activist explained the principles and
practices of Kwanzaa or *Matunda ya Kwanza,* the seven-day First
Fruits festival.

I wore my green, red, and white "You Better Sleigh" Christmas
sweater and stood on the stage to tell people how much I appreciated everyone's support. People used the time to write personalized
messages of support on our holiday postcards during the event to get
word about my candidacy to others in the district. We had our eyes
on the polls. At the same time, we were happy to be able to provide a
free and culturally relevant event for our community. Guests talked
to us about how expensive it usually is to have their kids' pictures
taken with Santa and how hard they have to search just to find one
who's Black. Others told us they were happy to have the opportunity
to learn about Kwanzaa and to just be in good company with a good
DJ, celebrating together.

I ushered in 2020 riding high from the excitement of the holiday
event, certain that I was going to win my seat that year. I could picture the moment I found out I'd won. I had a vision of myself walking out of my small office in my campaign headquarters wearing a

purple dress, crying with joy while people ran up and embraced me. I told myself that all I had to do was be patient and keep working and that vision would become a reality. Then came COVID-19.

.   .   .

IN EARLY MARCH, THERE was plenty of news about the coronavirus, but it still felt far away from where we were. Missouri hadn't shut down. I was a national surrogate for Bernie Sanders's campaign for U.S. president, the second time around, and I'd been on a tour speaking at rallies for Bernie around the country and now all over my state. That month alone, I'd done several dozen over the span of a few days. On March 9, the day before our Missouri presidential primary, we had a full day of events in the district that I spoke at. It was huge, and the people who showed up were on fire with enthusiasm.

When I walked onstage to introduce Bernie, I could feel the electricity in the room as progressives from all over the state and beyond experienced the rush of being together with like-minded people. I felt that rush myself, and after I gave my speech, I made my way through the crowds shaking hands, hugging people, talking excitedly with those in the crowd. Afterward, many of us who attended the rally marched through the streets of downtown in the falling rain to Bernie's nearest campaign office, where I gave several more speeches about all the work we'd done together in support of his candidacy. That next day, Joe Biden defeated Bernie and all the other candidates in the primary.

Two weeks later, I was sitting in my house when I started to feel sick. My head hurt. I was dizzy and feverish. I couldn't catch my breath, but I used my inhaler, took some vitamin C, and felt well enough to sleep through the night. I woke up the next day and felt fine, but the symptoms soon returned and were worrisome enough to send me to urgent care.

As an asthmatic and a longtime nurse, I knew that not being

able to get my breathing under control was potentially deadly. I was uninsured, and I spent the next hours back and forth between home, the urgent care where I had to pay the up-front cost of $100 to be seen, and the emergency room. I was eventually admitted to the hospital and released a few days later. Back home, I didn't feel much better, but I hesitated going to the hospital a second time because I worried about the bills from two emergency room visits and two hospital admissions.

But when my good friend Victoria Dooley, MD, a family medicine physician from Michigan, called to check on me the day after being released from the first hospital stay and heard my labored breathing and broken sentences, she took it upon herself to call an ambulance to my home. I needed a regular schedule of high-dose steroids, which I received while hospitalized, but I was lonely there. Because of newly instituted COVID-19 protocols, I couldn't receive visitors during either stay. I called my family when I could, but my breathing was so labored that I could barely speak. Every night, I feared falling asleep, wondering if my body would continue to breathe on its own without my focused effort and whether I would wake up in the morning. I didn't sleep for several nights.

After a few days, I was released again. Zion and my dad, in their KN95 masks, picked me up and brought me home. I was so worried about potentially getting them sick that I didn't even speak during the car ride. Zion had moved closer to his school's campus, and Angel had moved out on her own, so I lived alone. But my dad and Zion stayed and cared for me for the two months that I ended up being sick with COVID. Every other day they brought me food, orange juice, vitamins, and tea. My bedroom was on the second floor of a multistory town house, and I soon realized I couldn't manage the stairs without straining my lungs. I would leave my bed to make tea or soup downstairs, and then I would be too weak to move again for hours. So I put an extra-high air mattress in the first-floor living room and moved downstairs. I couldn't understand why I wasn't getting better as the days and weeks went on. I might have a good morning, but then the extreme fatigue, tremors, body aches, and labored breathing would come rushing back. I'd had the flu and pneumonia before. This was something else entirely.

I continued to campaign, first from my bed and then from the air mattress. The state locked down, and all in-person events were canceled anyway. When I felt up to it, I wrote posts that we could post on social media, I attended fundraising events online, and I spoke to my supporters on Zoom. This transition to virtual took some effort. I was too sick to do my own hair, so I bought a couple of wigs and scarves that I wore. I put on lipstick to prevent people from noticing how sick I was. I would still take calls, make decisions, strategize with the team from my bed, even through the labored breathing and pain. Otherwise, I rested.

I wasn't sure when I'd get better. The prospect of quitting the race entered my mind on more than one occasion. But I desperately wanted to avoid a repeat of my last attempt at winning the seat, when a car crash rendered me unable to give my campaign the final push that it needed. This time, I was going to stay in the race. I was going to get better.

By the time I recovered, we were nearly two months out from the August 4 primary. We stayed the course. In early July, our polling showed that I was trailing Clay by twenty points. I'd been behind by as much at the same point in the 2018 race. But that was about to take a turn.

The incumbent organized two mailers intended to cut me and my campaign down. One flyer was printed with the phrases "trust matters" and "character matters." It was a flagrant attempt to drag my name through the mud with lies and distorted truths. For example, contrary to what that mailer said, I had in fact voted for Barack Obama in 2008. Like so many Americans, I'd supported Obama's historic win and sat in awe with my father before the television watching the president-elect's victory speech in Grant Park.

The flyer also claimed that I'd been evicted three times and that the State of Missouri had once suspended my nursing license. These were true, but using this information in this way illustrated to me just how out of touch Clay's team was. They had no idea what it meant to be low income and resource poor. I'd had my license suspended in 2013 because my state income taxes were beyond what I could manage. I had a monthly payment plan, and the bill due skyrocketed when the state changed the third-party credit agency it worked with for collections. When it came time to renew my license, because of this, it was taken hostage while I negotiated payment arrangements.

And, yes, I had been evicted three times. First, when I was with DeVon. Second, when I was accepted into nursing school and asked to be allowed out of my lease but was denied. And third, when the property management company told me I had been seen on TV at the Ferguson protests, and my neighbors were afraid I would bring the protests to their door. These matters were the consequences of living in poverty—I didn't have the money to fight the evictions. But these did not reflect my character or voters' ability to trust me.

Clay's strategy backfired. People flooded my campaign office with messages of support, particularly from those who had planned to either vote for him or sit out the election entirely. Our office had reopened during the early summer after the lockdown was lifted, and one day, a woman came running in the front door of our storefront office in North Oaks Plaza. "Where is she?" she asked breathlessly. "I need to talk to Ms. Bush." She wanted me to know that she, too, had been evicted, and when she saw Clay's mailer, she felt personally attacked. "What he said here is that something is wrong with me and people like me."

Why hadn't he used his position in Congress to address the problems of too-high rents and joblessness and the other limitations that led to people being put out on the streets, instead of blaming them for being evicted? In the twenty years that he had held that office, why hadn't Clay addressed the problem of people with stretched paychecks being punished by having their professional licenses suspended?

Clay's other flyer featured a photograph of me with my friend, Palestinian American human rights activist Linda Sarsour. "Cori Bush stands with BDS, and BDS stands with her," it read, referencing the international boycott, divestment, and sanctions movement that encourages people to educate themselves about the Israeli state's ongoing abuses against Palestinian citizens and to hold Israel accountable for those abuses. The flyer accused me of having "an anti-Israel agenda." The framing was hateful and dishonest. My personal faith, as a pastor, is rooted in the same Judeo-Christian and Abrahamic traditions shared by Christians, Muslims, and Jewish peoples alike.

I am not anti-Israel. What I am opposed to are human rights abuses. I'm against the outright theft of Palestinian land and livelihoods by Israeli settlers. I stand on the side of equity and equality in the United States and globally. I endeavor to work against all supremacist systems. In my years as an activist, I had long spoken out in support of St. Louis's Palestinian and Muslim community members and their family members' fight for self-determination and dignity in the Middle East. I went to mosque for prayer. I, alongside Jewish community members in my district, decried U.S. complicity in Israel's human rights abuses. I can be critical of the Israeli government and still love and support the Israeli people the same way I can be critical of our own government in the United States and still value and hold dear my country and our people.

I never once tried to hide these allegiances. I wanted my campaign to show that you can still be who you are, still hold true to your political commitments, and run for office. I wanted my campaign to challenge the conventional wisdom that you have to be unquestionably, uncritically pro-Israel in order to win elections in this country. Gatekeepers might act as if such deference were "the American way," but that wasn't how I wanted to win the seat.

A new sense of peace came over me. I knew the tide had changed. Suddenly voters who never cared much about an electoral race before felt personally attacked by Clay's tactics, and they came to stand with me.

On August 4, 2020, I woke up singing the *Rocky* theme song, which had been circling on a loop in my mind. "Won't be long now / Getting strong now . . . / Flying high now." I was certain that we would win. I felt no fear, no anxiety. I arrived at my campaign office by 6:00 a.m. and added that song, "Gonna Fly Now," to our day's playlist. My team was ready, too. As we drove onto the North Oaks Plaza parking lot, headed toward the campaign office, there was a long line of folks waiting to receive their polling assignments and merchandise. Everyone in the car yelled out in excitement, seeing the line extend past several of the plaza's stores, "We're gonna win!"

We poured into a van and drove from polling place to polling place all day long after first making a stop at my polling place so that I could vote. As I talked to voters, I didn't try to persuade them or even try to gauge where they stood. I was there to thank them and show them my love. I casually chatted with people as they stood in line at the polls. Kids wearing my purple "Cori Bush for Congress" T-shirts came up and grabbed me around the waist, offering me their hugs as hellos. It was electric, and the energy buoyed me even further.

As the afternoon softened into the evening's dusk, we returned to the office to ready for our watch party. Everyone settled into their various tasks, and I told my team that I didn't want to hear about early numbers. "Don't tell me," I said. "I don't want to hear any numbers until the reporting reaches eighty-ninety percent. If we're not in a position where we know something for sure, don't tell me." Everyone nodded.

I left our storefront and walked to another shop in the plaza to have my makeup done for the night. I sat calmly while my makeup artist, Tara Lowery of Blush on the Boulevard, powdered my face, shadowed my eyelids, and lined and colored my lips. When I walked back over to our office, there were just ten minutes before polls were scheduled to close. Many people were already there, in the parking lot in front of the campaign office, dancing to the music of the DJ on site from Streetz 105.1. Just across the street, we could see a polling station. People were jumping out of cars and running to the line.

Minutes later, I was in the middle of a conversation with a supporter when two members of my team approached me, worry radiating off them. "We need to talk to you," one said, interrupting. They led me to the small room that was my office and closed the door, asking me to sit down. "The race was called," the campaign staffer said, deflated. "You lost." I didn't understand. The words didn't make sense to me. At this point, the polls had been closed for only about twenty minutes. We could still look across the street and see people waiting their turn to vote. I took a deep breath.

"What's the percentage?" I asked. "We can't have more than 1 percent of precincts reporting." The staffer nodded and said, "One percent." They had been watching Twitter and taken someone's baseless post—not the Associated Press or *New York Times* election coverage—as fact. I was furious.

I'd spent so many nights watching results come in on my dad's races, and I'd been through my own previous congressional races. I knew the night would be a roller coaster of emotions if I hung on every premature declaration out there. Now I was on edge.

I shooed everyone out of my office, gave my campaign manager, Isra Allison, my phone, and sat down again. I could feel the anxiety welling up inside me. After getting my makeup done, I'd planned to change into the purple dress I'd brought with me. I wanted to match my supporters in their campaign gear as I thanked them for their support later that evening, and I wanted to see my vision realized. But now I felt I couldn't change into that celebratory gown or regain my festive, confident spirits.

I left on my T-shirt and jeans and took a deep breath, willing myself not to cry. "God would not have me do this again just to be humiliated," I told myself. Sitting there alone, I pulled out my iPad and turned on a movie, trying to let the story line distract me from my thoughts. There weren't many people I could see at that moment, especially not my kids. I did not want to worry Zion and Angel; they were having fun. But I was glad when my sister, Kelli, and my five-year-old nephew Kyrie came into my office to sit with me. She cheered me as only a sister could, and my nephew's smile melts my heart every time. The time passed quickly while we were laughing and reminiscing, talking about everything except the election. That's when Dominique Alexander, the president of Dallas's Next Generation Action Network and a supporter of my campaign, poked his head in the door. "I don't know what y'all are doing in here," he said. "But whatever it is, keep doing it."

Dominique came back about an hour later, silently gave us a thumbs-up, and left again. My dad came in and joined us for a while, and at some point a notification popped up on my iPad: "Cori Bush just won the city." I knew that at least in that part of the district I was on top. "Wait. What is happening? This is more like it!" I was immediately energized like Skittles had been shot into my veins. The next time a notification appeared on my screen minutes later, it was from a reputable source, and it took my breath away: "Cori Bush won."

My sister and I stared at each other, and I called out for my campaign manager. "Issy! Verify it before I get too happy!" She walked away for a few seconds and then came back and assured me that the win was ours. Kelli and I yelled in excitement. People and cameras swarmed the space. Someone yelled out, "You just won, what do you have to say?" My response was: "I have to pee!" I was stressed and had been holding it in for hours. I grabbed my dress from its hook behind the door and ran to the bathroom to change. Before I walked back into the room to celebrate, I looked at myself in the mirror. My hair was in long, medium-sized box braids, the front twisted back and away from my face, and I looked happy. We had done it. I closed my eyes and took a deep breath, letting the satisfaction and sense of gratitude move through me.

I opened the bathroom door to a crowd of people with cell phone cameras, patting me on the back. They accompanied me into the open space in our campaign office, where I was greeted by people cheering and crying with joy, grabbing each other into big, whole-hearted hugs. They gave each other daps and high fives. Supporters who didn't even know each other held hands and jumped up and down for joy. The activists who'd been with me on the streets of Ferguson chanted with fists in the air. News media scrambled to get to the office, caught off guard by my win, and suddenly in need of footage. My team and I thought we were prepared, but when the moment arrived, our uncontainable joy left us flustered. It took a moment to remember where we'd put the microphone I needed for my victory speech.

I'd won and was able to breathe a bit knowing the November general election would pose less of a challenge in this largely Democratic district. I was going to Congress.

I looked out over the crowd and saw my dad nearby, shaking as many hands as he could, tears streaming down his face. "You did it," he said as I made my way toward the lectern. He emphasized the word "you," though all along he'd been right there beside me. Still, he wanted me to feel the sense of accomplishment, the glory that accompanies a hard-won success.

"You did it," he said. "You did it."

Conclusion

IN THE THREE MONTHS leading up to the general election, as I was getting used to the idea that I was heading to Congress, I started receiving advice. I should temper my expectations. As someone newly elected to the seat, I wouldn't be able to accomplish much. I wasn't yet going to have the important relationships or the clout that I needed to move major policy, seasoned politicos told me.

But just after my win, members of the group whom many have dubbed "the Squad," including Alexandria Ocasio-Cortez, Rashida Tlaib, Ayanna Pressley, and Ilhan Omar, and others whom I didn't yet know started calling me. They introduced themselves, gave me tips, and helped me get ready for the role. They were all newly elected, and they wielded their influence as a group and individually, and they all hit the ground running. I didn't see why I couldn't do the same.

I was elected to bring change, and I wasn't going to sit around. I was going to bring it. Many members of Congress called to congratulate me, even those who opposed me in the primary. One thing that stuck out to me was a question that I was asked several times: Would I be a show horse, or a workhorse, people wanted to know. I decided that I didn't want to be any type of horse. But if you must call me one, I'd bring the best qualities of both and be a show-work horse, I said.

I decided to use those months before my swearing-in to work on whatever my community needed. My campaign team and volunteers coordinated with census workers to host events outside grocery stores and in parks around the district, encouraging people to submit their forms. I later learned that our outreach efforts helped our district secure at least a million additional dollars in federal funding. We traveled the state and held voter registration events. During a three-day tour, we were joined by Democratic candidates for offices around Missouri, all of whom were excited about building progressive power and getting our people to the polls.

We knew we wanted the watch party on election night to be a community celebration. By the time Tuesday, November 3, arrived, we were ready. For our primary win, we were hopeful but nervous. This time, we could truly enjoy ourselves, watching the returns come in with a sense of ease and joy. We gathered in the North Oaks Plaza parking lot in front of our campaign office. We danced to the Streetz 105.1 DJ's music again, old-school R&B and hip-hop, gospel, and some new rap music. My family, friends, activist family, and supporters were all there. It was a great feeling having my mom and brother there this time, particularly because they had been unable to attend the primary election watch party.

As progressives, we needed the lift that my win provided. We had suffered the many disappointments of the Trump years, as well as the backlash that followed our organizing in Ferguson. We had come together on this campaign to do something incredible, and now many in the district expressed they had a reason to have some cautious faith in change becoming a reality.

Once the race was officially called, I climbed to the podium. A huge Black Lives Matter flag was mounted behind me. I wanted it to be clear that I still planned to speak out against police brutality, that I was not going to hide who I was now that I'd won. I was the same Cori. And I wanted my story to help people feel seen.

I wanted it to be known that you can be a regular, everyday person and do what others deem impossible. Past traumas don't have to hold you back from achieving your goals in life. Victims and survivors of assault, low-wage workers, single parents, people living with disabilities, folks who are unhoused or transient, people on EBT, WIC, or any other form of state assistance, people with credit issues, those who are incarcerated or were formerly incarcerated, those who are LGBTQIA+, and members of every marginalized group.

We must not allow people to put us in the box that they put their own selves into due to insecurities, fear, envy, or their own shortcomings. Let them address those limitations in their lives, if they choose. When people say that you can't achieve something because you don't look, sound, or dress the part—or because you don't have the money, a specific kind of educational background, or the political ties that are a part of some unwritten rule book—tell them, "Maybe YOU can't do it, but YOUR limitations don't apply to me." I walked in faith knowing my God hadn't placed limits on His purpose for my life.

I opened my victory speech with my memories of trying to escape DeVon all those years ago. "I was running," I said. "I was that person running for my life across a parking lot, running from an abuser. I remember hearing bullets whiz past my head, and at that moment I wondered, 'How do I make it out of this life?'" I knew the unfortunate truth.

My story, and the nightmares that I had lived through, mirrored the experiences of too many of my soon-to-be constituents and people nationwide. And I wanted the people listening to know that I had lived as they did, and I knew what it meant to be a survivor of domestic and sexual abuse, to be marginalized, unhoused, and broke, and I was going to be fighting for them. "I was uninsured. I've been that uninsured person, hoping my health-care provider wouldn't embarrass me by asking me if I had insurance. I thought, 'How will I bear it?'"

I looked out into the audience, my face wet with tears. I looked at my children, Zion and Angel, now young adults. "I was a single parent. I've been that single parent struggling paycheck to paycheck, sitting outside the payday loan office, wondering, 'How much more will I have to sacrifice?'" I was speaking my truth, even ad-libbing some of it, and I didn't mince words.

My heart was opened by the magnitude of what we'd done together. I wanted to let those gathered know that I could feel the hurt in our community. I wanted them to know that it was my hurt as well and that that hurt fueled my fight.

. . .

SO AS THE FIRST Black woman, nurse, and single mother to have the honor to represent Missouri in the United States Congress, let me just say this. To the Black women. The Black girls. The nurses. The single mothers. The essential workers. This. Is. OUR. Moment.

Six years ago, St. Louis captured the eyes and ears of the entire world during the Ferguson uprising. We could not stand the injustice any longer, so—in the tradition of every one of our ancestors who fought for a better world—we organized for Michael Brown Jr. We organized for four hundred days, side by side, arm in arm, St. Louis strong. And now in the face of a global pandemic and relentless attacks on our right to vote, we organized all the way to the ballot box. We mailed in our ballots, we voted absentee, we reached our families, friends, neighbors, and peers—and we showed up. St. Louis strong.

For years, we've lived under leadership that shut us out of our own government. For years, we've been left out in the cold: protesting in the streets, sleeping in our cars or tents, working three part-time jobs just to pay the bills. And today, today, we, all of us, are headed to Congress— St. Louis strong!

My message today is to every Black, Brown, immigrant, queer, and trans person, and to every person locked out of opportunities to thrive because of oppressive systems: I'm here to serve you. To every person who knows what it's like to give a loved one that "just make it home safely, baby" talk: I love you.

To every parent facing a choice between putting food on the table and keeping a roof over their head: I'm here to serve you. To every precious child in our failing foster system: I love you.

To every teacher doing the impossible of teaching through this pandemic: I'm here to serve you. To every student struggling to the finish line: I love you.

To every person living with disabilities denied equal access: I love you.

To every person living unhoused on the streets: I love you.

To every family that's lost someone to gun violence: I love you.

To every person who's lost a job, or a home, or health care, or hope: I love you.

It is the greatest honor of my life to accept the responsibility to serve every single person across Missouri's First Congressional District, as your first-ever Black congresswoman-elect. This is our moment.

Tonight, we the people are victorious. We, we the people are going to Congress. Because we the people have committed to a vision of America that works for all of us. An America that treats every person with respect. That recognizes health care as a human right. That believes every person deserves food to eat, a home to live in, and a dignified life. Our America will be led not by the small-mindedness of a powerful few, but by the imagination of a mass movement that includes all of us. That is the America we are fighting for.

Your congresswoman-elect loves you, and I need you to get that because if I love you, I care that you eat. If I love you, I care that you have shelter and adequate safe housing. If I love you, I care that you have clean water and clean air and a livable wage. If I love you, I care that the police don't murder you. If I love you, I care that you make it home safely. If I love you, I care that you are able to have dignity and have a quality of life the same as the next person, the same as those who don't look like you, who didn't grow up the same way you did. Those who don't have the same socioeconomic status as you. I care.

· · ·

I FELT THE SUPPORT at my back of the movements for social, racial, and economic justice that came before me. I felt ready to serve those who had gotten me to that moment.

Sure, I had plenty of questions about what would come next. I had a lot to learn. But that night, I had strength and confidence. I had come so far, and I knew to trust myself and trust God, just as I had always done.

Acknowledgments

Over the years, a wide community of people have helped to lift me up and bring me to where I am today, and without them, this book would not have been possible.

First my parents, Barbara Blakney and the Honorable Errol Earl Bush, who have been an inspiration to me my whole life, showered me with unconditional love, and lent a hand when times were hard. My sister, Kelli, who has been my ride or die since we were kids, and my brother Perry, who always brought laughter into the room, I am fortunate to also call my friends. My niece, Khaliah, and nephew, Kyrie, who warm my heart every time I see them. My aunt Patricia Blakney, who has been an angel to me my whole life, and my aunts Sherry, Earline, and Ernestine. My uncles Fred and James, who I can always count on for the jokes to give me grief about something. To my many cousins and my late grandparents Ulysses and Beulah, J.D., and Vera, Tommy and Momma Woodson, like so many in my wider family, of whom there are too many to name.

My beautiful babies, Zion and Angel, give my life joy and meaning every day because they are the most beautiful parts of it. I have watched them grow into fine young people, and everything I do, I dedicate to them.

My heart, Cortney, the love of my life, has stood by me and offered me his love, reading these pages alongside me as they've come together, and helping me through the entire process of sharing my most vulnerable moments. Every meal he cooked, every tear he wiped, every hug he gave helped me complete this book.

My friend Stephany Rose Spaulding has also read drafts, offering wise remarks and encouragement to help me push through the difficult moments. My longtime dear friend Kenyatta Patrick Griffin, who has been my family since high school and whose daughter Imani I am proud to call my goddaughter. My friend Yolanda Collier was there throughout nursing school. We leaned a lot on each other. I would like to thank my friend Pastor Daphne Rice, as well as her parents, Apostle Lee and the late Apostle Doris Rice. My friend LaShonda Obiakor walked through many days of this journey with me, as we struggled together. Allean, who reintroduced me to Jesus Christ and who helped take care of my kids at daycare while I had to work, and her husband, the late Herman Keys, who would sing to my infant daughter every day. My late spiritual mother, Sylvia Vinson, who first told me to write my story, as well as Pastor Leonard Barber and Apostle C.N., who forever changed my life.

I owe a debt of gratitude to many in the political sphere, especially those who believed in me early on, when few others did. In particular, the late Hazel Erby; my friend Amy Vilela, who goes above and beyond to help everyone; Kristine Hendricks, who took a lot of hits after endorsing me; John Theodore, who nominated me to Justice Democrats; Bruce Franks Jr., from protests to politics we did together along with Rasheen Aldridge. Nina Turner, Dr. Victoria Dooley, and Bernie Sanders.

The creation of a book is a collective effort, and many people have poured their labor into it, helped to make it what it is.

My chief-of-staff Abbas Alawieh is my right hand. He plays a crucial role in my day-to-day, in almost every aspect of my work and life. Without him, there would be no book.

Lynese Wallace, my deputy chief of staff and legislative director, has likewise been an invaluable partner throughout this process, offering her sharp guidance.

Thank you to Dani McClain, who worked intimately with me—over the course of countless hours of interviews and months of work together on the page—and helped me tell my story in my own voice. Without her, too, this book would never have come into being.

I want to say thank you to Julia Pacetti, who connected me to my incredible team of literary agents, Esther Newberg and Zoe Sandler—who championed me and my memoir from the beginning.

And I want to thank my team at Alfred A. Knopf for getting behind my book and offering me a publishing home. Reagan Arthur, the publisher, and Maria Goldverg, my editor. Thank you to Kathy Hourigan, Victoria Pearson, Peggy Samedi, and Mike Collica, who produced and shepherded my book with delicacy. And thank you to my publicity and marketing team—Erinn Hartman, Jess Purcell, Amy Hagedorn, Sarah New, Laura Keefe, and Matthew Sciarappa.

I want to thank my entire campaign team, from 2015 to the present, for the work they do on my behalf, every volunteer and supporter—you know who you are, those of you who have carried me in my races.

Thank you to the Ferguson Frontline and all the Ferguson activists, my second family, who fought out there with me every day, for so long, for what we knew was right. To icon Dr. Angela Davis and Dr. Fania Davis, who publicly supported me before many knew my name. To Dr. David Ragland, for everything throughout the years.

Thank you to the people of St. Louis, for believing in me, and for being my home.

Your congresswoman loves you.

A Note About the Author

Cori Bush is a registered nurse, a community activist and organizer, a single mother, and an ordained pastor. She is serving her first term as the St. Louis congresswoman. Bush is the first Black woman and first nurse to represent Missouri; the first woman to represent Missouri's First Congressional District; and the first activist from the movement fighting for Black lives to be elected to Congress.

A Note on the Type

This book was set in Adobe Garamond. Designed for the Adobe Corporation by Robert Slimbach, the fonts are based on types first cut by Claude Garamond (ca. 1480–1561).

Typeset by Scribe,
Philadelphia, Pennsylvania

Printed and bound by Sheridan Printing, a CJK Group Company,
Brainerd, Minnesota

Designed by Michael Collica